K·I·S·S

DK

The Only Guides You'll Ever Need!

THIS SERIES IS YOUR TRUSTED GUIDE through all of life's stages and situations. Want to learn how to surf the Internet or care for your new dog? Or maybe you'd like to become a wine connoisseur or an expert gardener? The solution is simple: Just pick up a K.I.S.S. Guide and turn to the first page.

Expert authors will walk you through the subject from start to finish, using simple blocks of knowledge to build your skills one step at a time. Build upon these learning blocks and by the end of the book, you'll be an expert yourself! Or, if you are familiar with the topic but want to learn more, it's easy to dive in and pick up where you left off.

The K.I.S.S. Guides deliver what they promise: simple access to all the information you'll need on one subject. Other titles you might want to check out include: Playing Guitar, Living With a Dog, the Internet, Microsoft Windows, Astrology, and many more to come.

GUIDE TO PLAYING

Golf

STEVE DUNO

Foreword by Colin Montgomerie
Consistently ranked #1 golfer on the European Order of Merit

A Dorling Kindersley Book

Dorling  Kindersley

LONDON, NEW YORK, SYDNEY, DELHI, PARIS,
MUNICH AND JOHANNESBURG

Dorling Kindersley Publishing, Inc.
Editorial Director: LaVonne Carlson
Series Editor: Beth Adelman
Copyeditor: Kristi Hart

Dorling Kindersley Limited
Editorial Director: Valerie Buckingham
Senior Editor: Bridget Hopkinson
Project Editors: Caroline Hunt, Julie Oughton

Managing Art Editor: Stephen Knowlden
Senior Art Editor: Heather McCarry
Designers: Justin Clow, Carla De Abreu

Jacket Designer: Nealosh Cobourne
Picture Researchers: Jamie Robinson, Mariana Sonnenburg
DTP: Louise Waller
Production: Sarah Coltman, Louise Daly

Library of Congress Cataloging-in-Publication Data

Duno, Steve.
    The KISS guide to playing golf / Steve Duno.--
1st American ed.
        p. cm. -- (Keep it simple series)
        ISBN 0-7894-5978-7 (alk. paper)
        1. Golf. 2. Golf--Rules. I. Title. II. Series.
GV965 . D86 2000
796.352--dc21

                                                          99-050662
                                                          CIP

Dorling Kindersley Publishing, Inc. offers special discounts for bulk purchases for sales promotions or premiums.
Specific, large-quantity needs can be met with special editions, including personalized covers,
excerpts of existing guides, and corporate imprints. For more information, contact Special Markets Department,
Dorling Kindersley Publishing, Inc., 95 Madison Avenue, New York, NY 10016 Fax: 800-600-9098.

Color reproduction by ColourScan, Singapore
Printed and bound by Printer Industria Grafica, S.A., Barcelona, Spain

For our complete catalog visit

www.dk.com

Contents at a Glance

PART ONE

PART TWO

PART THREE

PART FOUR

PART FIVE

CONTENTS

PART ONE *Before You Pick Up a Club*

CHAPTER 1   Our Oldest Game   22

CHAPTER 2   How and Where the Game Is Played   34

CHAPTER 3   The Basic Rules   50

PART THREE *The Short Game*

Foreword

I AM DELIGHTED TO BE IN A POSITION to welcome you to the best game in the world – golf. Steeped in history and time-honored tradition, golf is a fascinating, challenging, sociable sport that allows people of all ages to compete with the common aim of achieving their personal bests. The simple pleasure of executing a perfect shot or playing the best round of your life produces a natural high for professionals and amateurs alike. You'll soon discover how easy it is to develop an undying passion for this marvelous game.

You may have decided to take up golf for one of many different reasons – for the exercise, the social contact, or perhaps you just want to be out in the fresh air for a few hours a week. Whatever your reason, this book will tell you everything you need to know about golf, from the rules and etiquette of the game to choosing your equipment and learning the essential skills. If you have any questions, you'll discover an ocean of information that should satisfy your every query, and if you want to explore the world of golf further, there's a great list of web site addresses – including my own (www.colinmontgomerie.com)!

As a professional golfer, I have always been fascinated by the methodology of teaching and learning golf and have, over the years, produced videos and instructional material for numerous books and magazines. My current projects include a number of junior golf programs and plans to open a series of teaching academies in the UK and Europe. My aim for all of these enterprises is the same as that of this book – simply to help each individual golfer develop and improve upon his or her natural ability.

I inherited my love of golf from my father at an early age, while my mother taught me the importance of 100-percent commitment. The combination of these two factors – and a lot of hard work – led ultimately to the fortunate situation I now find myself in. Not only do I get paid for enjoying my hobby, but golf has given me the opportunity to meet people from every conceivable walk of life. The thing I love most about this game, though, is knowing that when I meet fellow golfers the world over, we will immediately have a common bond – a language that crosses all boundaries.

I do hope that this book inspires you, either to take up golf from scratch, or to help you sort out those niggling problems that may have been holding you back. It could be the beginning of a very special, lifelong love affair.

COLIN MONTGOMERIE, MBE

Introduction

CONGRATULATIONS! *You've taken up the world's most popular recreational pastime. Welcome to the game I love. Challenging and beautiful, the game of golf enables people of all skill levels to compete and to succeed. Now that you are one of us, I want to welcome you to what I think will be a lifelong love affair – an exhilarating, frustrating, and rewarding relationship*

THE OLD COURSE, ST. ANDREWS, SCOTLAND

that becomes, to those who are dedicated to it, a way of life more than a weekend sport. You will know what I mean when you hit your first crisp fairway wood off of the manicured turf or knock a pitching wedge to within five feet of the flagstick. There's just no other sport like it.

The goal of this book is to help ease you into the sport as painlessly as possible, leaving you with golf skills you can quickly put to work. It won't happen overnight, but if you remain patient, practice diligently, and heed my advice, you should be having fun on the course in no time. Just keep it simple and you'll be fine.

And don't worry, I'll take you along slowly, starting with the simple skills and gradually moving you along into the more advanced areas of the game. Sooner than you think, you'll be able to hit the ball with confidence and get out onto the course with friends to finally experience what so many millions already have: the thrill of playing one of history's oldest and grandest games.

PERFECT PUTTING STYLE

Like many of today's golfers, I first began playing golf as an early teen but temporarily put it aside in favor of the more popular team sports: baseball, football, and soccer. It wasn't until much later that I rekindled my love affair with the game. And in some ways I think that's appropriate, because golf is a game as much of the mind as it is of the stroke, and I probably appreciate the mental aspects more now that I'm an adult.

Since renewing my passion for golf, I have learned a myriad of things that, hopefully, I can pass on to you. I'll give you advice on all aspects of the game, from buying equipment and taking lessons to grooving the perfect swing and mastering the intricacies of course strategy.

My aim in this book is to take you, the novice golfer, and turn you into a decent player – one who can hit the ball well and score consistently. I also hope the book will inspire you to continually improve your skills. Don't be satisfied with the status quo; always strive to play a better, more complete game. Even the world's top golfers try to improve every day, taking lessons and playing endless practice rounds to make that happen.

Feel free to take your time with this book. Read and reread until everything becomes clear. Then go out to the practice range or the golf course, and try out what you have just learned. Don't rush. After all, golf is not a frantic game, but one that calls for patience and skill. Think of it as a craft or the making of a fine wine. All good things come to those with the maturity and composure to take things one step at a time.

STEVE DUNO

TIGER WOODS, AN INSPIRATION TO MILLIONS OF GOLFERS

What's Inside?

THE INFORMATION IN the K.I.S.S. Guide to Playing Golf *is arranged from the simple to the more advanced, making it most effective if you start from the beginning and slowly work your way to the more involved chapters.*

PART ONE

In Part One I'll give you very basic information about the game, including its history, objectives, rules, terms, and etiquette. You'll need this information before heading out onto the course so you'll know what people are talking about out there.

PART TWO

In Part Two I'll teach you the fundamentals of the game, including the science of ball flight, basic equipment needs, the grip, proper setup techniques, and the ABC's of the golf swing. This is an extremely important section, so read it carefully!

PART THREE

Part Three discusses the importance of the short game and why it is so vital to racking up good scores. I'll cover putting, chipping, pitching, and sand shots in detail. I'll also explain why the short game can be an especially potent weapon for beginners.

PART FOUR

Part Four is dedicated to the player who has mastered the fundamentals and wants to take his or her game to the next level. Key swing tips, troubleshooting, speciality shots, and course strategy are all discussed here.

PART FIVE

In Part Five I'll discuss practice techniques, handicapping, lessons, and equipment upgrades. I'll also take you beyond the golf course and show you how to improve your knowledge and appreciation of the game by attending professional tournaments, watching golf on television, and taking fabulous golf vacations.

The Extras

THROUGHOUT THE BOOK, *you will notice a number of boxes and symbols. They are there to emphasize certain points I want you to pay special attention to, because they are important to your understanding and improvement. You'll find:*

Very Important Point

This symbol points out a topic I believe deserves careful attention. You really need to know this information before continuing.

Complete No-No

This is a warning, something I want to advise you not to do or to be aware of.

Getting Technical

When the information is about to get a bit technical, I'll let you know so that you can read carefully.

Inside Scoop

These are special suggestions that come from my own personal experience. I want to share them with you because they helped me when I was learning the game.

You'll also find some little boxes that include information I think is important, useful, or just plain fun.

Trivia...

These are simply fun facts that will give you an extra appreciation for the history and uniqueness of the game of golf.

DEFINITION

Here I'll define words and terms for you in an easy-to-understand style. You'll also find a Glossary at the back of the book with all the golfing lingo.

INTERNET

www.internet.com

I think the Internet is a great resource for golfers, so I've scouted out some web sites that will add to your enjoyment and understanding of the sport.

PART ONE

THE ROYAL & ANCIENT CLUBHOUSE, ST. ANDREWS

BEFORE YOU PICK UP A CLUB

NO LONGER just a game for doctors taking time out from the surgery, businessmen making high-powered deals between holes, and Florida retirees, golf has become a national pastime for the masses.

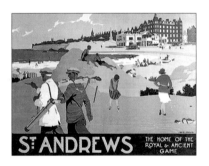

People young and old are *discovering* that you don't need lots of money and a wardrobe of questionable taste to get into the game. What you do need are patience, a basic *understanding* of the rules, a little sense of history, and a desire to walk a few miles while smacking a little ball around with you as you go. And, of course, a book. This one will do nicely.

Let's get started by looking at the history of the game and the basics of how it's played. I promise *I'll keep it simple!*

Chapter 1

Our Oldest Game

Whether you know it or not, you have just joined a very special band of crazed devotees. Golf is not merely a sport, but an age-old tradition going back for centuries and extending straight into the heart of American and European history. Just like you, golfers over the centuries have enjoyed sweet successes and bitter disappointments in the hope that a perfect round of golf is just around the corner...

In this chapter...

✓ Welcome to the club

✓ A simple history of the game

✓ Now that you're hooked, it ain't that easy

✓ A game for life

Welcome to the club

GOLF PROVIDES THE CHANCE *to excel at an exciting sport and the opportunity to get away from the hustle and bustle of everyday life. When you're out on the golf course, you get to experience a few precious hours in beautiful, peaceful surroundings, with only one delightfully difficult task at hand: to somehow hit a small white ball around a lush, green golf course with as much precision and grace as possible.*

The ideal shot

No matter what your skill level, each round of golf offers you the opportunity to hit that ideal shot, the one you know is perfect from the moment it leaves your club face. Arcing beautifully down the closely mown grass of the *fairway*, the ball lands perfectly, perhaps even finding its way onto the *green* and into the hole after a few tentative bounces or a long, serpentine roll. The ball homes in on its small, hollow target like a guided missile, as if it had a mind of its own.

■ **The fairway** *is usually bordered by either long grass, known as semi-rough, or completely uncut grass, called rough. It can also be surrounded by challenging obstacles such as trees, bunkers, or water hazards.*

The perfect round

All golfers play for that moment, and for the chance to improve their skills over time so that they might one day play that perfect, nearly unattainable round of golf. The occasional perfect shot, and the quest for the elusive pure round, keeps us coming back for more, year in and year out.

Falling in love with the game

Once you get out onto the rolling fairways and experience the highs and lows that only golf can provide, you will be hooked. After that, the desire to improve will take over, compelling you to do whatever is necessary to lower your scores and play better. A marvelous addiction this game of golf, and a tough taskmaster as well. Falling in love with it means finding yourself squeezing in quick practice sessions during lunch and getting up at 6 a.m. on Saturdays in hopes of playing a round before the rest of your family realizes you're gone. Get hooked on golf and you will find yourself reading every magazine and book on the subject, hoping they might help lower your scores by a shot or two. You will buy all the latest miracle equipment and, yes, actually watch hours of golf on television (much to the dismay of your family, who will wonder how on earth you can stay indoors on such a pretty day).

■ **Many golf courses** *have beautiful surroundings that range from wild coastline to lush parkland.*

You're hooked!

Whether you are a salesperson, rocket scientist, housekeeper, or president, you will find your mind reliably wandering to the game throughout the day, when you probably should be concentrating on other things. Thoughts like, "If only I had hit that third shot on the 5th hole straighter!" or "Boy did I nail that long putt on the 9th!" will course through your head at the most inopportune moments. When that happens, you'll know you belong to the club, and that years of frustration and joy await you.

The chance to play like the pros do

Golf is different from other sports. It takes longer and is rarely played with more than four people in a group. It can be played alone, as well, for in golf you really don't compete against other players, but against the course itself. It might also be the only sport that allows even the average player, every now and then, to perform as well as the best professional golfer in the world. Anyone, at any given time, can step up to a golf ball and hit a pure, sweet shot that goes exactly where it is supposed to go, just as a pro might. Few of us, though, could ever hit a 95-mph fastball into deep left field or throw a 60-yard pass for a touchdown. The chance to perform a perfect sporting act is very seductive to most of us, and is what brings most golfers back to that 1st tee time and again. The golfing gods every now and then throw you a beautiful bone and keep you hooked.

The inner game of golf

Golf is a thoughtful game. Unlike baseball or football, which often require you to instinctively react to what is happening on the field, golf requires you to consciously initiate your every action and to think hard about what comes next. It takes time and patience, much like a chess game or making a piece of fine furniture. This thoughtful, artful aspect of golf is what makes it so alluring and at the same time so difficult.

A lifelong interest

Once you start playing the game, you will take almost as much pleasure in recalling your failures as in boasting of your victories. You will sit around with friends and crow over that great shot you smacked over the pond or mourn about the sand bunker it took you four shots to get out of. And, as always, the "what ifs" will simmer in your brain, compelling you to come back again and again for more in hopes that something special might one day happen. That feeling will not go away with time, but will, instead, remain as strong as ever for as long as you care to play the game. After all, golf can be played for life – unlike other sports, which become increasingly difficult for older people to participate in. Just visit any golf course on a sunny weekday morning and you'll discover what all those retirees are doing while you slave away at your job, wishing you were playing golf.

Trivia...

Believe it or not, the first golf balls were made of feathers tightly packed into a hand-stitched leather covering. Called featheries, they took a long time to make and were very expensive to buy. A feathery did not travel nearly as far as today's balls do, giving the game of golf a very different character from the one it has today.

One step at a time

By buying this book, you have shown a desire to join the golfing community and to make a serious effort to learn the fundamental skills needed to get around the golf course. Congratulations! All of us golf-crazed fanatics welcome you with open arms and encourage you to learn the game from the ground up, at a comfortable pace.

Remember to take your time and to not jump into the deep end of the pool too quickly. Mastering this game will require determination, practice, and, above all, patience.

A simple history of the game

MOST HISTORIANS AGREE THAT *the game of golf originated in Scotland nearly a thousand years ago, with bored Scottish farmers and shepherds hitting small round stones into rodent burrows with sticks. Documented court records from 13th-century Scotland show that more than one king, seriously concerned about farmers and soldiers spending too much time playing golf, handed down decrees limiting the amount of golf played in their kingdoms.*

■ **There is little** *documentary evidence of golf prior to the middle of the 15th century. This manuscript illustration from the Flemish Book of Hours (c.1520) displays some of the first true images of the game.*

Exclusive beginnings

Mary Queen of Scots and James II were both avid golfers in the 16th and 17th centuries, and the famed Old Course at St. Andrews in Scotland has been in operation since the 17th century. The first rules of golf, set down by the Scots in 1744, predated the American Revolution by more than 30 years. Now that's old!

Golf crosses the Atlantic

Golf came to the United States in the late 19th century, with a number of magnificent courses built in the East, including Shinnecock Hills on Long Island, Pine Valley in New Jersey, and Winged Foot in Westchester, New York. At first the sport caught on with the wealthy, who saw to the expansion of the game through the early 20th century, primarily as a way to flaunt their moneyed status and compete with European aristocrats. More and more prestigious courses were built, and interest soared.

INTERNET

www.dmcsoft.com/sgts/

If you want to make a pilgrimage to the birthplace of golf, Tayleur Mayde's web site offers golf vacations to Scotland's legendary courses.

Golf hits the TV screen

By the late 1920s golfing competitions began to capture the attention of the public, with players such as Walter Hagen, Bobby Jones, and Gene Sarazen winning tournaments once dominated by European players. With the development of homegrown golf stars such as Sam Snead, Ben Hogan, and Byron Nelson in the late 1930s, America's love affair with golf was firmly entrenched. With the introduction of television, golf truly came into its own. Millions of fans could now tune in on a Sunday afternoon to see Arnold Palmer and his armies of fans charging up the 18th fairway to yet another victory, or to see the newcomer Jack Nicklaus challenging Palmer for dominance on the professional circuit.

■ **Television** *generates million-dollar advertising and sponsorship deals for many professional players.*

Everyone's welcome to play

■ **Tiger Woods,** *the youngest winner of the Masters Tournament, has inspired millions of players.*

No longer just for the wealthy, golf in post-war America saw a tremendous upsurge in popularity among the middle class, who played the game not on exclusive private courses, but on the many public courses being built to meet the rising demand. Once a game of the elite, golf is now fast becoming a pastime enjoyed by players from all economic and cultural strata. From rural Texas to bustling cities such as Chicago and New York, golf is gaining popularity each year, especially among the young, who, after watching Tiger Woods and his great success, no longer see golf as boring or uncool.

Be part of the recreation of choice

Professional golf is alive and well today in the United States, with the PGA (Professional Golfers' Association), LPGA (Ladies' PGA), Senior, Nike, and other tours providing venues for some of the most talented players in the world. The Canadian, European, and Asian Tours also produce some of the world's most talented players, who, through competition here and overseas, show that they are as good or better than our own homebred golfers. On the recreational side, in this country alone more than 30 million Americans play golf regularly, and the golfing industry generates billions of dollars in revenue each year. From the President to the kid next door, golf has truly become the recreational sport of choice. And now you are part of it!

Now that you're hooked, it ain't that easy

YES, GOLF IS ONE *of the most exciting and rewarding sports you will ever attempt to play. And yes it's great to be outdoors in the sunshine with good friends or alone, surrounded by trees and birds and rolling green hills. Unfortunately, golf isn't the easiest sport to play well, and as such can often dissuade some beginners from sticking with it long enough to master its challenges. Why is this?*

Simply focus your mind

First, as I mentioned earlier, golf is not a reactive sport like baseball or football, in which your actions depend primarily on what others on the field are doing or on the position of the ball.

In golf the ball sits before you motionless, waiting for you to get the ball rolling, so to speak. When you're playing baseball, the ball is thrown at you and you simply react to it, attempting to hit it with a bat. Very little thinking takes place; you simply allow your reflexes to take over. In golf, however, you start all the action. You look down at that little white ball and think, "I have to swing this club, strike that tiny ball perfectly and send it way out there to a specific target." With beginners, far too much thought and concern are thrown into the equation, often resulting in a badly hit shot. Golf is difficult, then, because of nerves and because the entire outcome of each shot depends solely on you being able to strike the ball perfectly, every time. It can be quite unnerving, especially with others watching.

■ **No two golfers** *have the same swing although different techniques share the same key elements. The classic swing is smooth, controlled, and perfectly timed.*

It's harder than you think!

Apart from the mental challenge of the game, golf requires you to perform an extremely difficult act, over and over again. That act, of course, is to hit the ball with the club face perfectly so that the ball goes exactly where you want it to. Now think about it:

The standard golf ball is exactly 1.68 inches in diameter. The average club face has anywhere from four to five square inches of area, but only about one square inch of that is the sweet spot. The club face is on the end of a shaft whose length varies from 32 inches all the way up to 45 or more.

You have to swing that club back over your shoulders, then down and around in a precise arc so that the tiny sweet spot on that club face will squarely smack the small golf ball sitting on the tee or in the grass. Talk about a needle in a haystack!

Accuracy is everything

The room for error is minuscule in comparison to baseball, for instance, which uses a much bigger ball and a bat with a much larger sweet spot than the one on a golf club. Although the baseball is thrown at you very fast, you don't have to hit it to a particular spot, you just have to hit it somewhere within the boundaries of a large playing field. In other words, there is very little room for error in hitting a golf ball well. When you combine that with the pressure of being watched by others, as well as the need to hit the ball perfectly dozens of times during the round, you can begin to see why golf is not exactly the easiest sport to master!

■ **The pressure** *of being under scrutiny is never greater than at a professional golfing tournament.*

Slowly does it

To overcome these seemingly impossible obstacles and begin to play well, you must do two things. First, keep it simple!

Learn the game at a pace you can handle, and don't get in over your head too quickly.

Too many beginners buy a set of clubs, hit balls for a few days at a driving range, and then jump onto an 18-hole course, not having the slightest chance of playing decently. Think about learning to drive a car: Did you jump into the driver's seat and immediately pull out onto the highway? Probably not. So why would you expect to do that with golf? Rookie golfers who try to play too soon often give up in frustration. Instead, you need to learn the game from the ground up at a nice, easy pace, making sure you understand each step before moving on to the next. By doing so, you won't feel as much pressure or become nearly as angry at yourself.

Stick with it

Golf, perhaps more than any other sport, is a game of delayed gratification. It takes a good while to become skilled at it, not only because hitting the ball is difficult, but because many of us take up the sport well into our adult years, when some of our innate, youthful learning skills have been

■ **Young golfers** *often perfect their skills in far less time than adults.*

diminished. Kids learn golf seemingly overnight, because their bodies and minds are little learning machines. We older types find learning new physical and mental skills to be much more difficult, and so we must stick with it longer.

1920s GOLF POSTER

Patience and practice make perfect

The second thing you need in order to play golf well is, of course, gobs of patience. Don't expect to be setting records on the golf course for at least a few years. The game has many subtle aspects that take a while to grasp; without patience, you won't get your scores down any time soon. Golf is multifaceted, with numerous areas that require varied skills on your part. The long game, for instance, requires strength and timing. The short game requires good feel with the hands. Putting demands excellent nerves and aiming skills. On-course strategy requires a sharp, focused mind and an ability to spot where the biggest dangers are on each hole. Each aspect of the game must be understood, practiced, and perfected in order for you to excel. If you hit the ball a mile but can't putt to save your life, you won't do well. Likewise, if you have an elephant-size ego, you won't survive this most humbling of games.

Patience, and the desire to learn and practice all parts of the game, will be your greatest allies on the course, so go slow and don't get frustrated with yourself in the beginning!

A game for life

TRUE, GOLF MIGHT NOT *be the easiest game to learn. What it has that many other sports do not, though, is the ability to generate in its fans a lifelong passion, an allegiance of sorts that never seems to diminish but instead grows stronger over the years. Many of us stop playing team sports soon after we leave high school or college, either because they become too strenuous for us or because we just don't have the time or the motivation to continue. Golf seems to escape that fate with most of its enthusiasts, who continue to play the game well into old age.*

■ **Ben Hogan** *is regarded as one of the greatest players of all time. He won 62 U.S. Tour events from 1938 to 1959.*

Simply stay calm

Golf is not a macho sport. It is, instead, a pastime that, though often humbling, fosters a feeling of great accomplishment when some small victory is achieved. You will never beat the golf course, but you will make fewer mistakes every once in a while, resulting in a good score and a feeling of fulfillment. Sheer strength and emotion won't cut it on the golf course the way they can in other sports. Instead, grace, humility, and your ability to reason, focus, and relax become the deciding factors.

Golf, to be played well, calls for a level of calmness and maturity rarely needed in other sports.

■ **A friendly handshake** *between Fred Couples (left) and Ian Woosnam (right) marks the end of play in the 1993 Ryder Cup.*

You've taken up the challenge

No two rounds of golf are ever the same, even when they're played on the same course. Changing weather and course conditions, as well as your own frame of mind, combine to create a new experience each time, ensuring that something unexpected will undoubtedly happen whenever you swing a club. The challenge, unpredictability, tradition, and beauty of the game of golf are what has made it so appealing to so many for so many centuries. If you stick with it, you'll find yourself enjoying the game for many, many years to come, well into your retirement years. Golf is truly a game for life, and you have taken the first step on a very challenging, gratifying trip. So sit back, relax, and read on, rookie!

INTERNET

www.worldgolf.com

A huge web site with information on golf tournaments and courses around the world. World Golf also offers a good section on the history of golf.

A simple summary

✓ Anyone can enjoy playing golf, no matter what your age or level of athleticism. That's because your real opponent is the course and not other players.

✓ Golf originated in Scotland about a thousand years ago, and its popularity exploded in the United States after World War II.

✓ Golf is a difficult game to play, because every action must be initiated by you. That means you control all the possible outcomes of your shot, and that can make a player nervous!

✓ It's important to give yourself time to learn how to play the game well. Learn at your own pace and don't rush out to tackle difficult courses before you're ready, because you'll just get frustrated.

✓ Golf can be a lifelong passion. People play golf well into old age, and many take up the sport later in life.

Chapter 2

How and Where the Game is Played

THE GOLF COURSE CAN BE YOUR enemy and your friend – sometimes both on the same day during the same game. As I mentioned in Chapter 1, the course is your only opponent, and it can be a formidable one. But it is also beautiful, dotted with trees and undulating hills and, often, running water. It's time to meet your opponent, understand all its various parts, and begin to fathom its subtleties.

In this chapter...

✓ The object: simply put the ball in the hole

✓ Different designs and fees, same purpose

✓ The driving range: where the real work is done

A TENSE MOMENT ON THE PUTTING GREEN

The object: simply put the ball in the hole

THE OBJECTIVE OF EVERY *golfer who steps onto a golf course is to get a little white ball into each of the 18 holes on the course, one after another, taking as few shots as possible. Sound simple? Well, it is and it isn't. First, all of the holes have different lengths and designs, offering you endless challenges and obstacles in your attempts to home in on that little cup with the flagstick jutting out of it. Some of the holes are short while others are medium or long, requiring more shots to get to the putting green at the end.*

From tee to green

Every hole has what is called a par, which is the number of shots it would take a good player to go from *tee* to green. For instance, a par-3 hole, usually about 85 to 230 yards long, calls for you to hit your tee shot directly onto the green, where you would then be allotted two more shots to put the ball into the *cup*. The cup is located somewhere on the green and marked by a long flagstick, which is just a plastic or metal pole with a numbered flag on it (the number tells you which hole it is). On a par-4 hole, usually about 230 to 460 yards long, a good player is allotted two shots to get onto the green, and then two putts to put the ball into the cup. On a par-5, usually more than 460 yards long, a good player is allotted three shots to get onto the green and two putts to find the cup.

> ### DEFINITION
>
> *You've probably noticed by now that the word **hole** is used to mean both the hole in the ground that you hit the ball into and the entire area from the tee to the hole in the ground. So when you "play the 10th hole," it means the whole hole, and not just the hole at the end. Got it? If this is getting a little too confusing, you can also use the word **cup**, which just means the hole in the ground that the ball drops into.*

> ### DEFINITION
>
> *Here's another of those double-use words. The **tee** is the designated place where you begin your quest for each hole. It's also the little wooden or plastic pedestal you stick in the ground to hold up the ball on the tee. That first shot off the tee is called the tee shot.*

■ **Tees** *come in many shapes, sizes, and heights to suit each of the clubs in your bag. Tees can be made of plastic (above), wood, or rubber. Professional players favor wooden tees as they don't damage the club face.*

Choose your weapon

As you progress down each fairway, the distance to the flagstick gets shorter and shorter. That means you want to hit the ball as far as possible on your tee shot, but on subsequent shots you want to work on accurate placement over shorter distances. This requires you to use a different club for each shot. Club faces are made of either wood or metal, and the different materials affect how far and how high the ball will go.

■ **Metal woods** (right) are more forgiving than wooden woods (far right) and are better suited to less experienced players.

Iron or wood?

For instance, on a long par-4 hole you might use a driver or a 3-wood for your first shot, a 4-iron or 5-iron for your second shot, and then a putter for your third and fourth shots.

Generally, a higher-numbered club such as a 9-iron will hit the ball higher up into the air but with less distance than a lower-numbered club, such as a 4-iron or a 3-wood.

(I know this stuff with the clubs can get pretty complicated, and I promise I will tell you all about them in Chapter 6.)

How many clubs to carry

Each player is allowed to carry up to a maximum of 14 clubs in his or her golf bag. The choice of which clubs you carry is up to you and the type of game you play. All you need to know right now is that you cannot have more than 14 in your bag and that you cannot use any of your playing partner's clubs during a round. You can, of course, carry fewer clubs if you choose to; this would limit your shot options but lighten the load a bit. Are you beginning to see how many variables are involved in playing this game?

INTERNET

www.igogolf.com

The International Golf Outlet sells a lot of everything to do with golf, including clothes. There are pictures of everything, so you can see before you buy.

■ **The classic set** *of 14 clubs comprises a driver, two fairway woods, eight irons, two wedges, and a putter.*

The obstacles

As you advance down the course toward the hole you are playing, many obstacles and challenges will appear that have the potential to inflate your score. It's the course's job, you see, to make it as difficult as possible for you to plop your ball into its holes. You might have to hit your ball over a lake or pond, out of some tall grass or a sand-filled bunker, around a pesky tree, or into a stiff wind. Any or all of these can make your round of golf a formidable task, testing your shot-making skills as well as your ability to think your way around the course.

■ **The bunker shot** *holds a special fear for the average golfer, but many professionals would prefer to play a ball from sand than from the rough.*

Scoring the game

At the end of your round, you add up the shots you took on all 18 holes and that is your total score. The fewer shots you've taken, the better. In golf, you see, the idea is to score as low as possible. A very good golfer can normally shoot par, which on most 18-hole courses is about 70 to 72 shots total. The average golfer in the United States will shoot about 20 to 30 over par, or 90 to 100 shots total. When you first begin playing, though, odds are that your scores will be higher than this. That's normal so don't feel bad if you shoot a score higher than your weight for the first few dozen rounds!

Start at the tee box

Now let's take a look at a typical par-4 hole and how it might be played by a good golfer. Let's say that from tee to green the hole is 385 yards long. At the very beginning of the hole is the tee box, which is a relatively small area where you must start your play.

The tee box has a marker on each side, usually about ten yards apart. The tee box is two club-lengths deep, or about eight to nine feet. You have to tee up your ball somewhere inside this ten-yard by nine-foot box.

You do not have to be standing inside the tee box itself. Your feet can be outside of it as long as your ball is inside.

The reason the tee box is relatively large is to give you the option of teeing up in different areas according to what kind of shot you want to make.

For example, the fairway in front of you might turn slightly to the left, making it advantageous to tee up as far to the right as possible for the straightest possible line to the hole. A right turn would call for you to tee up on the far left of the tee box. Also, certain parts of the tee box might not be level. You will want to avoid those parts and find a nice, flat area to tee up in.

Tee markers

Every hole will have at least three different tee boxes, positioned at different distances from the putting green. The closest tee box is normally marked by red tee markers. Beginners and those who cannot hit the ball very far should play from them. The next tee box is marked by white tee markers. This is where most golfers play from. The farthest tee box is often marked by blue tee markers. This is where a very good golfer would play from. Sometimes a course will have another tee box even farther back than the blue markers. This would be used by

■ **The rule book** *states that a ball can be placed up to two club-lengths back from the tee markers. These red, white, or blue markers indicate the distance of the tee box from the putting green.*

experts, or by professionals during a tournament. For now, consider using the red or the white markers, unless you want to torture yourself! Just keep it simple, okay?

The view from here

■ **Fairway bunkers** *are strategically positioned to trap the unsuspecting golfer. Some, as shown here, border the entire length of the fairway.*

If we were standing in the tee box looking out on our fictitious par-4 hole, we would see the fairway stretch out before us. It might bend to the left or right or be perfectly straight. It might be level, uphill, or downhill. It could have a stream, pond, or lake placed in or by it, and it could have trees bordering it or within its boundaries. It could even have one or more fairway bunkers, pits of sand that will make your life as miserable as possible if your ball happens to wander into one.

The green, green grass...

The grass on the fairway will be closely mown, usually about three-eighths of an inch high – maybe more, maybe less according to the desires of the grounds-keeping crew. On each side of the fairway is usually a slightly longer strip of grass called the primary rough. This thin strip has grass that is usually close to an inch high. Beyond that is the secondary rough, a more expansive area of grass kept substantially longer than the primary rough – usually anywhere from two inches to over four or even six inches, depending on the course. Hint:

■ **The area of** *grass alongside the fairway is known as the primary rough. Here the grass is almost an inch long to provide a troublesome lie for any player making an errant shot.*

You need to stay out of the primary rough!

Beyond the primary rough might be an area deemed out-of-bounds (very bad to land in), or even the fairway of another hole.

From fairway to putting green

The fairway can vary tremendously in width depending on the course. Generally the narrower the fairway, the harder the hole is to play. On the PGA Tour, many of the courses have fairways that can be as narrow as 20 yards in certain areas. This makes keeping your tee shot in play a much harder prospect. An average course won't be that tight, although the width of the fairways will still have a major effect on what type of shot you will play off the tee. Bottom line:

You need to keep your ball on the short grass and out of trouble!

At the end of the fairway is the putting green, the object of your desires. Greens are often round or oval, but they can also have more unusual designs, including hourglass, horseshoe, square, or even pear-shaped. The grass on a putting green is the shortest on the golf course, usually no more than three-sixteenths of an inch long and often less, especially on higher quality courses. This allows the golf ball to roll smoothly toward the hole.

Beware of hazards!

Most putting greens are guarded by a variety of hazards or dangerous areas that you should try to stay out of at all costs. The most common type of hazard found around a green is the sand trap, sometimes called a greenside bunker, which is usually an irregularly shaped pit of sand. You'll want to stay out of those if you can. Other hazards that could be guarding a putting green include streams, ponds, lakes, high grassy areas, concave areas, groves of trees, or areas deemed out-of-bounds.

The putting green itself can be relatively flat or can have an undulating design to it, making putting the ball into the hole a real challenge. You might find yourself trying to make a putt that bends right or left, or travels up or down a steep incline, or both. The changing topography of a putting green is what makes this part of the game so difficult and so crucial. Groundskeepers regularly change the location of the flagstick, so your strategy on any given day must change to suit its location.

■ **Only an accurate drive** *down the center of this fairway will avoid the numerous sand traps that encircle and protect the green.*

DEFINITION

Getting your ball into the cup in one under par is called a **birdie**. *Even less common is an* **eagle**, *or two under par. Extremely rare is a double-eagle, or three under par on a par-5 hole. Also rare is the* **ace**, *or hole-in-one, which everyone dreams about making. The first time you make an ace, you will truly know what it means to be a golfer!*

"HOLE-IN-ONE!"

Making par

On this fictitious 385-yard par-4 hole we've been playing, the typical tee shot would be to the middle of the fairway, preferably out at least 200 yards. That leaves you with a 185-yard second shot to the green. Your second shot should land on a part of the green that affords you the best chance of getting the ball to the hole in no more than two putts, enabling you to make the hole in four shots, which is par in this case. If you get really lucky, you might even need only one putt.

All these shots have names, and if you've watched any golf on television you've probably already heard words like *birdie*, *eagle*, and *ace*. These are words you'll want to hear again – when you're describing your own game.

Variety and challenge

That's pretty much a typical golf hole. There are also par-3s and par-5s, but all holes have the same basic components and challenges, with the only differences being length and shape. Sound easy? Maybe. Now let's look at how golf courses can differ and which might be better suited to your level of skill and your wallet size.

Different designs and fees, same purpose

FORTUNATELY, THERE IS A WIDE variety of golf courses for you to play on. Some are extremely expensive and exclusive while others are relatively inexpensive and open to the public. Some are long and difficult while others are short and fairly easy.

In addition to 18-hole courses of 6,000 to 7,000 yards (a typical full-length course), there are shorter 18-hole layouts of between 4,000 and 6,000 yards, as well as nine-hole courses of various lengths.

Whatever your need, there is a course waiting for you and it's probably nearby. All you have to do now is a little research.

Open to the public

The most commonly frequented type of course is the public course, which, as you might expect, is open to anyone with the appropriate fee and attire. Public venues are either municipal courses (called "munis") run by the city, or daily fee courses run by a private company. Most public courses require you to have the proper attire, which might mean simply pants and a shirt for one course but a collared shirt and slacks for another. Usually, though, if you're clothed, you'll get into a public course.

Munis and daily fee courses tend to be reasonably priced, usually charging between $15 and $30 for 18 holes of golf. These are the courses that most golfers play on, meaning the courses are usually crowded, especially on a summer weekend.

If you are just learning, it's always preferable to play at an off time — say a weekday morning during the spring or fall — so you can take your time and not feel pressured by the more experienced, faster-playing golfers.

High-end daily fee courses

There is a growing number of public courses offering slightly higher quality conditions and amenities than those available at municipals or run-of-the-mill daily fee courses. Located everywhere, these high-end daily fee courses offer the average golfer with some extra money to burn a taste of what it might be like to play at a ritzy, well-kept country club. For about two to five times the cost of a regular public venue, these expertly designed and manicured layouts will knock your socks off. These courses almost certainly will have a more stringent dress code than your neighborhood muni or daily fee course, so dress accordingly.

Strictly private

About 30 percent of the courses in the United States are private clubs, allowing only dues-paying members and their guests to play. In addition to the privilege of playing on the course, members and guests have the added benefits of clubhouse amenities, including restaurants, social functions, and personal services such as private lessons, club repair, locker room, massage, and even shoe shine. To get all of this requires a rather hefty initiation fee (usually many thousands of dollars), plus exorbitant monthly dues.

■ **Every golfer dreams** *of playing at the magnificent Augusta National Golf Club, birthplace and home of the U.S. Masters Tournament.*

Unfortunately, most of us can't afford this luxury although many of us will be lucky enough to be a guest at a private club at some time in our lives. Private clubs are usually a joy to play on not only because of the impeccable conditions but also because fewer golfers play the course.

Trivia...

Shinnecock Hills Golf Club in Southampton, New York, was the first country club in the United States to allow women to join. It opened in 1891, welcoming both male and female members.

Private goes public

Some private clubs looking to make extra revenue will open up play to the public on a limited basis, sometimes on the weekends or five days a week during the best weather months. These semiprivate clubs are more expensive than the average public course but can be a delight to play on, as they are normally in great shape and have fewer golfers on them than do the munis or daily fee courses. Dress codes for these courses are usually fairly strict, so be sure to find out in advance if a collared shirt and slacks are called for.

The last resort

The last type of course you can play on is the resort course, for golfers who like to play while they're on vacation. These wonderful venues are often located in warm places such as Hawaii, Florida, Arizona, South Carolina, Mexico, and The Bahamas. (I'll tell you more about golf vacations in Chapter 24.) Resort courses offer country club-type golfing facilities and superior hotel accommodations, as well as things to do for the kids and any nongolfers who might have come along. The course itself is usually reserved for hotel guests only, which helps keep crowds down. Prices can vary from reasonable to outrageous, so plan accordingly!

INTERNET

www.resortsonline.com

There are hundreds of links to golf resorts around the world on this site. Information is provided by the individual resorts.

■ **Golf vacations** *have become popular in recent years. This Jamaican resort boasts perfectly-tended courses, spectacular views of the Caribbean, and glorious sunshine throughout the year.*

Half the holes

In addition to 18-hole courses, there are many nine-hole courses for you to hone your game on. A normal round of golf on a full-size 18-hole course will take you upwards of five hours (unfortunately, due to slowpokes).

A round on a nine-hole course often takes less than half of that. This will enable you to have some fun and learn the game even during the week, perhaps before or after work.

You can usually squeeze in a two- or three-hour block of time for nine holes much more easily than a five- or six-hour block for 18 holes.

Fewer golfers play these abbreviated courses on the weekends, too, so you can scoot down to the course Saturday morning, play nine holes and then get back home to help with weekend chores or take the kids to soccer or Little League. Also, many beginners do not have the endurance to play a full-size 18-hole course at first, making the shorter nine-hole venues a necessity.

Speciality courses

Some nine-hole courses are exactly half the length of a normal full-length course.

Usually measuring about 3,000 yards, nine-hole courses often have four par-4 holes, four par-3 holes, and one par-5 hole, making for a nice mix and a good challenge.

Others, known as executive par-3 courses, are comprised entirely of par-3 holes of varying lengths and levels of difficulty. Often measuring less than 1,200 yards total, these smaller courses can be played over a long lunch break or on the way home from work, usually in an hour or less depending on the crowds. The executive par-3 is the course of choice for a complete beginner who needs to master the fundamentals, including the short iron shots, shots close to the green, and putts. Even experienced players love stopping by a par-3 course to work on their short game and practice approach iron shots to the greens.

Finding the right course

Chances are that wherever you decide to play the bulk of your golf you'll have a great time. Just make sure the course is affordable for you so that you can play regularly and improve steadily. Also, look for a course that doesn't get deluged with golfers at the times you can play. Nothing can put a damper on learning the game faster than hordes of golfers in front of and behind you on the course.

How to investigate

To locate courses near you, talk to employees at your local golf store, read local newspapers, buy guidebooks to golfing in your area, and even look in the Yellow Pages. Don't worry: As you become more involved in the sport, you will learn more and more about the courses in your area. Soon you'll know every course within a two-hour drive of your home!

■ **The Yellow Pages** *provides a complete listing of munis, daily fee courses, and private clubs in your local area.*

The driving range: where the real work is done

IF YOU ARE A BEGINNER, odds are that you will soon be spending hours at the local driving range, and for good reason. Once there, you can take your time and hit as many balls as you want without the worry or embarrassment that can come on the course. You can stay for ten minutes or four hours and practice hitting with any club in your bag as many times as you want.

The local driving range is the perfect place to learn how to make consistent contact with the ball — an absolute necessity if you want to play decent golf on the course.

■ **There are an estimated** eight million golfing enthusiasts in Japan, but only a small percentage of these will ever have the opportunity to play on a course due to the shortage of space. The country has more than 4,000 driving ranges, though, many of which are multi-leveled structures or located on top of other buildings.

What to expect

A typical driving range has at least 40 to 50 individual stalls separated by metal or wooden barriers to prevent errant shots from striking the people on either side of you. A large, green artificial turf mat, usually about six feet square, is on the floor of the stall with a metal tray next to it for holding the practice balls you buy from the front desk or get out of an automatic vending machine. A bucket of 50 to 75 balls usually costs anywhere from $4 to $6 and should last you at least half an hour – if you don't rush yourself.

The mat usually has a small rubber tee sticking out of it somewhere close to the edge of one side. You can place a ball atop this and hit it with any club in your bag even though the tee is normally used for the longer clubs, particularly the driver. Most players hit their iron shots straight off of the mat since that most closely resembles hitting from the grass.

Aim for a target

At the driving range, you hit balls out into a large grass or dirt field, which usually has signs placed at measured distances from your stall. When you look out, you can see markers indicating 75, 100, 125, 150, 175, 200, and 250 yards. These will help you quickly learn how far you can hit balls with each of your clubs – something all golfers must know in order to play effectively. Some driving ranges also have simulated greens with flagsticks set up out there at different distances, enabling you to shoot right for the hole.

Whether or not a flag is set up, it is important to actually choose a target when you're hitting balls at the range, to ingrain a feel for playing real golf.

If you simply start pounding balls out into the field without ever focusing on a target, you will never learn to control your shots effectively and will most likely shoot wild on the course. So take your time at the range and always choose a target.

Make each shot matter

It's a good idea to go to the driving range as often as possible while learning to play golf. Perfecting the proper swing and making good, consistent impact with the ball is difficult, and repetition is essential to the process. It's corny but true: Practice makes perfect.

Make sure you don't get into the habit of hitting ball after ball like a machine gun when practicing at the range.

Instead, pretend you are playing a round of golf and that each shot really matters. Take your time and think about each swing carefully. Watching how the ball flies and how far it goes will teach you a lot about golf mechanics and ball flight and better prepare you for the course.

Short-game skills

Many driving ranges also have one or two greens set aside for patrons to practice their short games. If your driving range has these, make sure to spend as much time there as on the range itself. Too many beginners spend all their time banging away with their drivers while ignoring their short-game skills. You should spend at least half your time working on the short shots and on putting as you do hitting full swings with your woods and irons. (Part 3 will discuss this all-important aspect of the game.)

There's nothing like the real thing

If you are lucky enough to belong to a private club or play at a high-end public course, chances are you will have access to a natural grass driving range. These are preferable to the artificial turf ranges because they more closely approximate real playing conditions. Some things are just that simple.

When you're hitting at a grass driving range, you must be considerate about how much damage you do to the grass. When hitting shots with irons, for example, you'll almost always take a chunk of grass out of the ground below and directly in front of your ball. This is

■ **A divot** *is the piece of turf displaced by the club head during a swing. Whether at the driving range or on the course, all divots should be replaced immediately to preserve the condition of the grass.*

called a divot. Taking too many of these will temporarily ruin the turf in your designated practice stall, which means the groundskeepers will have to close it down and re-seed. To minimize this, you should make sure to hit each ball as close as possible to where the last ball was struck. This way, the divot patch you end up taking out of the ground will be concentrated to one small area, instead of spread around.

A lesson or two

Most driving ranges offer reasonably priced group or individual lessons for the beginner.

You should strongly consider taking a few introductory lessons to make sure that your fundamentals are correct, you have the proper equipment, and you have some well-defined short-term and long-term goals for your game.

Without some initial guidance, you might end up going in the wrong direction for months without realizing it. Once bad habits are ingrained in your game, it will be very hard to get rid of them, so don't hesitate to seek out help from the driving-range professional right away. (For more on taking lessons, see Chapter 21.)

Regular practice

Wherever you decided to practice, make sure you do so regularly, especially in the beginning. To learn a new skill, your body and brain need to develop *muscle memory*. The golf swing is a complicated series of muscle actions that have to be performed over and over before they become automatic. That, of course, should be one of your main golfing goals: to not have to think about swinging but instead to just let it happen, leaving your brain to think about course strategy instead.

DEFINITION

Muscle memory is a physical phenomenon that enables your body to perform an action repeatedly in exactly the same way every time without consciously thinking about it.

A simple summary

✓ The objective of golf is to get the ball into each of the 18 holes on the course, one after another, taking as few shots as possible.

✓ Each hole has a par, which is the number of shots it would take a good golfer to get the ball from the tee to the hole.

✓ Golf courses have a number of obstacles designed to make the game harder, such as sand bunkers, ponds and streams, wooded areas, and sections that are out-of-bounds.

✓ There is a golf course in every area and for every budget. Some courses have 18 holes and some have nine. The shorter courses are great for beginners and for getting in a quick game.

✓ A driving range is an excellent place to practice your game. Make sure you practice both your long and short shots as well as your putting at the range.

✓ Always aim for a target when you're shooting at the driving range so you can practice both distance and control.

	Name		White Yards	Par	Yellow Yards	Stroke Index
2	Devil's Den					
3	Golden Valley	391	4	380		
4	The Rookery	494	5	454	11	
5	Pook's Hill	165	3	158	9	
6	Witchcraft Bottom	410	4	410	15	
7	Highwayman's Hide	492	5	446	1	
8	Ringshall	190	3	181	5	
9	Knob's Crook	400	4	390	13	
OUT	Cottons	179	3	175	3	
		361	4	340	17	
		3082	35	2934	7	

TIME

Chapter 3

The Basic Rules

BEFORE YOU GET BEHIND the wheel of a car, you first have to learn the rules of the road, what the traffic signs mean, and what penalties await you if you break the rules. The same goes for golf, which has a hefty number of rules and terms you need to understand and abide by. This chapter is going to get a little bit sticky, but please bear with me. Knowing the rules is important for any game.

In this chapter...

✓ The rule book

✓ The eight most important rules of golf

✓ Still more rules

✓ Keeping score

The rule book

THE UNITED STATES *Golf Association (USGA) publishes an official rule book each year. About 100 pages long, this inexpensive, pocket-size paperback should be required equipment for all golfers. Buy one at your local golf shop and read through it carefully. Make sure you are sitting down before you do so, though, because it is rather complex and filled with clauses, subclauses, and various easily misunderstood golf minutiae, and its list of do's and don'ts seems nearly endless. The reason for its density is simple: The game of golf has evolved over many hundreds of years and, much like our Constitution, the rules need to be amended or reinterpreted every so often to deal with changes in course or equipment design or in the overall way the game is played.*

■ **Scotsman** *Duncan Forbes was instrumental in drawing up the first rules of golf in 1744.*

Although most of your golfing will require you to know only the basic rules and penalties, it's probably a good idea to have a rule book handy.

Resolving disputes

■ **A rule book is** *essential for reference when a query presents itself during the game.*

In addition to specifying every single rule (and believe me, there are many), the USGA rule book gives accurate, official definitions of everything involved with the game, including equipment, the type of game played, and specific parts of the course. Having a copy with you on the course can often help put to rest any argument that might pop up over some little-known rule. So pick up a copy and keep it in your golf bag, just in case you or a playing partner run into a problem.

INTERNET

www.usga.org

The official web site of the United States Golf Association includes a complete rule book, an explanation of the handicap system, tournament structures, and a virtual tour of the golf museum.

The eight most important rules of golf

ALTHOUGH YOU SHOULD EVENTUALLY familiarize yourself with everything in the rule book, in the beginning you need only remember some very basic and important rules – the ones that define the very core of golf and that need to be respected and obeyed in order to maintain the integrity of the game. Many recreational players often do not heed them, as there are no such things as golf police or referees out there enforcing the rules.

If you break a rule, you are obliged to call the penalty on yourself.

Can you imagine that happening in the NBA or the NFL? I don't think so! You should still choose to obey the rules of golf out of respect and honor for the game and its traditions. The following are what I consider to be the eight most important rules you need to remember while out on the course.

Rule 1: Play the same ball, tee to green

You have to play the same golf ball from the tee box of a hole all the way to the flagstick on the putting green. The only exceptions to this rule are if you lose or damage your ball, if an animal or person steals it, or if someone accidentally plays your ball and doesn't realize the error.

Rule 2: Play the ball as it lies

Simply put, you have to hit your ball from wherever it ends up. For example, if you hit your tee shot into a hazard instead of the nice cushy fairway, you cannot pick it up and move it onto the short grass. You must accept the situation handed to you. Fate plays a major role in golf.

However, there are exceptions to this rule. Some situations do allow you to move your ball to a better position. For instance, if your tee shot ends up on top of a sprinkler head, you are allowed to move the ball to a better spot, or *lie*. If your ball is embedded in the ground, you are also allowed to pick it up and move it to a better position. In both cases, you are also allowed to clean the ball before replacing it.

DEFINITION

The spot where your ball rests on the course is called the lie. It can be a good lie or a bad lie, depending on how the ball is sitting and what it is sitting on. A good lie, for example, is a flat piece of closely mown fairway, while a bad lie is high grass on a hill.

In bad weather, many local courses will implement a rule that allows you to pick your ball up, clean it, and then replace it onto a drier spot close to its original position. Called "lift, clean, and place," this rule is only enacted when conditions are extremely muddy and difficult. Although "Play it as it lies" sounds simple, it is probably the most violated rule in the game.

Many a golfer will approach his or her ball after the tee shot, find it sitting in high grass or a divot, and nonchalantly move it to a better lie. Don't be one of these cheaters!

Rule 3: Don't touch the hazard surface

A hazard is not a fun place to be. If your ball finds its way into one, it will be difficult or even impossible for you to get it out and back into play. But touching the surface of the hazard before you try to shoot your way out of it (called grounding the club) would unfairly give you extra information about what is required to get yourself out of this mess.

Many different types of hazard can be found on a golf course. A bunker, also called a sand trap, is probably the most common as well as the easiest to hit out of (if you practice). But when you're setting up to hit your ball out of the bunker, you cannot push your club head onto the sand because this might give you an idea of its consistency, helping you decide on what type of shot to play. Remember, the bunker is supposed to be a punishment of sorts.

Trivia...

St ANDREWS — THE HOME OF THE ROYAL & ANCIENT GAME

The first uniform code of golf rules was written in 1897 by the Royal and Ancient Golf Club of St. Andrews (R&A) in Scotland. Before that, each golf club had its own rules for play. Since 1984 the USGA and the R&A have jointly administered the rules of golf worldwide. They jointly publish Decisions on the Rules of Golf *every year, and once every four years a Joint Decisions Committee meets to review these rules.*

■ **Bunkers** *are carefully sited by course architects to "trap" any wayward shots. For this reason bunkers are rarely found in the middle of the fairway.*

Next is the water hazard, which is always marked by yellow stakes. A water hazard sits somewhere between the tee and the hole. Rivers, streams, ponds, lakes, or even oceans are often located on or next to golf courses and can swallow golf balls. If your ball goes into a water hazard and you decide to try to hit it out (usually not a good idea), you cannot touch the surface of the water with your club before the shot. If you do try to hit out of the water, no penalty is incurred but your chances of successfully hitting out of water are very low. You could end up swatting at the ball ten or 15 times and getting soaked in the process!

■ **Yellow stakes or lines** *mark the edge of a water hazard on the course.*

Most sane players will take relief from the situation, meaning they are allowed to remove the ball from the water and place it in a more playable position. However, there is a price to pay for this relief, and that price is one penalty stroke. In other words, you must add one stroke onto your total score. For instance, if your second shot goes in the water, the relief penalty stroke – your third shot – is the act of taking the ball out of the water, and so score-wise your next shot is your fourth shot.

WHAT TO DO IN WATER

Once you have picked the ball up and added the penalty stroke, you can do either of the following:

a **Drop the ball behind the water**
Drop the ball anywhere behind the hazard on an imaginary line running from the hole to the point where the ball first entered the water.

b **Re-play the shot**
Go back to the spot where you originally hit the shot and play it again.

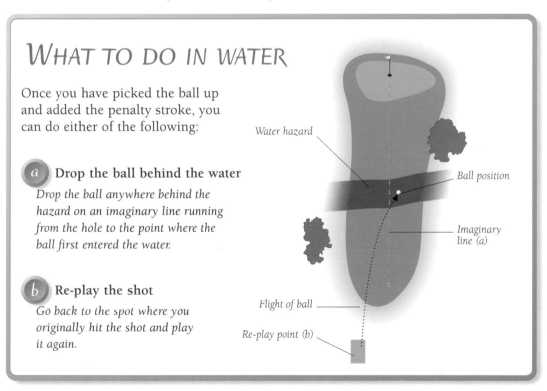

Water hazard

Ball position

Imaginary line (a)

Flight of ball

Re-play point (b)

LATERAL WATER HAZARD

A lateral water hazard, always marked by red stakes, is located on the sides of the hole and will not be positioned between you and the flagstick. Often a meandering stream will border a hole and be considered a lateral hazard. Sometimes a lateral hazard will not even have water but might simply be a dry river bed, gully, ditch, swamp, or some other type of ball-eating mess. Either way, it will be marked with red stakes or a red line spray-painted onto the grass.

Like the regular water hazard, you are welcome to hit your ball out of it if you can, provided you do not ground your club. Or you can do <u>one</u> of the following:

a **Drop the ball behind the water**

Drop the ball anywhere behind the lateral hazard on an imaginary line running from the hole to the point where the ball first entered the water.

b **Re-play the shot**

Go back to the spot where you originally hit the shot and play it again.

c **The two-club drop**

Drop the ball within two club-lengths of the point where the ball last crossed the margin of the lateral hazard.

d **Two-club drop opposite the water**

Identify a point on the opposite side of the lateral hazard (but no closer to the hole), and drop the ball within two club-lengths of that point.

For any of these options, you must penalize yourself one stroke. When you do pick the ball up to move it, though, you are allowed to clean it off.

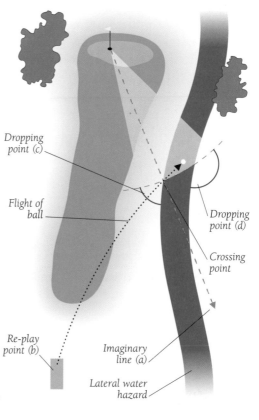

Dropping point (c)

Flight of ball

Re-play point (b)

Dropping point (d)

Crossing point

Imaginary line (a)

Lateral water hazard

REPLACING A LOST BALL – IT'S SIMPLE!

If your ball has been forever swallowed up by the hazard and you must bring out a new ball, the process is simple:

1 Locate the closest spot that allows complete relief from the hazard, and mark it with a tee. This spot could be a few inches or several feet away. Complete relief means that both the ball and your feet are clear of the hazard.

2 Measure out from that spot either one or two club-lengths (away from the hole you're shooting for, never toward it) depending on the situation. For instance, you use two club-lengths when getting relief from a water hazard but only one when getting relief from a sprinkler head or a cart path. Remember to use the longest club you have (usually your driver) to measure this distance. Mark that spot with a tee.

3 Now you're ready to drop the ball. To do so, stand where the marker tee has been placed, hold your ball out at shoulder height and arm's length, and drop the ball straight down without spinning or tossing it at all. It's really that simple. Wherever the ball ends up is where you hit it from, unless it rolls closer to the hole or back into the hazard. If this happens, you have to drop it again.

Rule 4: Going out of bounds

If you hit your ball out of bounds, you must hit the shot again from the same spot and also add a penalty stroke to your score. Like every field of play in every sport, a golf course has clearly defined boundaries. In golf, out-of-bounds is marked either by a series of white stakes placed about 25 yards apart or by a boundary fence. Any golf hole located on the perimeter of a course will have out-of-bounds markers clearly visible on the left or right side of its fairway. Golf holes located well inside the perimeters of a course will not, however, mean that you could hit your ball into the fairway of another hole.

If you are unlucky enough to hit your ball out-of-bounds, you are penalized not only one stroke, but also the distance that you hit the ball. Called "stroke and distance," this means you must drop your ball (or re-tee if the shot was a tee shot) as close as possible to the place you were standing when you first hit it out-of-bounds, and then make the shot again – after penalizing yourself one stroke.

So, if you hit your first shot out-of-bounds, the shot you re-hit will actually be your third stroke.

This is why hitting out-of-bounds is so undesirable: Your second shot will end up really being your fourth – and you won't have gotten anywhere!

Rule 5: If you lose a ball...

If a ball you hit is lost, you must go back to your original hitting position and hit another ball and also add one penalty stroke to your score.

When you first start playing golf, many of your shots will unfortunately veer left or right of your target and often end up in high grass, bushes, ravines, or some other area famous for gobbling up golf balls. When this happens, you must go back to the spot where you hit the original shot, hit again, and add one penalty shot to your score. This means the second shot you hit will actually be your third stroke.

If you hit a ball that appears to be lost, don't immediately go down to where you think the ball might be and start looking.

■ **Only five minutes** *are allowed to find an errant ball, after which time it is officially declared lost. Usually, it is easier to play a provisional ball from the same spot than attempt to find the original one.*

The better course of action is to inform your playing partners that you think your ball might be lost and that you intend to hit another ball, called a provisional ball, from the same spot.

Doing so will help save you the time of looking for your first ball, failing, then having to walk all the way back to your original position to hit again.

After hitting the provisional ball (which you hope this time will end up someplace where you can find it), you should go down to where you think the first ball might be and look for it. You have exactly five minutes to look and can ask your playing partners for help. If you do not find it, you must play the provisional ball. However, if you actually find the first ball you hit, you must play it instead of the provisional ball even if the provisional ball is in a much better spot.

Rule 6: An unplayable ball

If you hit your ball into an unplayable lie, you must penalize yourself one stroke. Eventually, you will hit a shot that ends up inside a bush, stuck under a tree root, or buried deep inside a bunker. This is known as an unplayable lie, which means you just cannot hit a shot. You are the one who decides if a ball is unplayable; you can actually take a swing at anything if you want to. But usually it is a much better choice to declare the ball unplayable and take the one-shot penalty rather than try to hit a miracle shot from an impossible position.

GETTING OUT OF AN UNPLAYABLE LIE

If you hit your ball into an unplayable lie, here are the relief options open to you. Each, by the way, carries a one-shot penalty.

a Drop your ball within two club-lengths of the spot where the ball lies, making sure it does not end up any closer to the hole.

b Draw an imaginary line between the hole and where the ball lies, and drop your ball on a point on that line which is behind the ball's present position. You can go as far back as you want but never closer to the hole.

c Hit another ball as close as possible from where the original shot was played.

Rule 7: Artificial obstructions

You are entitled to relief from artificial obstructions on the golf course, without penalty. An obstruction is simply anything on the course that gets in the way of you hitting your ball. If you find yourself behind a tree, you are out of luck, as this is considered a natural obstruction – it's part of the course itself. If you find yourself behind an artificial obstruction such as a rake, lawn mower, or golf cart, however, you get to move either the obstruction or your ball out of the way without incurring any penalty at all.

■ **Golf carts are artificial** *obstructions from which golfers are entitled to relief without penalty.*

There are two types of artificial obstructions on a golf course. The first, known as a movable obstruction, is typically something like a soda can, rake, cigarette, or candy bar wrapper. Movable items such as these can simply be removed, and then you play your ball where it lies. If the object is actually touching your ball, however, you should first mark and lift your ball, remove the item, then return your ball to its original position.

The second type is known as an immovable obstruction. Bleachers, temporary structures, sprinkler heads, and large trailers are examples of artificial obstructions too large and heavy to be moved by a player. If your ball rolls under an immovable obstruction (or so close to one that you are unable to take a proper swing), you can obtain relief with no penalty at all (whew!).

■ **A sprinkler head** is an immovable obstruction for which you are allowed a free drop if your ball rolls near the edge and becomes unplayable.

To do so, first figure out the closest spot where there is absolutely no interference to your ball and stance. Mark that spot, then measure out from it (no closer to the hole) one club-length and mark this new spot. Standing at the second spot, drop your ball and play it where it comes to rest. If the dropped ball rolls up to or underneath the immovable object again, just repeat the dropping procedure until you get a playable lie.

Walls, fences, or stakes that define out-of-bounds on a course are not considered artificial obstructions, unfortunately. If your ball comes to rest next to or underneath one of these, you must either play the ball as it lies or obtain relief from an unplayable lie, incurring a one-shot penalty in the process.

Rule 8: Loose impediments

All loose impediments can be moved without penalty. Unlike obstructions, loose impediments are naturally occurring objects such as branches, leaves, or stones that are not firmly embedded in the ground and not actually sticking to your ball. If any of these objects are in the way of you making a decent swing, you can simply remove them, provided you do not move your ball in the process. If you move the ball, you incur a one-stroke penalty.

Anything still growing cannot be considered a loose impediment. That means you can't yank a clump of grass or a small plant out of the ground if it is in the way. A worm, snail, or some other kind of little creature is considered a loose impediment, however, and can be moved (gently, please!).

There are some exceptions to this rule.

 Twigs, leaves, and stones *are deemed natural objects that can be easily removed without penalty.*

No loose impediments can be removed from a hazard such as a bunker, pond, or stream.

A replaced divot, no matter how poorly it has been placed back into position, cannot be considered a loose impediment, although a completely detached divot can be. Loose soil on the fairway cannot be moved, but soil or sand on the putting green can be. Dirt adhering to your ball cannot be removed without penalty, unless the ball is on the green or some other rule is in effect that allows you to clean your ball (such as a locally established rule or a rules situation allowing you to move and drop your ball). Got that?

Still more rules

YOU DIDN'T THINK YOU'D get away with just those eight, did you? Although I think those eight rules are the most important, there are a number of other important rules that you must be aware of, including the following:

1. You are limited to a maximum of 14 golf clubs. If you accidentally break one, you can replace it provided you do not delay play. If, however, you break a club in anger, you cannot replace it.

2. You cannot give or take advice from your playing partners.

3. You must tee up your ball within the prescribed teeing area.

ORIGINAL GOLF RULES FROM 1744

4 The order of play on the first hole is determined by drawing lots. On subsequent holes, the player with the best score for the previous hole tees off first. The player with the next-best score goes next, and so on. In the event of a tie on a hole, the scores from the hole before that determine the order of play. Anywhere else on the course, the order of play is determined by whoever is farthest from the hole. The player farthest away goes first, the second farthest goes next, and so on.

5 You may not fix any spike marks that are between your ball and the hole on the putting green. The spikes on the soles of golf shoes can leave marks, but they are just another hazard to be endured. You may fix them after you put your ball into the hole, however. The next group passing through will appreciate it.

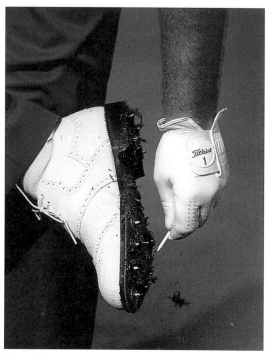

6 You must not putt while another player's ball is in motion.

7 You cannot remove dew or frost from the putting green.

8 You are allowed to wait a full ten seconds to see if a ball teetering on the edge of a cup is going to drop in. After that, you must make another stroke. If the ball drops in on its own after the allotted ten seconds, you must count that as a stroke.

■ **Golf shoes with spikes** *are an essential part of the golfer's equipment but can cause considerable wear and tear to the green. No matter how bad the damage, however, you are not allowed to repair the marks until after the ball has been putted.*

9 If your ball moves after you have positioned your body in preparation to swing, you must penalize yourself one stroke and place the ball back in its original position. If, however, the ball moves before you are in your swing position, you incur no penalty and simply place the ball back in its original position.

10 If your ball lands in *casual water*, you are entitled to relief without penalty. The most common form of casual water is a puddle of rainwater on the fairway. Just determine the closest point that avoids the condition and then measure out one club-length from there, no closer to the hole. Drop your ball from that point and play on. If, however, your ball is in a puddle of water inside a bunker, you cannot obtain relief, as your ball is already inside a hazard. You will just have to resign yourself to getting wet!

■ **Large puddles** *may interfere with play but, unless the puddle of water is in a bunker (as above), you may remove your ball without incurring a penalty.*

11 If your ball lands in *ground under repair*, you are entitled to relief without penalty. The relief procedure is identical to that for casual water.

12 If your ball embeds or plugs itself into soft or muddy turf on the tee box, fairway, or green, you are entitled to relief without penalty. Simply lift and clean the ball, then drop it as close as possible to its original position. This does not apply to a ball that plugs or embeds itself in the rough or anywhere else other than the tee box, fairway, and green.

DEFINITION

Casual water *is a temporary accumulation of water not officially declared a water hazard, such as a puddle.*
Ground under repair *is any area on the course under construction and marked as such by the groundskeeper.*

■ **Winter Rules** *are the set of codes that come into effect during extreme weather conditions.*

If your ball embeds itself outside of these areas, it's tough luck! Sometimes during bad weather, however, a golf course will invoke what are called winter rules, which often allow a player to lift, clean, and replace a golf ball that has become embedded in the rough or has collected mud or grass on it because of the dismal conditions. For you to take advantage of this, the course officials must clearly post a "winter rules in effect" sign.

13   Once your ball is on the putting green, you are allowed to mark its position.
You should do so for two reasons: First, it will enable you to clean your ball,
preventing any adhered dirt from interfering with the ball's roll and perhaps
causing a well-struck putt to miss the hole; second, very often a ball located
close to the hole will interfere with the putting line of someone whose ball
might be farther away. By picking up your ball, you reduce the chances of
interfering with that person's putt.

MARKING YOUR BALL

1   **Place the marker**

*Position a marker or a small coin directly
behind the ball so that it is nearly touching
and pick up the ball.*

2   **Replace the ball**

*Tap the marker down so that it lies flat, clean
the ball with a towel, and return the ball to its
original position to putt.*

14   Once you are on the putting green, you must have the flagstick removed. If
your putted ball strikes the flagstick, you incur a two-stroke penalty. You can
either have the flagstick removed entirely before you putt, or you can have it
attended, meaning a playing partner stands next to the flagstick and pulls it
out just as you stroke your putt. If you choose to have the flagstick attended,
make sure your playing partner checks that it is not stuck in the hole. If he or
she can't get the flagstick out and away by the time your ball gets to the hole,
you will be penalized two strokes. Off the green, you have the choice of having
the flagstick in or taking it out. Some players, when taking a high shot to the
hole from just off the green, like to have the flagstick left in to act as a
backboard for a fast-moving ball. Others prefer to have the flagstick removed.
It's all up to you when you're off the green.

15   You must not play your ball from the wrong putting green. If your ball does
come to rest on any green other than that of the hole being played, you must
drop your ball at the nearest point of relief, usually the fringe of longer grass
surrounding the green.

Keeping score

EVERY GOLF COURSE *gives players a scorecard.*
Having one on hand is a good idea, not only to keep track of
how you are doing but also to learn about the course itself. The
scorecard tells you exactly how long each hole is, what its par
is (that is, how many shots a good player should need to put
the ball in the hole), and how difficult a hole is in relation to
all the others on the course. Some scorecards even supply you
with the layout of each hole, and perhaps even in context of the
entire course – a great aid in deciding just how to play each
one. The map shows you the general layout of the hole, as well
as where hazards, trees, and out-of-bounds areas are located.

> ## Trivia...
> *Until 1951, if a player's ball*
> *blocked your line on the*
> *green and prevented you from*
> *having an unobstructed*
> *pathway to the hole, you*
> *would have to chip over your*
> *opponent's ball to get to the*
> *hole. The rule governing this*
> *circumstance, called a stymie,*
> *was changed in 1951 for the*
> *sake of fairness and to*
> *prevent divots on the green.*

Because every hole has several tee boxes set up at various distances
from the hole, the yardage for each is clearly marked on the scorecard.

The distance to a hole marked on the scorecard is to the exact
middle of the putting green; this may not actually be the distance
to the hole on any given day, however, because the
groundskeepers usually move the hole
each day to keep you guessing and
to prevent one specific area of a
green from becoming overused.

Scorecard

Course map

■ **Study your scorecard** *carefully before*
going onto the green: as well as being a
record of your score it contains valuable
information about the course.

Also listed on the scorecard are two numbers: one is the slope and the other is the course rating. The slope number helps rate how difficult a course is in relation to other courses. The higher the number, the harder the course. An average slope would be somewhere around 113, and a high slope would be around 150 or more. Stay off of courses with high slopes for now; they will give you fits! The course rating is the score that a golfer who typically shoots par would score on that course. The average course usually has a par of around 72, so a golf course with a course rating of 66 would be considered very easy compared to one with a difficult course rating of 76. In the beginning, try to stick to courses with ratings under 70.

Marking a scorecard

On the scorecard there is room for you to write in your name and the names of your playing partners. One of the curious things about golf is that, officially, you do not keep your own score but rather you keep the score of your playing partner. When a professional plays a round of golf, he or she actually records his or her partner's score. At the end of the round, players sign their names to the card they have been in charge of and then hand it over to the partner, who checks it for accuracy and then also signs it. During a tournament, the card is then handed to the scoring officials. This method ensures honesty and also encourages each player to pay attention to his or her partner's game. When you play a friendly round of golf, things are a bit more laid back. You should still think about keeping your partner's score as well as your own, though. This enables you to check for errors and also gives you a concrete record of how you and your friend(s) did.

INTERNET

www.golfcourse.com

A directory of thousands of courses in the United States that includes brief course descriptions, fees, yardage, slope, par, and course rating for every course.

No cheating!

It is very easy to cheat while playing golf. A player can move his or her ball a few inches in order to get a better lie or can blatantly lie about his or her score on a hole. There are no referees or umpires running around the golf course keeping tabs on you.

Nevertheless, be honest out there and play by the rules. The integrity of the game relies on you policing yourself.

If you deserve a penalty, levy it upon yourself and inform your playing partner. It's the right thing to do.

In addition to writing down your overall score on each hole, consider recording how many putts you took on each green. This helps you keep track of your putting progress over the months.

Hopefully, you'll begin to see the number of putts go down over time. In addition, you might consider writing down how many fairways you managed to get onto with your tee shots, as well as how many greens you were able to get onto with your second shot on par-4s, or your third shot on par-5s. The fewer putts and the more fairways hit per round, the better you are doing. You'll enjoy seeing your progress as you play more and get the hang of this game.

A simple summary

✓ It's a good idea to read the USGA rule book and to keep it handy in your golf bag in case a question arises during play.

✓ Although there are no referees in golf, you can show your respect for the game and for your fellow players by following the rules.

✓ Fate will always be your partner in a round of golf. You must play the same ball all the way from tee to green on each hole, and you must play your ball wherever it lands.

✓ In certain circumstances you are allowed to pick up your ball and either move it or drop a new ball. You're never allowed to move your ball closer to the hole, and in most cases you must penalize yourself one stroke for circumventing fate in this way.

✓ A scorecard is handy whether you plan to keep score or not. It tells you how long each hole is, what the par is, and how difficult the course is. Many scorecards also supply little maps of each hole.

✓ Keeping track of total shots, putts, and how you did on your first and second shots will help you chart your progress.

Chapter 4

The Last Friendly Game

ETIQUETTE, DEFINED AS "courteous and polite behavior among group members," plays a big role on the golf course. Unlike other sports, golf continues to maintain a high level of sportsmanship among both amateur and professional players. As a beginner, you should honor and emulate this attitude.

In this chapter...

✓ Who goes first?

✓ Respecting other players

✓ Pick up the pace

✓ How to use a golf cart

✓ What's that you're wearing?

✓ Play an honest game

BROAD SMILES FROM TIGER WOODS AND MARK O'MEARA

Who goes first?

AS I EXPLAINED in Chapter 3, the player with the lowest score on the previous hole has the *honor* on the next. If the score was tied, the player with the lowest score on the hole before that one goes first, and so on. You continue in score order at every tee. Once you're on the fairway, the player farthest from the flagstick hits first. On the green, the player farthest from the hole putts first.

If you're ready to play, you're first to play

Although the rules do state that the player farthest from the hole always hits first, very often players in a group will agree to play ready golf, which means that the player who is ready to take a shot should do so, even if he or she might be closer to the hole, provided no one is in the way.

■ **If you and your playing** *partners decide to play ready golf, just make sure you keep your eye on everyone's position so no one gets hit accidently.*

Respecting other players

GOLF DEMANDS THAT YOU *maintain a healthy respect for your fellow players – much more so than is normally expected in other sports. Apart from common courtesy, one important reason for this is that golf requires a very high level of concentration, and any distractions at all can mean the difference between a great shot and a poor one.*

Too good to be true

Crowds roar at sporting events all over the world, and athletes are expected to perform despite the noise. But not in golf. Everyone is quiet and still. Even the television commentators at pro tournaments whisper on the sidelines. That's the nature of the game, and it actually can be one of its more enjoyable aspects. Imagine spending four or five hours walking in a beautiful park with a bunch of your friends, each one of you striving to be as polite and considerate as possible. Heaven! How many times a week is life like that?

■ **Concentration** *is so important in golf that fellow players and spectators know to respect the rule of silence when a stroke is being played.*

SSShh!!!

VIP

When one of your playing partners is preparing to make a shot take care to remain as quiet and still as possible.

Stop any conversations you might be having, and make sure you aren't fiddling with your clubs or making any distracting movements. There is nothing worse than a player to the side of you suddenly taking a practice swing just as you are about to hit your shot. Make sure you are well off to the side and out of harm's way, as well, because worrying about whacking you with a golf club could cause one of your partners to hit a poor shot. Additionally, watch where your shadow falls, especially early in the morning or late in the day. Make sure it does not fall in front of your opponent's shot.

Repair divots and ball marks

Always fix all your divot and ball marks on every hole. When you're using an iron to make a shot, you will invariably cut a small piece of turf out of the ground and send it flying about ten yards. If it's not quickly replaced, the bare spot left behind will leave the players after you with a potentially terrible lie. When you one day hit a perfect shot only to find your ball inside an unrepaired divot mark, you'll know why it's vital to replace divots! The solution is simple: Fit the divot back into its original spot, then step gently down on it. The grass will re-root itself in a few days.

■ **Replace divots** *and tread them down carefully. If divots and pitch marks are not dealt with immediately the grass on the green or fairway can take weeks to recover.*

Watch your shot

VIP

Always wait until the group ahead of you is clear before making a shot.

For example, if you know you usually hit your first shot about 225 yards off the tee, don't hit your tee shot until the group ahead is at least 250 to 275 yards ahead. Nothing is more obnoxious or dangerous than flying a fast-moving golf ball right into a group of players out in the middle of the fairway, so take care to respect the safety of others.

"Fore!"

And now the moment you've probably been waiting for: If a shot you hit seems to be veering toward another group of golfers, you should immediately yell "Fore!" to let them know an errant shot is headed their way. Likewise, if you hear someone else yell "Fore!" you should duck and cover your head to prevent injury.

■ **Shout "Fore!"** *as loud as you can if you see your ball heading towards other golfers. Nothing hurts more than a golf ball to the head!*

Pick up the pace

ONE OF THE MOST annoying aspects of golf today is the slow pace of play that many of us set on the course. An 18-hole round of golf should ideally take less than four hours, but nowadays it often takes more than five. Although having too many players out on the course can contribute to slow play, the most common reason a round takes so long is that some players just cannot keep up the pace. Too many players take too long deciding what club to hit and what type of shot to take. Many players will take far too many practice swings before hitting. And sometimes a beginner will play a course that is too hard or long, resulting in enormous delays and flaring tempers. (Yes, I do remember I said everyone is supposed to keep their temper in check on the golf course. But there is nothing more annoying than having a player in front of you hit 10, 12, or 14 shots on every hole.)

Speed it up!

Picking up the pace is easy. First, be ready to make your swing as soon as it is your turn. While walking up to your ball, you should already be deciding on what club to use and what type of shot to hit. As soon as you have decided, pull out the right club and wait for your turn. When it comes, take one or two quick practice swings, then let it rip! Next, make sure your level of skill matches the course you play. If you are just starting out, don't tackle a 6,500-yard par-72 course. Instead, play a par-3 nine-hole course or a short, easy 18-hole course. And if you find yourself hitting eight, nine, or ten shots to get to a hole, have the courtesy to pick up your ball, admit that the hole has beaten you, and move on to the next hole. The group behind yours will be forever grateful.

Use the provisional ball

If a ball you hit looks as if it is going to be hard to find, hit a provisional ball before running off to find the first one. If you do not hit a provisional shot and fail to find your first ball, you will have to walk all the way back to the place where you hit the original shot and hit again. Hitting the provisional saves you from having to walk back.

■ **Searching for a ball** *often wastes so much time that it is better to hit a provisional shot immediately.*

Making the turn

In between the *front nine* and the *back nine*, most players head off to the clubhouse for the restroom and to buy food or beverages. After all, they've already been walking around for more than two hours, lugging a bag of golf clubs. Unfortunately, too many players decide to take a 20-minute break at this point, causing delays at the 10th hole that can sometimes be incredibly long. It becomes very difficult to fit those players back into the carefully choreographed order of players coming up behind them. Most golf courses start players at eight- to ten-minute intervals off of the first tee. Take a group out of the rotation and then try to squeeze them in 20 minutes later and you get gridlock. To help speed up play, you should *make the turn* as quickly as possible.

DEFINITION

An 18-hole course is divided into the front nine *holes and the* back nine *holes. When you finish the 9th hole, you* make the turn, *in golf jargon, and head to the back nine.*

Considerate play

Don't go into the restaurant, order a big meal and languish for an eternity.

Instead, consider bringing your own food and quickly purchasing a beverage in the restaurant, or taking a water bottle along with you. Use the restroom, then get back onto the course!

Also, when you approach the putting green, place your golf bag or cart as close to the next tee as you can to save yourself time afterwards. A player who leaves his or her bag on the far side of the green has to cross the green, pick up the bag, then cross the green again on the way to the next tee. If all of your playing partners do this, as much as 45 minutes can be added to your round. Have some empathy for all the groups behind you, and leave your golf bag on the side of the green closest to the next tee!

Don't linger on the green

After you and your playing partners have all sunk your putts, leave the green immediately. Do not stand around talking about that hard putt, the price of beer, or anything else. And do not stand on the green to record your score. Instead, do so on the next tee. This way the group behind you will be able to shoot for the green much sooner.

■ **Make sure you only mark** *your scorecard once you've moved off the green and are on the next hole.*

Let faster groups play through

If you and your group are playing significantly slower than the group behind you, have the courtesy to allow them to play through. In other words, step aside on the next tee and offer them the opportunity to go ahead of you. They will be grateful and you won't feel so pressured to hurry up.

How to use a golf cart

GOLF WAS MEANT *to be played on foot. However, not everyone can walk around an entire course, and there's no reason people who aren't able to do all that walking can't also enjoy a round of golf. If you decide to use a motorized golf cart, keep it on the cart path as often as possible to prevent damage to the course. If the fairways are hard and dry, you can drive on them. If they are soft and muddy, however, keep off.*

INTERNET

www.mrgolf.com

This is the homepage of Mr. Golf Etiquette, who will tell you everything you need to know about playing by the rules and being courteous on the golf course.

Cart etiquette

Park the cart on the side of the fairway and walk over to your ball instead of driving right up to it, which can leave deep ruts in the soft turf.

Never drive a cart onto or near any green.

When approaching a green, make sure you park the cart on the side nearest the next tee. And finally, refrain from driving the cart anywhere near a player who is getting ready to make a swing. If you are driving on the cart path and see someone close by who's about to take a shot, stop immediately and wait until they are done.

■ **Golf carts** *are not allowed near the green and most clubs have clearly marked signs to show when the cart should be driven off the fairway.*

What's that you're wearing?

GOLF HAS A LONG reputation of being a game where people wear plaid pants (perhaps in homage to kilts that the game's founders wore?), pastel-colored shirts, hats with pom-poms on top, white shoes, and other clothes that no one would want to be buried in under any circumstances. This is most definitely not a requirement of the game. Still, while many courses have relaxed their rules concerning what players must wear on the course, most private and a good number of public venues will require you to wear some version of proper attire. This dress code does not require you to have bad taste, but it may require a shirt with a collar and neat, unripped long pants. Some courses will also require you to wear slacks instead of jeans.

■ **Unsuitable attire** *may well find you turned away from the golf club so make sure you abide by the local dress code.*

It's simple: no shirt, no play!

All courses will expect you to wear a shirt of some type, as well as pants, shorts, or a skirt. (Some insist that only women can wear skirts.) Don't expect to be able to walk onto the course in a bathing suit. Additionally, some courses now prohibit the use of metal spikes in your golf shoes, claiming that they damage the greens too much. Instead, they require players to use softer plastic or rubber spikes.

When calling a golf course to make reservations, ask what the dress code is.

In restaurants if you show up without a jacket and tie, they make you wear the lime green tie with the size 42 maroon jacket. This is humiliating, but it's not as humiliating as being forced to buy an overpriced shirt or pair of pants in the pro shop just so you can play a round of golf.

■ **With a touch of humor,** *this Spanish sign clearly states the club's strict dress code.*

Play an honest game

AS I'VE ALREADY MENTIONED, golf is the only sport that requires you to be your own referee. You don't have to, of course. You could cheat on every shot and lie about your score on every hole. But then you wouldn't really know how you're progressing as a golfer, and I'd like to think you're the kind of person who would feel bad about that too. Always play an honest game. Let your partners see you playing by the rules and expect the same from them. Otherwise it's just not golf.

A simple summary

✔ The player with the lowest score on the previous hole shoots first off the tee. If the score was tied, the player with the lowest score on the hole before that one goes first, and so on. Once you're on the fairway, the player farthest from the flagstick hits first. On the green, the player farthest from the hole putts first.

✔ Courtesy and consideration should rule in golf. That means being quiet and still when your partners are taking their shots.

✔ If you're using a golf cart, keep it on the designated paths and try to stay off the grass. The groundskeepers will thank you, and so will your fellow players.

✔ It's important to maintain an efficient, steady pace on the course so you don't drive the group behind you crazy. If you really must play slower, let the group behind you play through.

✔ While many courses have relaxed their dress code, many still have some basic standards for attire. Call ahead to find out what constitutes proper attire so you don't get turned away from a course for wearing shorts or a tee-shirt.

✔ Honesty really counts when it comes to golf. If you don't play an honest game, you're not really playing golf.

PART TWO

TEED UP AND READY FOR PLAY

LEARNING THE FUNDAMENTALS

WHEN THEY'RE FIRST starting out, most beginners look upon the act of hitting a golf ball as a near *magical* occurrence, an incredibly hard combination of movements that might take years to master. The truth is that although hitting a golf ball isn't the easiest *skill* to master, it needn't be as hard as most rookies make it out to be, provided you keep it simple, take things one step at a time, and strive to *understand* just what is needed to hit the ball consistently every time.

This part will walk you through those steps, providing clear, concise definitions and directions so that mastering these new skills will be as *simple* as possible. Follow my advice, and I'll have you swatting that little white ball like a professional!

Chapter 5

How and Why a Golf Ball Flies

A WELL-STRUCK GOLF BALL is a thing of beauty. Leaving the club face at well over 100 miles per hour, this small bundle of energy rockets out like a missile and heads for its intended target. Even an average golfer is capable of hitting his or her tee shot 200 or more yards. How is this possible? The answer is simple, my dear Watson: physics.

In this chapter...

✓ When ball meets club face

✓ The spin

✓ Impact and compression

✓ Buying your balls

✓ Hit down to get the ball up

✓ Power and accuracy

GOLF BALL FLYING OFF THE CLUB FACE AFTER IMPACT

When ball meets club face

WHENEVER THE FACE OF *a golf club hits a golf ball, a tremendous amount of potential energy is released. That energy is converted into velocity and lift, sending your little golf ball soaring up into the air. But where does all this energy come from? There are two answers to that question: the construction of the golf ball and the velocity of the golf club head.*

> **Trivia...**
> The number of dimples on a golf ball can vary depending on the manufacturer, but typically there are between 350 and 500.

USGA golf ball guide lines

First, let's take a look at the makeup and construction of a typical golf ball.

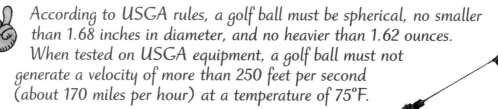

According to USGA rules, a golf ball must be spherical, no smaller than 1.68 inches in diameter, and no heavier than 1.62 ounces. When tested on USGA equipment, a golf ball must not generate a velocity of more than 250 feet per second (about 170 miles per hour) at a temperature of 75°F.

The same ball must not travel farther than 280 yards when hit by the USGA's robotic ball-hitting machine, within a six percent tolerance. Adding that extra six percent to 280 yards gives us a distance of about 300 yards, making most drives by John Daly and Tiger Woods illegal! Except that these guidelines are imposed on the ball, not the players. The USGA draws up guidelines to prevent competitive golfers from using a ball designed to travel significantly farther than most other balls. The limits on velocity and distance are enforced in an attempt to even out the playing field, so no one has a "super ball" that would give them an unfair advantage.

■ **The robotic club-swinging device** *used by the USGA and other golf governing boards to test golf balls is affectionately referred to as "Iron Byron," after the great U.S. golf champion Byron Nelson.*

THE CONSTRUCTION OF THE GOLF BALL

The inside of a golf ball is where much of the magical velocity is born. The ball is usually made in either a two- or three-piece design, and its components contain tremendous amounts of potential energy.

Surlyn, a relatively hard, synthetic, rubber-like substance, is often used to cover less expensive balls, as well as those designed to spin less, travel farther, and last longer. Natural balata, once used to manufacture the covers on golf balls, has now been replaced by a synthetic version. Synthetic balata, much softer than surlyn, is used by better players who want a softer-feeling ball and one that will spin more, enabling them to purposely turn the golf ball left or right according to the shot at hand.

Most amateur golfers tend to use a two-piece ball, however, because they spin less (minimizing errant shots) and last longer.

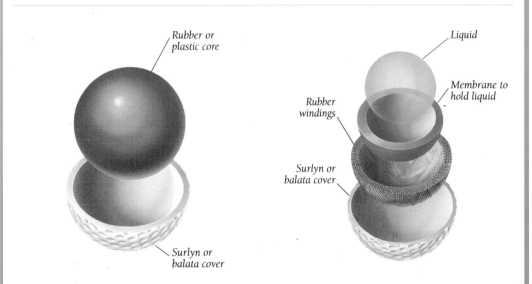

Rubber or plastic core

Surlyn or balata cover

Liquid

Membrane to hold liquid

Rubber windings

Surlyn or balata cover

Two-piece ball

A two-piece ball typically consists of a hard synthetic rubber or plastic inner core and a thin, resilient, durable outer covering made of either surlyn or synthetic balata. The core produces incredible rebounding energy, while the cover gives the ball its unique low spin and durability, making it the more popular choice for beginners.

Three-piece ball

A three-piece ball has either a small, synthetic rubber or liquid core surrounded by a layer of thin rubber windings capped off by a surlyn or balata cover. Most professional golfers use three-piece balls because they have a softer feel and are more workable than most two-piece balls (in other words, you can more easily turn the ball right or left).

Dimples and compression

A golf ball also has hundreds of dimples on its cover. These dimples enable a spinning ball to generate lift, much as an airplane wing does, to get the ball up in the air. Golf balls come with a number indicating compression, which is how densely the ball's inside components are packed. Ranging from a soft compression of 80 up to a whopping hard 110, the compression of a ball has less to do with distance than with the feel. A 100-compression ball will feel relatively hard off of the club face, while an 80- or 90-compression ball will feel softer. Although distances may actually vary somewhat, most amateurs will notice more of a difference in feel than in distance off the tee.

The speed of the club

The other ingredient in the speed and distance of a golf ball is actually the golf club. Basically, the faster the head of the club is traveling when it makes contact with the ball, the farther and faster the ball will travel, provided the face of the golf club is square to the target line. Club-head speeds of the average golfer are typically between 80 and 110 miles per hour, while professionals can hit in excess of 160 miles per hour. When they make contact with a lively little ball, watch out!

The speed of your club head depends on two things: the length of the club and the force you put into swinging it. If you grab a short club (say a sand wedge) and take a lazy half-swing at the ball, you will probably generate a club-head speed of only 40 or 50 miles per hour. Choose a driver, however, the longest club in your bag, and swing it hard, and you'll generate two or three times that speed. That, combined with the driver's small degree of *loft*, will cause the ball to travel much farther and lower than will a sand wedge.

DEFINITION

Loft *is how high up in the air a club will send your ball flying. Every club has a degree of loft, which is the angle the club makes with the ground. For example, a driver's face is nearly vertical – that is, it's perpendicular to the ground when you hold the club straight up and down. A sand wedge is the club with the most extreme loft, which means the face of the club is at a very wide angle to the ground. The lower the number of a club, the less slant, or loft, of the club face.*

Bigger can be better

Surprisingly, the type of material the club head is made of has much less effect on distance than you might think. If the swing speeds are equal, a 44-inch-long driver with a steel head will hit a ball about as far as a 44-inch-long titanium driver. The real advantage of the titanium is its lighter weight, which means the titanium club head can be much larger than a steel head of the same weight. The larger club head provides for a much bigger sweet spot, or effective hitting area, on the face of the club. This is especially helpful for amateurs, who often do not hit the ball with the exact middle of the club face. Even if your ball makes contact an inch to the left or right of the sweet spot it will travel relatively straight, with less distance lost than with a steel-headed club. Also, a club with a titanium head – being lighter – can be swung faster, resulting in more distance.

KNOWING YOUR DISTANCE

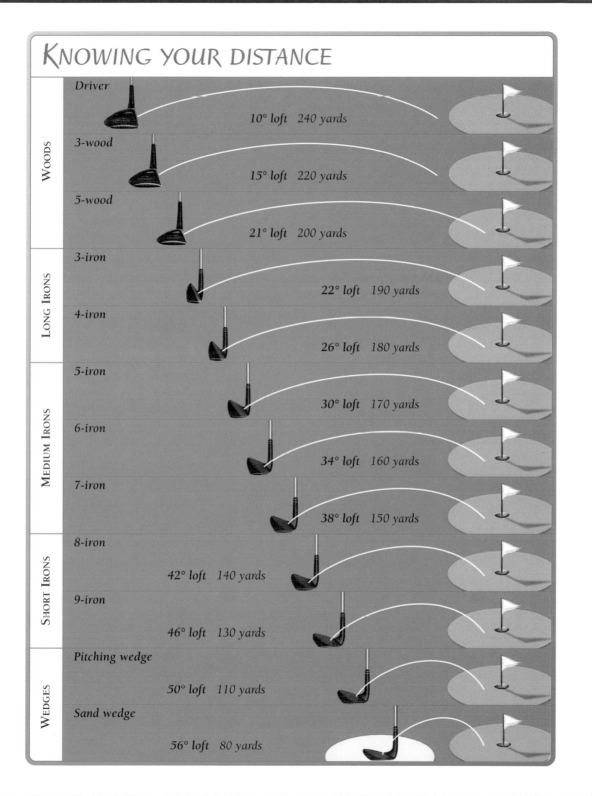

WOODS	Driver	10° loft 240 yards
	3-wood	15° loft 220 yards
	5-wood	21° loft 200 yards
LONG IRONS	3-iron	22° loft 190 yards
	4-iron	26° loft 180 yards
MEDIUM IRONS	5-iron	30° loft 170 yards
	6-iron	34° loft 160 yards
	7-iron	38° loft 150 yards
SHORT IRONS	8-iron	42° loft 140 yards
	9-iron	46° loft 130 yards
WEDGES	Pitching wedge	50° loft 110 yards
	Sand wedge	56° loft 80 yards

The spin

IT'S PRETTY OBVIOUS *that a struck golf ball moves through the air. But it also spins on its own axis as it moves. This is similar to the way the Earth rotates on its axis and also moves around the sun in its orbit. Golf balls can spin backwards and sideways, and the results are very different.*

Backspin creates lift

Backspin

No golf ball could ever get up into the air without backspin. The backward spinning of the ball, in combination with the hundreds of dimples, creates lift, making it possible to launch a ball high up into the air. Without backspin, the ball would never get more than a few feet off the ground.

After being struck by the club head, a golf ball will not only have forward momentum, but will also be spinning backward due to the loft of whatever club was used. A club with a small amount of loft (for example a driver, which can have anywhere from seven to 12 degrees of loft) will impart a small amount of backspin, resulting in a low, boring ball flight. A pitching wedge, however, which usually has about 48 degrees of loft, will impart a large amount of backspin to the ball, resulting in a much higher ball flight.

Sidespin

Sidespin may also be generated when a golf ball is hit, particularly with the longer, lower-lofted clubs. Sidespin can be your friend, but it can also be your great enemy on the golf course. When the club face hits a ball at an angle (instead of squarely), sidespin is generated. If you are a right-handed golfer and you hit the ball with a club face that is turned slightly to your right instead of at right angles to your target line, the ball will spin clockwise and fast in addition to spinning backward. If a golf ball spins clockwise fast enough, it will curve to the right. Known as a *slice,* most of the time this errant shot will end up in trouble. If, on the other hand, a right-handed golfer hits a ball with the club face turned slightly left of the target line, the ball will spin counterclockwise, causing it to curve to the left. Known as a *hook,* this shot will also often end up off the fairway and in some sort of trouble.

DEFINITION

A slice is a golf shot that sharply bends to the right after being hit (by a right-handed golfer). A hook is a golf shot that sharply bends to the left after being hit (by a right-handed golfer). A fade is a golf shot that is deliberately turned slightly to the right (for a right-handed golfer). A draw is a golf shot that is deliberately turned slightly to the left (for a right-handed golfer). For a left-handed golfer, just reverse the terms.

The higher the loft the lower the sidespin

Sidespin usually is reduced in the higher lofted clubs, as the large amount of backspin they generate tends to cancel out much of the sidespin. As the loft of a club decreases, however, the effects of sidespin increase. That is why you are more likely to hit a slice with a driver than with a pitching wedge.

Fading and drawing

Better players use sidespin to their advantage. If, for instance, the fairway on a particular golf hole makes a sharp turn to the right, a good right-handed player will purposely generate some clockwise spin on the ball, thereby turning it onto a path that fits the shape of the hole. This controlled type of slice is called a *fade*. Or, if a fairway turns to the left, a good right-handed player might put some counterclockwise spin on the ball to turn it slightly to the left. This controlled type of hook is called a *draw*.

In the beginning don't worry about creating sidespin. Just hit the ball as straight as possible, which means with as little sidespin as possible.

Your job as a beginner will be to keep your ball in fair play on every hole. When you begin to shoot some low scores, you can start thinking about working the ball to the left or right, according to the design of the hole.

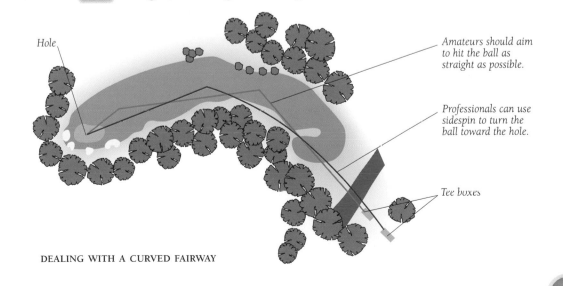

Hole

Amateurs should aim to hit the ball as straight as possible.

Professionals can use sidespin to turn the ball toward the hole.

Tee boxes

DEALING WITH A CURVED FAIRWAY

Impact and compression

THE MOMENT THE GOLF ball is contacted by the face of your golf club, amazing things happen. This moment is called impact. At impact, the ball will compress substantially for a microsecond or so before jumping off the club face. This flattening of the ball is the secret to how far it can travel. When the ball rebounds from this compression, an incredible amount of energy is released, causing an explosive reaction. The ball zooms up and out toward its target.

How far does it go?

The amount of compression that occurs dictates the distance the golf ball will travel. The reason it goes farthest when hit by a driver, then, is simple: There is more compression due to the high speed of the swing for this longest of clubs. When the speed is combined with the driver's small amount of loft, the golf ball really gets a quick, long ride. In comparison, a pitching wedge generates a much lower swing speed and compresses the ball less. That combined with the wedge's much higher degree of loft, causes the ball to travel higher and about one-half to one-third the distance.

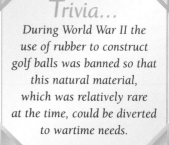

Trivia...
During World War II the use of rubber to construct golf balls was banned so that this natural material, which was relatively rare at the time, could be diverted to wartime needs.

Golf clubs with more loft will spin the ball more at impact because of the angle at which the club face contacts the ball. The clubs with the least amount of loft (the driver and the putter) will impart the least amount of spin to the ball.

With a driver, less spin means a lower, longer shot with more roll after the ball touches down; with the putter, little or no spin enables you to keep the ball on the green rolling toward the hole.

■ **Pros like Tiger Woods** *have incredible club-head speeds, often in excess of 120 miles per hour, which explains why they can hit the ball much farther than the average golfer.*

Buying your balls

CHOOSING A GOLF BALL used to be fairly easy. Professionals chose a high-spin, three-piece, balata-covered ball, while the rest of us went with a rock-hard, surlyn-covered, two-piece ball that cost less and lasted longer. Today, though, things have changed. There are so many golf ball varieties that choosing the right one isn't easy. Let me give you some details and guidelines to help keep it simple.

What's out there?

In general, you can place today's golf balls on a left-to-right scale, with the far left being the soft, expensive, high-spin, three-piece, control-type balls that the pros use, and the far right being the hard, inexpensive, two-piece, low-spin, distance balls that many amateurs and beginners use. In the middle of the scale are the multipurpose balls that offer a golfer a reasonable amount of control and feel while still providing ample distance off the tee.

> **INTERNET**
>
> www.golfballzone.com
> www.cheapgolfballs.com
> www.virtual-fairway.com
>
> *All three sites sell reconditioned golf balls, which are used balls that have been improved in some way. Look for balls with new covers as opposed to ones that have merely been cleaned.*

Choosing the right ball for you

This scale relates nicely to golfers' different skill levels. Beginners should usually start off at the far right end with a low-spin distance ball to help keep their shots in play. As your skills improve, though, the type of ball you use can move slowly but surely to the left. When you get better at controlling the flight of your ball on the course, you'll probably want to switch to a ball that responds better to your inputs – just like a race car driver prefers a sportier, more responsive automobile, while the average driver wants a car with safer, more predictable characteristics. A great golfer wants to spin the ball a lot, to hold the greens and to curve the ball left or right, according to the shape of the hole. He or she isn't concerned as much with squeezing every last yard out of a drive. These are the attributes of a high-spin, three-piece ball, the expert's choice. A beginner wants to maximize distance and hit straight shots, qualities found in low-spin, two-piece balls.

To start, go out and get a good supply of inexpensive two-piece golf balls with surlyn covers. They'll spin less and go farther, two attributes you as a beginner will need.

Also, they'll cost about half as much as three-piece balls – an important factor to consider for any rookie golfer, who will (trust me on this) lose dozens of balls during the first year or two of play. A dozen two-piece balls usually costs less than $20, compared with $30 or more for the high-spin balls. The surlyn cover on the two-piece, low-spin balls will last longer than the synthetic balata covers on high-spin balls, too. As an added plus, many manufacturers now make these two-piece balls with a soft yet durable cover, allowing a bit more spin during flight and a softer feel when putting.

Stick with a 90-compression ball instead of a 100, as this will give the ball a slightly softer feel at impact.

Number indicating compression of golf ball

HVC ▲ 90

You might even try an 80-compression ball, although most players find them to be a bit too soft at impact. Only after you begin to play a more consistent game should you consider going to a higher-spin ball, which will hold the greens better and enable you to shape your shots to the left or right, according to the situation at hand. But don't hesitate to try out a softer, high-spin ball just to experience the difference in feel.

And finally...

Just a few last points about golf balls, and then I'll stop.

1. Golf balls have a finite shelf-life and will begin to lose some of their resiliency after a year or so, resulting in a measurable loss of distance off the tee. Three-piece balls will suffer from this much more than two-piece balls.

2. Any golf ball will suffer a measurable loss of distance when the ball is cold. If you're playing on a particularly cold day, consider keeping a ball or two inside your jacket pocket. Handle the balls a bit while you're walking the course (no snickering, please) to keep the inner layers as warm as possible. Then just alternate balls from tee to tee, always using a warm one and placing the ball from the previous hole into your pocket to warm up.

3. Always mark your ball in an easily identifiable manner so you can distinguish it from other balls on the course. This will help prevent other players from accidentally (or purposely) playing your ball. Use a laundry pen or magic marker, and be creative. Use your initials, a funny face, your lucky number, or maybe the name of your dog.

MARKING YOUR BALL

Hit down to get the ball up

IT SOUNDS CRAZY, BUT with every club except the driver and putter, you must strike the ball with a slightly descending blow. This enables the built-in loft of the club head to send the ball up into the air. Hitting the ball with a descending blow also helps compress the ball more at impact, releasing more energy and driving the ball farther.

A common mistake for beginners

Many beginners try to lift or scoop the ball up into the air with their irons and fairway woods.

Hitting up on the ball, as it's called, is a big mistake and will only bring you missed hits and poor distance.

When swinging your irons and fairway woods, the very bottom of your swing arc should be just a fraction of an inch beyond the bottom of your ball. Watching a good player hit the ball with a 7-iron, for instance, you can see this for yourself. The good player's grass divots always start in front of the ball's position – never behind – meaning that he or she is contacting the ball first, with a slightly descending blow, and then contacting the turf in front of the ball. When this is done properly, the ball is momentarily squeezed between the club face and the turf, increasing compression and the resulting distance. Hitting up on the ball with your irons or fairway woods will cause the club head to miss the ball completely, or else make contact only with the top of the ball.

■ **Remember** *to hit down on the ball so that it is squeezed between the club face and the turf: this will increase compression and send the ball farther.*

91

The exception to the rule

Hitting with your driver is a different story. You want to hit a slightly ascending blow with it, to help get the ball up into the air. Most drivers have very little loft, which is why you have to raise the ball up off the ground about an inch or so for shots with your driver. And that is why some clever golfer invented the tee. Unlike with your other clubs, the bottom of your driver's swing arc should actually be an inch or so behind the ball. Because of this, you not only tee the ball up, but you also move the ball farther forward in your stance at a point opposite to or just inside the left heel (for a right-handed golfer). I know, this is getting pretty complicated.

Swing path of a driver

Tee

Driver creates 10 degrees of loft

■ **To compensate for its low loft,** *the driver must strike the teed-up ball with an ascending blow in order to send it high into the air.*

Just remember that when hitting the ball, the driver is the only club that requires you to hit up on the ball.

Power and accuracy

EVERY GOLFER WANTS *to cream the golf ball, plain and simple. There is no better feeling in the world than taking a smooth, graceful, long swipe at that terrified little ball and seeing it rocket down the fairway. Equally pleasing is seeing that same ball land accurately in the fairway or, even better, on the green.*

Getting it right

Achieving these two goals is what golf is all about. Even the pros struggle with them every day. For you, the beginner, the most important factor that will help create power and accuracy is simple:

You must make consistently good contact whenever you strike the ball.

This means you must:

 Contact the ball with the club head right on the sweet spot, that small central portion of the face. Striking the ball even an inch away from the sweet spot will result in much less power and accuracy.

 Hit the ball with a club face that is perfectly square, that is, perpendicular to the desired ball path.

3 Swing the club in such a way that impact occurs when the club head is traveling directly down the desired ball flight path.

Sounds difficult? Guess what? It is! But that is the beauty of golf: Every now and then everything falls into place and you hit that perfect shot. And when you learn to swing properly, everything will happen naturally without you having to think about it. When you get to that point, you'll hit the ball with power and accuracy, lower your scores, and play an enjoyable game of golf.

A simple summary

✔ A golf ball's energy comes from the velocity of the golf club head and the construction of the golf ball. Its construction enables it to spin fast and fly high and far.

✔ The loft of a club creates backspin when the ball is hit. This, combined with the dimples on the ball, is what makes a golf ball rise.

✔ One of the basic rules of golf is that with all clubs except the driver and putter, you have to hit down to get the ball up in the air.

✔ A key secret to power and accuracy in golf is to make contact with the ball directly on the sweet spot of the club face.

✔ Start out using a distance golf ball, which will spin less than other balls and go farther. When you're just beginning, you want less spin in order to minimize the effects of hooking or slicing the ball.

✔ Have at least a dozen balls in your bag at all times. Trust me: You're going to lose some.

Chapter 6

What Equipment Will You Need?

GOLFING EQUIPMENT has evolved quite a bit over the last 100 years. Both golf clubs and golf balls have changed dramatically in variety, design, and the materials used to make them. This chapter provides you with a soup-to-nuts primer on basic golf equipment and suggests what you as a beginner should consider buying so you can play the game right. Everything is included, so read on, and remember: try to keep it simple.

In this chapter...

✓ Clubs, clubs, clubs

✓ Custom-fitting

✓ What clubs should I buy?

✓ Your golf bag

✓ Clothes and accessories

A SELECTION OF IRONS

Clubs, clubs, clubs

TODAY, MANY DIFFERENT companies manufacture a dizzying assortment of golf clubs that cater as much to a player's sense of taste as to his or her needs. Everyone seems to rush out and buy the next "hot" club in the hope that it might dramatically improve their game. Although some designs work better than others for certain golfers, the bottom line is that it's less about the club and more about your own skills. That said, it is important to use clubs that fit your type of game and your body.

3-wood
5-wood
4-iron
6-iron
8-iron
Pitching wedge
Putter

THE TYPICAL BEGINNER'S SET

How much should you spend?

Visit your local golf shop and you'll be amazed at the variety of clubs available. The good news is that you no longer need to spend an arm and a leg to buy a decent set of high-quality clubs. A good beginner's set, including irons, woods, and a putter, needn't cost you more than $350. Most beginners shouldn't consider going out and buying an expensive set of clubs anyway because your constantly improving golf skills will probably require you to change some or all of your equipment at some point.

What about used clubs?

Another important point to consider before buying your clubs is that, quite frankly, you may find that golf is just not your game. If that happens, you don't want to be stuck with an expensive set of golf clubs that will probably end up sitting in your garage for ten years waiting to be sold at some future flea market. So it might be a good idea to buy a few used clubs at first (someone else's expensive clubs that they hardly ever used), or borrow some from a friend just to see how they feel and if the mechanics of the game suit you. Much of your introduction to the game will be spent at the driving range anyway, so having a full set of clubs won't be crucial at first.

As long as you have access to a 3-wood, a 5-iron, an 8-iron, a sand wedge, and a putter, you'll be able to get a good feel for things.

If you know that golf is going to be your chosen game, however, you can consider buying a full set of clubs. But just what exactly does a full set of clubs consist of? You are allowed to carry up to 14 clubs in your bag and no more. But that doesn't mean you can't buy more.

Choosing the right club for the right conditions

Part of the fun of the game is deciding which of your 14 clubs you will decide to use on any given day. This can change according to the conditions on the course you are playing and what kind of day you're having. For instance, a 5-wood and a 3-iron will hit a ball about the same distance, but the wood will hit a much higher shot that lands more softly and rolls only a short distance. In comparison, the 3-iron will hit the ball on a much lower trajectory, causing the ball to roll farther after landing. If you're shooting for a small green on a windless day, you might opt to use the 5-wood. But if you're shooting for a large green on a windy day, the 3-iron might be your best choice because its lower-trajectory ball flight will be less affected by the wind. The larger green will also accommodate the ball's longer roll. So you can see that choosing the right club for the right conditions is part of playing the game.

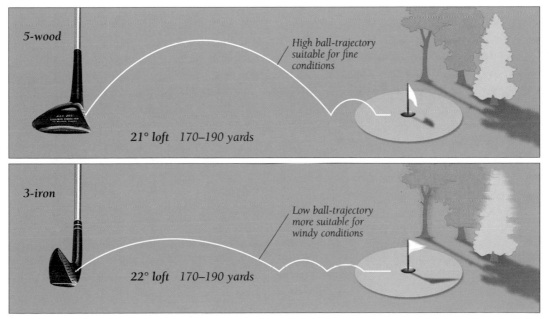

5-wood

High ball-trajectory suitable for fine conditions

21° loft 170–190 yards

3-iron

Low ball-trajectory more suitable for windy conditions

22° loft 170–190 yards

■ **The diagram above** *demonstrates the different trajectories of the 5-wood and the 3-iron. In windy conditions the 3-iron's lower trajectory will allow you to direct the ball more accurately.*

A CHOICE OF CLUBS

a Woods

Woods use a large, pear-shaped metal or wooden head to hit the ball. Woods also generally have longer shafts than irons do. There are two groups of woods. The first, drivers, typically have a large head and a deep, high face and are usually used to hit the ball off the tee. Drivers can vary in loft from seven degrees to over 12. The second, fairway woods, tend to be smaller and have a somewhat shallower face than drivers do. Fairway woods, often numbered, can vary from a 2-wood all the way up to a 9- or even an 11-wood. The higher the number, the more loft the wood has – just like the irons.

DRIVER **3-WOOD** **5-WOOD**

■ **The driver** is the longest and most powerful club in the bag. Fairway woods are safer options for the beginner.

b Iron woods

Iron woods are a comparatively new category of clubs that are a hybrid design, combining the best attributes of woods and irons. Available in different lofts, these clubs provide players with the precision of an iron and the power and high flight of a wood. Originally designed as an easier-to-hit alternative to the long iron (which can be difficult for the beginner to master), iron woods have a very low center of gravity (like today's shallow-faced fairway woods) and a shorter shaft than most woods on the market. This combination makes them easier for the beginner to swing.

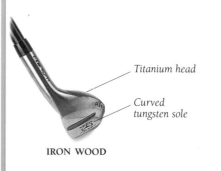

Titanium head

Curved tungsten sole

IRON WOOD

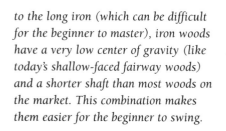

18° LOFT   **21° LOFT**   **24° LOFT**

■ **Iron woods** are easy to use and are an ideal choice for beginners.

DRIVER   **SAND WEDGE**

c Irons

Irons use a metal blade to hit the ball. The blade can be solid or cavity-back. Within this group are four subgroups. The long irons (typically numbered 1 to 3) are those designed to hit the ball a long way. Mid-irons (typically numbered 4 to 6) are for medium-range shots, and the short irons (typically numbered 7 to 9) are for shorter shots. The fourth subgroup contains the wedges. The high-lofted wedges (pitching, attack, sand, and lob) are used either to hit very short, high shots to the green or to get out of a hazard or some other type of trouble. The pitching wedge is the least lofted of the wedges, while the lob wedge has the most loft.

DEFINITION

A cavity-back iron is a type of iron that has most of the weight of the club head located around its perimeter to create a larger head and a larger sweet spot on the face. The back of the club head is essentially a large cavity, which reduces mass in the center and back of the head. Cavity-backs tend to be more "forgiving" of mis-hit shots.

Sweet spot

Heel

Toe

Grooves for spin

3-IRON   6-IRON

■ **Irons** *have grooves on the club face to give the ball spin.*

d Putters

Putters use different styles of metal heads to roll the ball along the green. There are many putter designs, including the traditional heel-shafted blade putter, the center-shafted blade, the mallet, and the semi-mallet. The putter is probably the most individualized club in the bag, and you'll have to try out a number of different designs before deciding on one. Nowadays, most are made of metal and often have a plastic insert built into the face that helps modulate the way a ball feels and acts when it is struck. Putters also come in a wide variety of lengths so you can choose the one that best fits your height.

IRON   PUTTER

■ **Putters,** *like the heel-shafted blade putters, bear little relation in design to the other clubs in your bag.*

TOE-AND-HEEL
PUTTER

OFFSET TOE-AND-
HEEL PUTTER

Custom-fitting

MORE AND MORE, TODAY'S *golfers are opting to have their clubs custom-fitted to their own shape, body type, and style of swing. A player well over six feet tall shouldn't have to play with the same off-the-rack clubs that suit someone much shorter. Likewise, someone with short arms and long legs will need a different fit than will a player with long arms and a short torso. You too may want to have your clubs adjusted to fit your body and playing style. Most good golf shops either provide the service or can refer you to a qualified fitter. Here are the most important adjustments to address when you're having a set of clubs custom-fitted.*

Shaft length

Obviously a child cannot use the same clubs as Michael Jordan. Your club fitter will determine the right length for each of your clubs. This can vary by as much as ten or 12 inches within a full set of clubs. For instance, most drivers sold today measure about 44 to 45 inches long, but the same person who uses that driver might need a 33-inch putter. Why? Because the way you stand and swing is very different when you're hitting a putt than when you're hitting a drive.

The average 5-iron measures about 38 inches long, while a sand wedge might be 35 inches or less. Generally, each iron in a set will decrease in length in about half-inch increments, going from the least-lofted long iron to the highest-lofted wedge. Woods, though generally longer than irons, will also decrease in length from the driver on down to the higher-lofted fairway woods.

Shaft flex

The stiffness, or flex, of your club shafts must be matched to the speed at which you typically swing your clubs. Called swing speed, this measurement varies tremendously from golfer to golfer. For instance, a child may have a swing speed of no more than 50 or 60 miles per hour with his or her driver, whereas a large, strong man might swing his driver at over 100 miles per hour. Some professionals can actually swing a club at over 160 miles per hour!

INTERNET

www.missilegolf.com

For something completely different, Peace Missile offers golf clubs made from Russian and U.S. nuclear missile parts.

Having the right flex in your clubs will enable you to achieve the most accuracy and distance possible for your swing speed. Too little flex and you won't get maximum distance; too much and your accuracy will suffer.

Shafts come in numerous flexes, including lady's, senior, regular, stiff, and extra stiff. Those of you who have an average swing speed of around 85 to 90 miles per hour should go with a regular flex shaft. Slower swingers should go with lady's or senior, while fast, strong swingers will need stiff or extra stiff. (Just to set the record straight, while the more flexible design is called "lady's," professional women golfers don't use them, and neither do good women golfers.) Your local golf shop will be able to measure your swing speed with a small device placed a few feet behind your ball.

TESTING THE LIE ANGLE

The lie angle of a club is the angle the shaft makes with the ground when the bottom of the club head is resting flat on the ground. Off-the-rack clubs come with a standard, factory-determined lie angle for each club in a set. These usually work out just fine for people of average height and arm, leg, and torso length. For unusually short or tall individuals or for those with other unique dimensions, the lie angle may need to be larger or smaller. The idea is that the bottom of the club head should be exactly parallel to the turf at the moment of impact. Try this coin test to ensure the club sits perfectly.

a Lie angle too upright

If the coin slips under the club toe to about halfway the lie is too upright and will result in poor contact and shots that go left of the intended target.

b Lie angle too flat

If the coin won't slip under the club toe, the lie of the club is too flat. This will also cause poor contact and shots that go right of the intended target.

c Correct lie angle

The perfect lie is found when the coin slips neatly up to one third beneath the club toe. If this is achieved the club is at the right angle for your height.

Although golf stores typically carry only standard-lie clubs, club manufacturers offer (by special order) clubs that are two degrees flat or two degrees upright. Most golfers are able to adequately use either the upright, standard, or flat lie angles. Regardless of the lie angle you need, well-stocked golf stores usually have a club fitter on the premises who will be able to determine what lie angles your clubs should have. Even if you need more or less than the special-order two-degree deviation, the fitter can help you adjust a set to your specific needs.

Grip size

Just as glove or shoe sizes vary according to the individual, so should the grip size on golf clubs. Unfortunately, many newcomers to the sport settle for whatever size grips are on the clubs when they buy them, even if they are too large or small for their hands. You needn't settle, though. Most golf equipment retailers will happily change the size of the grips on the clubs you buy, to ensure customer satisfaction. And why shouldn't they? You wouldn't buy a $400 suit or dress if the retailer refused to tailor it to your body, would you? Club fitters usually change the grip diameter by increasing or decreasing the amount of grip tape applied to the club shaft underneath the grip itself. For players with extremely small or large hands, however, the standard grip will need to be changed for one more suitable to the person's hand size.

VIP

Generally speaking, the larger the hand, the larger the grip required. If the grip is too small, your hands will whip the club around too fast, possibly causing a hook. If the grip is too large, you may not be able to use your hands properly in the swing, possibly causing you to slice the ball.

Ring finger touches the palm of the hand

THE SIMPLE GRIP TEST

To determine if a grip is the right size for you, grasp the club with your left hand (for a right-handed golfer) and note the position of the tip of your ring finger. If it lightly touches the palm of your hand, the grip is the right size. If the tip of your finger does not touch your palm, the grip is too big. If your ring finger digs into your palm or curls around and underneath the grip, the grip is too small. It's as simple as that.

What clubs should I buy?

IF YOU ARE SERIOUS ABOUT *learning the game of golf and are committed to buying a good working set of clubs, here are some simple guidelines for what you will need.*

Irons

Most beginners should consider buying a set of eight irons, from the 3-iron all the way up to a pitching wedge. And most matched sets include those as a matter of course. However, you probably won't be using the 3- or 4-irons right from the start, because they tend to take some time to master. Most beginners should also consider buying three additional wedges: an attack or gap wedge (which typically has about 52 degrees of loft, or four degrees more than a pitching wedge), a sand wedge (with about 56 degrees of loft), and a lob wedge (with about 58 to 60 degrees of loft). Including the pitching wedge, this means you would have four wedges in total. Until recently, it was rare to see golfers with more than just a pitching wedge and a sand wedge. Limiting yourself to these two, however, may limit the options for your short game.

INTERNET

www.golfsmith.com

This site has one of the largest assortments of clubs and other golfing equipment offered anywhere. You can buy new brand-name equipment and even purchase club components and assemble your own.

That's because the average golfer will hit the ball about 110 to 120 yards with a pitching wedge and about 85 to 90 yards with a 56-degree sand wedge. That leaves at least a 20-yard gap between the two.

To hit a shot of around 100 yards, a player would have to either "nuke" (hit a hard, committed shot) a sand wedge, or "baby" (play a short, soft shot) a pitching wedge, neither of which is easy to do with accuracy. Having a gap wedge in your bag takes care of this problem nicely; you can take a nice full swing and easily hit that 100-yard shot.

Likewise, if you were about 70 to 75 yards from the hole, you would be forced to halfheartedly hit a sand wedge. This cuts down on your accuracy and on ball spin, which is necessary to get the ball on the green. Having a lob wedge in your bag, however, would enable you to take a full swing, generate plenty of ball spin, and hit the ball just about 70 to 75 yards. For a beginner, these shorter shots in and around the green will be very common, because most of the time you won't hit your ball cleanly onto the green. So, strongly consider having these wedges in your bag. They will help your score!

Woods

You aren't going to like what I have to say now, but here goes. Forget about buying yourself that big, fancy, $400 driver for now. As a beginner, you'll have much better success using a 3-wood, which hits the ball higher and almost as far and is much easier to learn to use than the driver primarily because it is shorter. Most beginners do not generate enough club-head speed to hit a ball very far with a low-lofted driver anyway; many actually hit the 3-wood farther due to the extra loft.

Your beginning set of woods should include a 3-, 5-, and 7-wood to cover tee shots and fairway shots varying in length from 160 yards to over 200. Fairway woods are easier to hit with than long irons and they also hit the ball higher, which you need to do as a beginner. The 5-wood takes the place of a 2-iron (which few golfers now use), and the 7-wood takes the place of the 3- or 4-iron. Yes, you will have a 3- and a 4-iron in the set of irons you purchase, but you won't be using them until your game improves substantially.

Putters

As the most frequently used club in the bag, your putter is a vital scoring club. You'll need to take your time selecting yours. Most decent golf stores will have a small putting green inside for you to practice on, so grab a few different styles of putters and give them all a try. Also, if you have friends who play golf, ask to try their putters. Choosing a putter is a highly personal, subjective process; you have to like the way the putter feels, sounds, and looks. Yes, looks. Even the pros base their choice of putters partially on how they look when addressing the ball. When you find one that really seems to work for you, buy it!

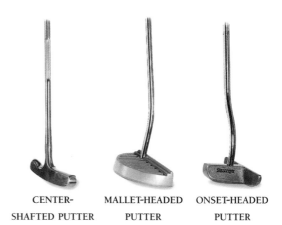

CENTER-SHAFTED PUTTER   MALLET-HEADED PUTTER   ONSET-HEADED PUTTER

■ **Putter heads** *come in a wide variety of shapes and designs so choose one that suits you for length and lie. Most putters have a visible sweet spot line or dot to help you guide your stroke.*

Counting clubs

Okay, so what clubs do we have so far? Of the irons, you'll at first want to use the 5, 6, 7, 8, 9, and pitching wedge (that's six clubs), and the attack (52-degree), sand (56-degree), and lob (60-degree) wedges. So far, that's nine clubs. Then we add the 3-, 5-, and 7-woods. That makes 12. Adding the putter brings the total up to 13.

Wait a minute, you say? You thought the USGA allows players to carry 14 clubs? They do, but that doesn't mean you have to use 14. Eventually, when you begin to make consistently good contact with the ball, you will want to buy a driver, bringing your total up to 14. And once you begin to hit your 5-iron with consistency, you'll be able to substitute your 3- or 4-iron in place of the 7-wood, especially when playing on a windy day. You need not do this, however; you may actually find that the 7-wood has become your favorite club and let those long irons collect dust in the garage.

Your golf bag

YOU NEED SOMETHING *to carry all those clubs around in, and that's your golf bag. Deciding what type of golf bag to use should be simple. Apart from personal taste, the choice will depend on whether or not you intend to carry your bag, use a pull cart, or regularly rent an electric or gas-powered golf cart. If you intend to walk the course most of the time, think about buying the smallest, lightest bag possible to prevent backaches, sore shoulders, and excess fatigue. A bag you plan to carry should also have a retractable stand built into it — one that uses lightweight metal or plastic legs that pop out as soon as you put the bag down. This feature makes club selection a breeze.*

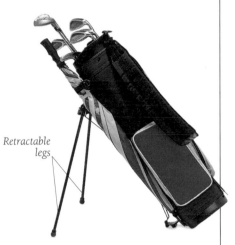

Retractable legs

GOLF BAG WITH STAND

The big bag

If you intend to use a pull cart exclusively, you can go for a heavier, more spacious bag that enables you to carry more accessories, food, water, and other items that might not be practical to take in a bag you have to lug around on your shoulder. The bag you buy for use with a pull cart must be able to fit properly onto the cart. Many golf bags have large pockets on three sides; invariably a bag like this will have access to one or more of its pockets either partially or totally obscured by the cart's frame or straps. Make sure the bag you buy does not have this problem.

■ **If you always** *ride in a powered cart, your bag can be as large and involved as you want it to be. After all, you don't have to lug it around.*

105

Club compartments

Whichever option you choose, your golf bag must be able to comfortably hold all your gear. Consider choosing a bag that has at least six club compartments separated from each other by full-length dividers. This will keep your clubs from getting all tangled during your round. Some bags have 14 separate compartments, one for each club. Also, make sure the top of each club compartment is covered with some type of soft material that won't mar or scratch the graphite shafts that are found on so many clubs sold today.

Divider

■ **Compartments**
prevent the club heads and shafts from being scratched each time you pull them from the bag.

Good storage space

The bag you choose should have several small to midsize, zippered pockets for holding a multitude of accessories, from shoes and gloves to water bottles, golf balls, and sandwiches. It should also have at least one large, zippered compartment for holding a jacket, a sweater, or rain gear.

Start out small and light

My best advice is to get the smallest, lightest bag that will comfortably and efficiently carry all the gear you need. This will give you the option of carrying it if you choose to – an option that will really get your heart pumping.

Walking the course is always preferable because it enables you to experience the game on a more intimate level.

Trivia...

The PGA Tour has a rule in effect prohibiting the use of carts during tournament play, claiming that walking is an essential part of the competition. But in 1998 professional golfer Casey Martin, afflicted from birth with a crippling disease that restricts blood flow to his left leg, sued for the right to use an electric cart during professional PGA Tour-sanctioned events. Casey won his suit and is now allowed to use a cart on the Buy.com Tour and in whatever PGA Tour events he qualifies for in the future.

Clothes and accessories

WHAT YOU WEAR on the course is pretty much up to you, provided you meet whatever dress code the course has established. Try to wear clothing that won't restrict your swing, regardless of the temperature. This often means going with layers instead of a big, cumbersome jacket.

WET-WEATHER GEAR

Come rain or shine

Make sure you have proper rain gear if you intend to play in inclement weather. During a light shower or mist, a water-resistant, windbreaker-type pullover will probably be sufficient. For a steady rain, though, a full rain suit may be necessary. Prices and styles vary tremendously, so shop around at various well-stocked golf shops in your area before you buy anything. When it's hot out, be sure to wear light-colored clothes to reflect the heat. Avoid wearing a tank top because walking in the hot sun for five hours will result in a pretty nasty sunburn. Shorts work well on a hot day. Just use sunscreen on all exposed skin to avoid getting too crispy. And drink lots of water!

The gloved one

Most golfers choose to wear a good-quality glove on their left hand (for right-handed golfers) to help strengthen the grip and to prevent blisters. Although most golfers opt for a leather glove because of its excellent grip and longevity, a number of synthetic gloves on the market will work quite well. If you choose leather, make sure to buy one that is made of soft, thin leather so you can really feel the grip of the club.

■ **It's a good idea** to keep an extra glove in your golf bag in case the one you are using rips or becomes soaked.

Avoid some of the cheaper brands that are made of inferior, thick-gauge leather as these won't give you the necessary feel. If possible go with a better quality glove.

Staying upright

Golf shoes are designed to give you the right amount of traction during your golf swing. Any slipping or sliding during this athletic move can cause a missed shot or even injury, so take your shoes seriously. Instead of wearing sneakers or street shoes on the course, go out and buy a good pair of golf shoes that are designed to grab the turf and keep your feet steady.

Shoe spikes

Most golf shoes have spikes on the soles. Once upon a time all spikes were made of metal and were screwed into the sole of the shoe. The problem is that metal spikes often leave holes and uprooted turf marks all over the green, which interfere

■ **Golf shoes** *come with either soft rubber dimples or sharp metal spikes, both of which are essential for gripping the turf during the golf swing. Comfort must also be taken into consideration as the average golfer will have to walk in excess of four miles.*

with putts. Nowadays, more and more golfers are switching to soft grips made of plastic or rubber. Soft spikes are much kinder to greens, and many course owners now prohibit the use of metal spikes because of the damage they do. Although soft spikes need to be replaced more often than metal ones, they are relatively inexpensive and easy to replace. It's up to you which you decide to use. Just remember that many courses won't let you play with metal. A good pair of golf shoes can cost upward of $100, so be sure to shop for a pair that is as comfortable as possible. Remember, you have to walk many miles to play 18 holes of golf.

Don't buy cheap or ill-fitting shoes as they will invariably cause blistered, aching feet. Take your time and choose a pair carefully.

Topping it off

You should wear a hat when you play to keep the sun out of your eyes and to help prevent sunburn. You'd be surprised how helpful a good hat brim can be in helping you follow the flight of a ball or see the undulations in a putting green. A basic baseball cap works well, although you might want to go with a full-brimmed straw hat if the sun is particularly strong. These hats will help keep the harmful rays of the sun off of your face, neck, and shoulders, too. If you're playing in the rain, a "bucket hat" designed to keep rain from dripping down your neck might be a good idea. SUN HATS

What else can you buy?

Part of the fun are all of the strange, unique little doodads you can buy and use both on and off of the golf course. From mysterious copper bracelets to a laser-guided putting helper, the list is almost endless. For now though you'll need only a few basic accessories. These include:

 A few dozen wooden tees. Make sure to buy the 2¾-inch variety, which will enable you to tee the ball up nice and high if you wish. Tees are cheap and can be purchased in large quantities.

A pitch-mark repair tool. This little two-pronged tool is used to repair ball marks made when your approach shot thumps down onto the putting green and leaves a depression in the grass. They cost less than a dollar in any golf store.

■ **Repair any pitch marks** *by pushing the repair tool into the turf around the indentation and easing the turf back toward the center of the hollow. Then tap the area gently with your putter to smooth down the surface as much as possible.*

A ball marker. You are allowed to pick up your golf ball when it's on the green to clean it or to get it out of the way of someone else's putt. When you do so, you must first mark its position with a small marker. Most players just use a coin, although some prefer poker chips. Be sure to have a few spare coins to use for this purpose. Just don't use anything bigger than a quarter.

An umbrella. You will eventually get caught in the rain. Be prepared by having a nice big golf umbrella when you play. Don't scrimp on this one; get an umbrella that is at least 60 inches across and is strong enough to resist heavy winds. Also, get one that is stylish and bright! Many golf umbrellas have a plastic stake at one end so you can stick it in the turf when you're getting ready to take your shot. Most golf bags have a built-in separate section for an umbrella.

GOLF UMBRELLAS

5 Towels. You should have at least one clean towel with you so you can clean off your grips and club heads during play. If you're playing in the rain, it pays to have two or three towels along.

6 A golf bag cover. When you're playing in the rain, water can run down into your golf bag and soak your grips, preventing you from properly holding the club. If your grips get too wet, your club might end up going farther than your ball! To help prevent this, carry a waterproof golf bag cover with you – one that can quickly be attached to the top of your bag to prevent any rain from dripping down your shafts and onto the grips. Most good golf bags come with a cover. If yours doesn't, you can buy one for a few dollars. One manufacturer even makes a tiny umbrella that fits right on top of your bag.

7 A small personal-belongings bag. While playing, you do not want to be encumbered by wallets, keys, rings, or other things in your pockets. Consider purchasing a small travel bag and storing your personal items inside it. Then just stow it away in one of the pockets of your golf bag.

BAG FOR ESSENTIAL ITEMS

8 Pencils. Make sure to have one or two tucked away in your golf bag in case you lose the one given to you with your scorecard. Also, consider having a magic marker on board to mark your golf balls.

■ **A small towel is necessary** *for keeping your clubs clean during play; and don't forget pencils for marking your scorecard.*

Be practical and keep it simple

That about covers the essentials. Of course, you'll develop your own list of must-have items just as the rest of us do. Feel free to carry anything you want to as long as you don't throw in the kitchen sink, which might slow you down a bit. Remember to be practical and keep it simple.

A simple summary

✓ To play the game right from the beginning, you must have the proper equipment.

✓ If you are not sure that golf is the game for you, think about buying a few used clubs at first or just borrow a few from a friend. After using them a bit, if you still like the game you can go out and buy a new set.

✓ You don't need to spend a fortune to get a decent set of beginner's clubs. Try not to spend much more than $350 for everything. Good beginner's sets are available for even less, so make sure to pinch those pennies at first.

✓ If you intend to carry your golf bag, buy a lightweight one with a retractable stand. If you'll be using a pull cart or motorized cart, you can opt for a larger, heavier bag with more storage space.

✓ Make sure to wear clothing that matches the weather you intend to play in. Dress in layers, and be sure to have a good-quality rain suit on hand.

✓ When you're playing in the hot sun, wear light colors and apply sunscreen. A visored hat is crucial, not only to keep glare away, but to prevent a sunburned face as well.

✓ Be sure to buy a comfortable pair of waterproof golf shoes.

✓ Always carry a towel, a pitch-mark repair tool, an umbrella, tees, a pencil, and a ball marker (or coins) with you on the course.

Chapter 7

Get a Grip

A CHAIN IS ONLY as strong as its weakest link and this certainly holds true for the golf swing. Most golfers agree that the single most important link in golf is the grip – how you connect the club to your body. In this chapter, I'll explain the three most popular grips and what they can do for your game. The one grip you won't find here is for your putter, which I'll deal with in Chapter 11.

In this chapter...

✓ How the golf grip is unique

✓ The three most popular grips

✓ Strong, neutral, or weak?

HANDS POSITIONED IN AN INTERLOCKING GRIP

How the golf grip is unique

THE GOLF GRIP IS DIFFERENT *from other sporting grips. Let's compare it to the way a baseball player grips the bat. In baseball, your hands must be placed one above the other with the bat held securely in your palms rather than in your fingers. When you swing a bat, you use a tremendous amount of wrist action. Your hands act almost independently of each other, swinging and snapping the bat around. With the golf grip, however, your hands must almost become a single unit instead of two independent forces working on their own. The reason for this is simple: A golf swing requires much more accuracy and timing than a baseball swing. The margins for error are smaller, as is the target area. In baseball, a relatively wide bat must strike a relatively large baseball well enough to propel it somewhere into a large playing area. In golf, a small club head must squarely strike a tiny ball well enough to propel it into a small, narrow target area.*

Trivia...

The famous golfer Sam Snead once summed up the difficulties of golf perfectly: "Golfers have to play all of their foul balls."

A good grip makes a good swing

A good golf grip enables you to keep control of the club while sensing the position and action of the club head. It melds the club to your arms, making them an extension of the shaft. A good grip doesn't put a stranglehold on the golf club but rather holds it lightly, to prevent muscle tension in your hands and arms that would ruin your flexibility and grace.

You should grip the club about as hard as you would grip an egg. Grasp too hard and you'll lose all of your feel – an essential part of the game.

You'll swing the club as if it were a sledge hammer instead of a scalpel. Think of the golf club as a surgical instrument and you'll be okay. Most beginners are not very impressed by the grip. They want to get right down to the swinging and hitting parts of the game. While this is understandable, it's also premature. Without a good connection to the club, you will never be able to hit the golf ball consistently with power and accuracy. So for now, take the time to really master holding the golf club. Perhaps no other part of the game is as important.

The three most popular grips

OVER THE DECADES, THREE *types of grip have become the most common ones in golf:*

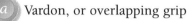 Vardon, or overlapping grip

b Interlocking grip

c Ten-finger, or baseball grip

All of them require you to place your left hand on top (toward the top of the grip) and your right hand on the bottom if you're a right-handed golfer (reverse this order if you're left-handed). The grip that is right for you will depend on the size and strength of your hands, as well as the grip's overall comfort. The only way to know which one is right for you is to experiment with all three.

> *Trivia...*
> *The Vardon grip, also called the overlapping grip, takes its name from Harry Vardon, a famous player from the late 19th to early 20th century who popularized its use.*

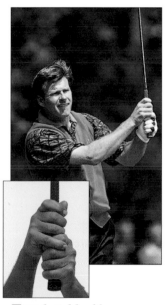

■ **Nick Faldo**, *like many pros, prefers the Vardon grip, as knitting the hands together can produce the most accurate swing.*

■ **Jack Nicklaus** *is a great exponent of the interlocking grip, which is a slight variation of the Vardon.*

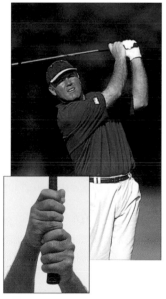

■ **Ronan Rafferty** *is one of the few pros to use the baseball grip in his game. Generally, this grip is used by younger players.*

THE VARDON GRIP

The Vardon grip is the most commonly used grip among both professionals and amateurs. Many believe the Vardon, or overlapping grip, is the most neutral of all the grips as it allows the hands to work as one cohesive unit. Nick Faldo, Sam Snead, and Curtis Strange are among the top players who use it.

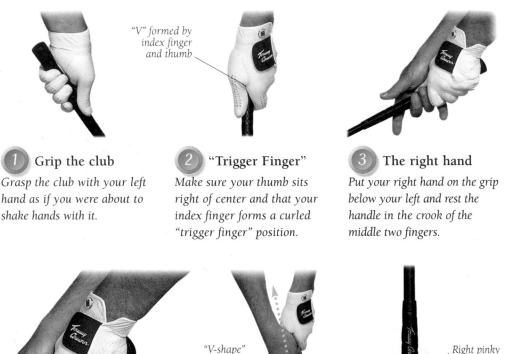

"V" formed by index finger and thumb

1 Grip the club

Grasp the club with your left hand as if you were about to shake hands with it.

2 "Trigger Finger"

Make sure your thumb sits right of center and that your index finger forms a curled "trigger finger" position.

3 The right hand

Put your right hand on the grip below your left and rest the handle in the crook of the middle two fingers.

"V-shape" points between right shoulder and right eye

Right pinky rides on top of left index finger

4 Overlap the fingers

Position your right pinky on top of your left index finger. Your right thumb should rest slightly left of the top of the club shaft. When you're done, the grip should effectively mesh your hands together into one unit. Check to see that the "V"s formed by your thumb and index finger point somewhere between your right shoulder and right eye.

THE INTERLOCKING GRIP

A simple variation of the Vardon grip, the interlocking grip is often used by golfers with smaller or weaker hands. Tom Kite, Tiger Woods, and Jack Nicklaus all use this grip, as do many of the world's top female players. Everything is identical to the Vardon grip except for the placement of the right pinky, which gets interlocked with your left index finger instead of laid on top of it. If you've tried the Vardon and found it to be uncomfortable, give the interlocking grip a try.

1 **Grip gently**
Rest the handle diagonally across the palm of your left hand, making sure your index finger points downward.

2 **Slot the fingers**
Bring your right hand below the left and slot the right pinky between the left index finger.

3 **Close the hands**
Rest the club in the crook of the two middle fingers of the right hand and close the right hand over the left.

4 **Firm interlocking**
The left thumb should be encased by the right hand. Make sure your fingers feel firm but not rigid.

Right pinky entwines with left index finger

THE BASEBALL GRIP

Used by children, those with small or arthritic hands, or players who consistently slice the ball, the baseball grip is sometimes called the ten-finger grip because you have all ten fingers touching the grip of the club. Only a handful of pros use this grip, and Ronan Rafferty is one of them. Despite its name, this grip is not really like holding a baseball bat. You do not wrap your thumbs around the club. Instead, you place them just as you would with the Vardon grip. The only difference from the Vardon is that you have your right pinky directly on the shaft instead of nestled into the groove between the left ring and index fingers. This grip will enable you to hit with more power, although controlling the club head can become more of a problem.

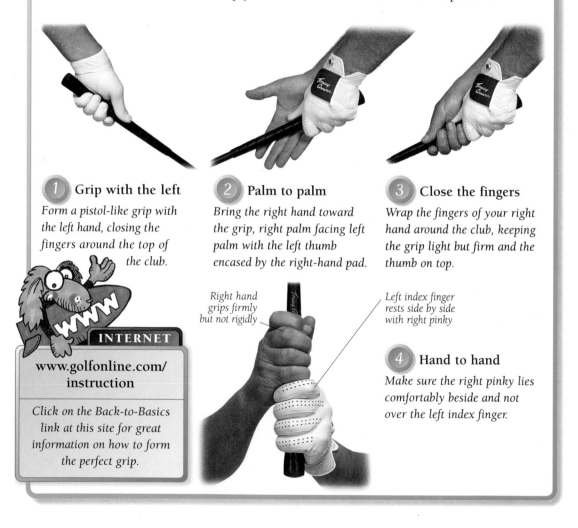

1 **Grip with the left**

Form a pistol-like grip with the left hand, closing the fingers around the top of the club.

2 **Palm to palm**

Bring the right hand toward the grip, right palm facing left palm with the left thumb encased by the right-hand pad.

3 **Close the fingers**

Wrap the fingers of your right hand around the club, keeping the grip light but firm and the thumb on top.

Right hand grips firmly but not rigidly

Left index finger rests side by side with right pinky

4 **Hand to hand**

Make sure the right pinky lies comfortably beside and not over the left index finger.

INTERNET

www.golfonline.com/instruction

Click on the Back-to-Basics link at this site for great information on how to form the perfect grip.

Getting a grip

Whatever grip you use, the handle of your club should run diagonally across the palm of your left hand (if you're right-handed), extending slightly beyond the heel of your hand and running across the palm to the middle of your index finger.

The handle should not be all in your palm or all on the base of your fingers, but rather should be balanced between the two. To test your position, lay your club across your palm. Next, close your hand slightly and suspend the club between the heel of your left hand and your index finger. You should feel the weight of the club head but also have the sensation that the club is perfectly balanced. You can see from this test that a very light grip is all you need to hold your club.

A light grip enables you to make a free and fluid swing. This is what gives you club-head speed.

THE PERFECT GRIP

b **Handle too high**
If the handle is too high across the palm you will end up with a misdirected ball.

a **The perfect position**
The perfect grip comes from holding the handle diagonally across the palm, from the top of the pad to the middle of the index finger.

c **Handle too low**
If the handle sits too low in the palm the angle of club shaft to club head to ball will be misaligned.

Strong, neutral, or weak?

ONE OF THE MOST *influential adjustments you can make to your grip is to rotate your hands slightly on the club. If, after forming your grip, you have about two knuckles showing on your left hand (remember, I'm talking about a right-handed golfer), that means you have a neutral grip, with each hand exactly on opposite sides of the club shaft. This type of grip will have the least effect on the flight of your ball and is used by the majority of golfers.*

If you have three or more knuckles showing on your left hand, you have a *strong grip,* one that has your hands turned clockwise more than the average golfer. This type of grip is often used to help a right-handed golfer promote a draw (a golf shot that is deliberately turned slightly to the left). If you have a grip that shows only one knuckle on the left hand, you have what is called a *weak grip,* often used to help promote a fade (a golf shot that is deliberately turned slightly to the right).

As you can see, changing the position of your hands on the club's grip can affect the flight of the ball significantly. That's because a slight twist of the hands will change the rotational positioning of the club head at impact.

DEFINITION

A strong grip is one where a right-handed player sees more than two knuckles of the left hand; it is used to turn the ball to the left.
A neutral grip is one where that same player can see two knuckles of the left hand when looking down at the grip itself while addressing the ball.
A weak grip is one where the player sees one knuckle of the left hand; it is used to turn the ball to the right.

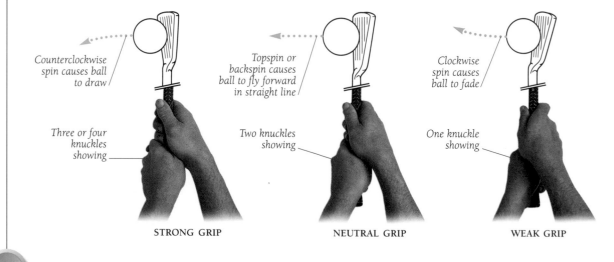

Counterclockwise spin causes ball to draw

Topspin or backspin causes ball to fly forward in straight line

Clockwise spin causes ball to fade

Three or four knuckles showing

Two knuckles showing

One knuckle showing

STRONG GRIP　　　　**NEUTRAL GRIP**　　　　**WEAK GRIP**

Building your own grip

As a beginner, you should start out using one of the three basic grips. Choose whichever one feels most comfortable to you and then stick with it, at least throughout your initial learning period. You can always change later. For now, try to maintain as much consistency as possible so you'll be able to pinpoint where you are making mistakes. As far as choosing between a weak, neutral, or strong grip, try starting out with your hands in a relatively neutral position, perhaps leaning a bit toward the strong. This will enable you to swing with power and help prevent the beginner's bane, the slice. Remember to hold the club lightly and to let your wrists bend naturally. Once you arrive at a comfortable grip position, try to hold the club that way every time to promote as consistent a swing as possible.

A simple summary

✓ The golf grip is your only connection to the club and thus to the ball. That means a good grip is vital to a proper golf swing.

✓ The purpose of the grip is to keep your hands and wrists relaxed enough to enable you to make a free and fluid swing. This is what gives you club-head speed through impact, eliminates any wrist action, and increases the amount of control you have over the club face.

✓ The three most common golf grips are the Vardon, interlocking, and baseball grips.

✓ Whichever grip you decide to use, you then must decide on whether to have a neutral, strong, or weak grip, determined primarily by the rotational positioning of your hands on the shaft. This will affect whether your ball flight bends to the right, to the left, or remains straight.

✓ Start out using the most comfortable of the three basic grips, and place your hands into a neutral position with about two knuckles of the left hand visible. Then, either make it slightly stronger or weaker, depending on which one feels more comfortable.

✓ Consider going for a stronger grip rather than a weaker one to prevent the dreaded slice, the bane of all beginners.

Chapter 8

Your Aim is True

GOLF IS LARGELY A TARGET SPORT. How precisely you aim at your target will detemine how successful you are. Accuracy depends greatly on how you aim your body and your equipment before you actually make the shot. The only way you stand a chance of hitting a decent shot is through proper setup and by the way you address the ball with your club. You must do both. This chapter will show you how.

In this chapter...

✓ Setting up for a good shot

✓ Proper stance

✓ Ball position

✓ Seeing the right pathway

✓ Take aim

✓ Practice makes perfect

THE 16TH HOLE AT CYPRESS POINT, CALIFORNIA

Setting up for a good shot

WHEN SOMEONE SPEAKS *of the setup in golf, they are talking about the way a player positions his or her body in relation to the ball right before the swing. Overall posture and the alignment of your shoulders, hips, knees, and feet in relation to the **target line** all play vital roles in how accurately your shot will come off. Where the ball is placed in relation to your body also plays a huge role in the outcome of the shot. All these factors combine to produce a sound, effective setup, perhaps the most important fundamental in golf.*

DEFINITION

*The **target line** is the imaginary line drawn from the ball to the target – the flagstick or the portion of the putting green or fairway that you're shooting for.*

See how the pros do it

If you watch professional golfers on television, you'll notice how meticulous the players are when they're setting up to the ball before every shot.

Pros don't just step up and swing; rather, they go through a mental checklist each time to make sure their bodies are situated in just the right way to hit the shot they want to hit.

You should try to emulate this when you're preparing to hit a golf ball, whether at the driving range or on the golf course. Each player has his or her own unique setup position, just as every person's swing looks different. That's okay, provided that you make sure you're following all the fundamentals. What are the fundamentals? Relax! I'm going to tell you about them now.

■ **Here, Nick Faldo is standing** *in the perfect setup position: his feet, hips, and shoulders are square to the club face, and the ball is correctly placed for a long club.*

Proper stance

BUILDING THE PROPER STANCE *for the golf swing is not hard. First,*
place your feet about shoulder-width apart, then bend your knees slightly. Don't
go overboard with this; just flex a bit. The objective is to create the feeling of
readiness in your body, as if you were about to jump up into the air or catch a
ball thrown to you.

Make sure your left foot (for right-handers) is turned outward about
20 degrees and your right foot is perpendicular to the target line.

Bend from the waist

Your weight should be evenly
balanced between your left and right
feet. You should also feel your weight
evenly distributed between your heels and
the balls of your feet. Bend slightly from
the waist, allowing your arms to hang
down in front of you. At this point if you
clasped your hands together, they should
be about eight to ten inches away from
your belt buckle. Use the distance of your
hands from your belt buckle as a gauge to
determine whether you are bent over at
the waist too much or not enough.

Positioning your head

Your head should be angled down slightly
but not too far. Don't let your chin rest on
your chest and don't hold it parallel with
the ground either. Ideally, you should
position your head so that you need to look
down slightly with your eyes to see the ball,

Arms hang down
in front of body

Hands about
eight to ten
inches from
belt buckle

■ **The setup** *is the one element of the game*
where the player has total control, so getting
it right is really down to you.

as if you were looking through bifocals. Make sure to keep your back relatively straight
instead of hunched. Practice this position a few more times to ingrain it into your
memory. After you're comfortable with getting in position and can do it automatically,
you're ready to practice it while you're holding a club, say a 7-iron.

Ball position

WHERE THE BALL is located in relation to your stance is crucial to a successful shot. This position does not remain static, but rather changes according to which club is being used. This is because each club is a different length and makes a different arc of contact with the ball. A sand wedge, for example, is the shortest full-swing club in your bag and will therefore require the ball to be much closer to your body than will a 3-wood. Quite simply, if it's too far away, your club won't be able to reach it.

PLACING THE BALL

The design of each of the clubs will determine where you set up the ball in relation to your body. The longer clubs, such as the driver, will need a ball positioned farther away from the body, whereas the shorter clubs, such as the sand wedge, will require the ball to be set up much closer to the body.

Another thing to consider is whether the ball should be played closer to your left foot, your right foot, or right in the middle of your stance. This again depends on the type of club used: As a rule the longer the club, the more to the left you should place the ball.

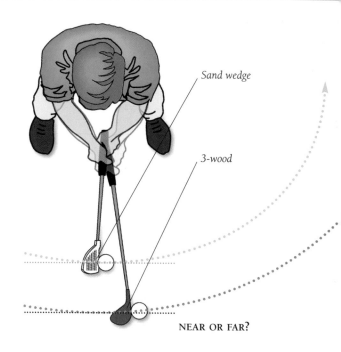

Sand wedge

3-wood

NEAR OR FAR?

Hitting with a sand wedge

When you hit with a sand wedge, the ball must be positioned closer to your right foot (if you're a right-handed person) and just an inch or two off center, while with a 3-wood it should be closer to your left foot. That's because the wedge is designed to contact the ball with a steep, descending blow as compared to the 3-wood's sweeping, more shallow angle of attack.

Hitting with a driver

The ball will be closest to your left foot when you hit with your driver. This is not only because of the driver's length, but also because the club should make contact with the ball on the tee after it has passed the bottom of its swing arc and has begun to ascend. As you can see, the length and arc of the club both play important roles in the positioning of the ball at address.

INTERNET

www.golftipsmag.com

Golf Tips magazine's site offers information on all the fundamentals, including setup, stance, and ball position.

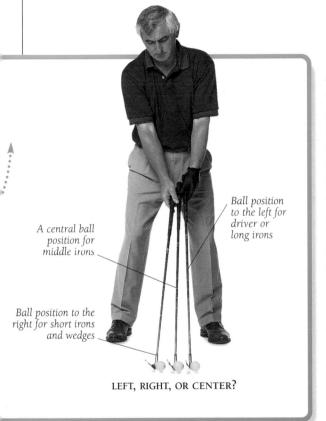

A central ball position for middle irons

Ball position to the left for driver or long irons

Ball position to the right for short irons and wedges

LEFT, RIGHT, OR CENTER?

A simple rule to remember

When you're hitting with your driver, position the teed ball even with your left heel (for a right-handed golfer). For fairway woods, the ball should be about an inch to the right of your left heel. For long irons, the ball should be another half-inch to an inch to the right. When you're using your middle irons (5-, 6-, and 7-), the ball can be positioned more to the center. Short irons and wedges should be played in the center of your stance.

How to find the right position

To get a good feel for positioning your ball, try this experiment. Grip your 3-wood as if you were about to take a shot, making sure your hands are no more than eight to ten inches from your belt buckle. Next, draw an imaginary line perpendicular to your left heel, and position the face of the club about an inch or so to the right of this line. That is the spot where the ball should be located when you address it with the 3-wood. Place a ball in that spot and leave it there. Then, repeat this procedure with a pitching wedge. Position its face slightly behind the midway point between your feet. Make sure your hands are again only eight to ten inches from your belt buckle. Now place a ball in that spot. Look at the positions of the two balls. As you can see, the proper ball position for a pitching wedge is not only well to the right of a 3-wood, but is also much closer to your body.

Seeing the right pathway

POSSIBLY THE BIGGEST error amateur golfers make when addressing the ball is poor alignment to the target. Most don't take the time to properly determine the correct line to the target, while others do so but fail to put their swing onto this critical pathway. Some just don't even consider the possibility of being able to hit a golf ball accurately, and so they just get up and swing away haphazardly.

Guiding your missile

VIP

That's a careless method and one that will prevent you from ever becoming a good golfer. Instead of thinking of a golf shot as a "shot in the dark," start thinking of it as a guided missile programmed to land exactly where it is told to.

If you align your body and club face properly, you will be 90 percent of the way toward hitting the ball right where you want it to go.

Getting your alignment right

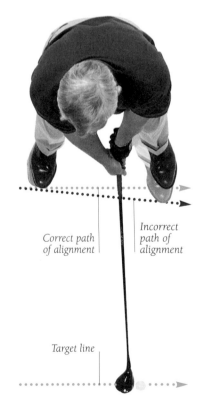

Correct path of alignment

Incorrect path of alignment

Target line

Many amateur golfers make the mistake of aligning their bodies toward the right of the intended target. Why? Because after aiming the club head exactly onto the right pathway to the target, most then incorrectly aim their feet, hips, and shoulders at the target as well. This causes the swing plane to shift slightly to the right of the target line even if the club head itself is correctly aligned. The pathway of the swing goes right causing the shot to do the same. Instead, think of parallel lines. The bottom edge of your club head is aimed directly at the target, and then your feet, hips, and shoulders are aligned parallel to but slightly left of the target line. If your swing plane is parallel to the target line, the club head will remain on the proper course and your shot will go where you intended it to. If you visualize these parallel lines whenever you step up to the ball, your aim will remain true.

■ **If you visualize** *your feet on an imaginary line parallel to the target line, you'll find it easier to hit a straight shot.*

Take aim

THE FIRST STEP IN AIMING is to stand behind your ball and see the target line. Then choose a secondary aiming point about two or three feet in front of your ball, one that sits directly on the line to your target. Any little mark, old divot, or blemish in the turf will do so long as you can see it plainly. Aim the bottom edge of your club head so it is perpendicular to the line leading to this secondary target. Your club head is now properly aimed.

Simplify your aim

Jack Nicklaus has always used this method, and most professionals use it today. A secondary target is chosen simply because it's close by and easily seen. Once established, the secondary target is all you really should concern yourself with. Worrying too much about the primary target sitting 100 or more yards away will only cause stress, which inevitably leads to a bad shot. Anyone can hit a ball to a spot only two feet away, right?

Lining up

After the club head is aimed toward the secondary target, verify that you're using the proper grip and setup. Then arrange your feet so they are parallel to the line to the secondary target. To do this reliably, do what many professionals do: Place a club down on the ground just in front of where your toes would be and aim it directly parallel to the target line. Then simply set your toes up to the club. Next, look down at your hips and make sure they appear to be on the same line as your feet. A good way to practice aiming your hips is to stick a club shaft or a yardstick through the two front belt loops of your pants and see which way the shaft points. If it draws a line that's parallel to your feet, you're in business. If it points left or right, you know your hips are not properly aligned.

Line of vision fixed on secondary target

Direct line to ultimate target

■ **Focus your aim** *on an intermediate target, like an old divot-mark or leaf, two or three feet in front of the ball along the target line – it's much simpler!*

Players often have no idea which way their hips are aimed; trying the yardstick drill will tell you what your hips are up to.

The square stance

Finally, make sure your shoulders are also on the same line as your feet and hips. To check this, you can hold a club up to your upper chest with crossed arms and see which way it points. If it points along the same lines as your feet and hips, you should be okay. If it doesn't, adjust yourself accordingly. This will give you a nice *square stance*, and a square stance gives you the best chance to hit the ball straight and true.

Later in the book I'll discuss ways you can adjust the square stance in order to bend the flight of your ball to the left or right. For now, though, stick with the square stance. It's the best way to learn fundamental aiming skills.

DEFINITION

When your club head is perpendicular to the target line and your feet, hips, and shoulders are all parallel to the same line, you are positioned in a square stance.

Practice makes perfect

PRACTICE THIS WAY OF *taking aim while you're at the driving range. Do it over and over again until you can achieve it quickly without any help from props or friends. Eventually muscle memory will kick in, enabling you to aim properly without any fuss at all. To verify that you really are aligning yourself properly, have a friend stand ten feet behind you and check out what you think is proper alignment. You may find that one or more parts of the aiming equation go off kilter every now and then, and having your friend check all of them will give you excellent feedback on this.*

Avoiding common mistakes

Of the mistakes amateurs make during alignment, the biggest two are probably a misaligned club face and a misaligned body position – that is, your feet, hips, and shoulders are aimed at the target instead of parallel to it. How can you avoid these mistakes?

Be sure to align the bottom edge of the club head, not the top edge (which on most clubs is sloped at a significant angle).

INTERNET

www.duffer.com

Check out this site for a complete listing of instructional golf books and videos that will help you learn proper alignment, as well as other important fundamentals.

Aligning the top edge of the club face perpendicularly to the target line will result in a closed club face and a shot that goes left. Improperly aligned feet, hips, or shoulders can be more difficult to diagnose and fix, so be sure to practice and check your stance regularly so you develop good alignment habits right from the start.

A simple summary

✓ Golf is a target sport. How precisely you aim your body and club face will determine to a large degree how accurately you hit each shot.

✓ Assuming the proper stance when addressing the ball is crucial to achieving the proper swing plane and hitting the ball consistently well. Assume a relaxed yet ready posture, one that feels as if you're getting ready to jump up into the air.

✓ Where the ball is placed in relation to your body at address will affect how you hit the ball. With wedges and short irons, play the ball midstance (for a right-handed golfer). For middle irons, play the ball slightly left of midstance. For long irons and fairway woods, play the ball about an inch or two to the right of your left heel. For the driver, play the ball even with your left heel.

✓ The longer the club you use, the greater the distance of the ball from your body should be. However, the distance from the end of the club's grip to your waist should generally stay about the same; about eight to ten inches is just right.

✓ When aligning your body in preparation for a shot, be sure to set your body on a line that is parallel to the target line instead of pointed directly at the target. Also ensure that your feet, knees, hips, and shoulders are all aligned parallel to the target line.

✓ Use a secondary aiming point located about a foot or two in front of your ball's position.

Chapter 9

The Pre-Shot Routine

ALL GREAT GOLFERS HAVE been able to enter into a "zone" of concentration on the golf course, enabling them to block out all distractions and think only about the shot in hand. Ben Hogan, one of the greatest golfers of all time, was famous for going into the zone while playing. More than once, he reached the end of a round and found he hadn't written a thing on his scorecard!

In this chapter...

✓ Sharpening your focus

✓ The power of the mind

✓ The benefits of repetition

✓ Visualize to realize

✓ Waggle that club

✓ A typical pre-shot routine

TOM WATSON FOCUSES ON THE SHOT AHEAD

Sharpening your focus

PART OF A GREAT *player's ability lies in his or her skill in staying focused on the moment, on the task at hand. If Ben Hogan hit a bad tee shot on the 14th hole, the aggravation of it would be out of his mind by the time he readied himself for his second shot, be it from the fairway or the rough.*

Ben Hogan knew that carrying regrets and anger over to the next shot would doom that shot to failure, so he simply learned how to let the frustrations go.

He knew that if he didn't, the anger would tense up his muscles and provoke negative thought patterns, almost guaranteeing another bad shot.

Letting those bad shots go

If you have played any golf at all, you know that forgetting all about a bad shot that happened just moments ago is a very hard thing to do. You just can't find a way to forgive yourself for hitting such a bonehead shot. "I should have used more club to get over that lake!" "It shouldn't take me three tries to get out of the bunker!" Everybody has these thoughts at one time or another, but holding onto them can doom the entire round of golf to come. Although we play golf for the emotional rush of hitting a pure shot right to the target, those same emotions can drive us to failure.

In addition to forgetting about a bad shot, good golfers have to be able to defuse any nervous tension during a big tournament. Think you wouldn't be nervous going into the final round of

■ **Until later on in his career,** *Ben Hogan's success lay in his ability to rid his mind of negative thoughts and focus on the shot ahead.*

the U.S. Open tied for first place with Tiger Woods? Think again. If that tension is left to fester inside you, it will kill any chance you have of making good shots.

The power of the mind

SO FAR I'VE TALKED *mostly about the physical aspects of golf, but you must also master the mental game in order to succeed in this most difficult sport.*

The key is to find some way of creating and entering the right frame of mind – a method that establishes a focused mindset, almost a hypnotic bubble that cannot be breached by prior bad shots, nerves, or annoying distractions on the course. In golf, this method is known as the pre-shot routine.

Trivia...

Toward the end of his career, golfing legend Ben Hogan began experiencing problems with his putting. Often he would set up and then freeze for what seemed like ages before taking a perfunctory putt, sending the ball offline and missing the cup. His pre-shot routine for putts had finally failed him; he could no longer clear his mind of doubt and began missing putt after putt. After his competitive career was over, he would play recreational rounds of golf from tee to green then simply pick his ball up off of the green without putting it into the hole.

Mental preparation

Watch an Olympic weightlifter just before he attempts to lift a really big weight. What does he do? He calms himself and tries to empty his mind. He then begins breathing slowly and deeply and starts to focus on the task at hand. Then he actually visualizes lifting the weight effortlessly above his head, allowing his mind to see the possibility of the event. Only then does he step up to the bar and do his thing. Without this type of mental preparation, he wouldn't stand a chance of success. He knows, as do most professional athletes, that the power of the mind is just as important as the power of the body. Good golfers go through this same type of mental preparation.

DEFINITION

*The ritualistic procedure performed before every shot is known as the **pre-shot** routine. Performing this identical series of preparatory steps before every shot relaxes the muscles and clears the mind, thereby increasing your chances of a successful shot.*

■ **Stress and frustration** *can affect the most professional of golfers. During major tournaments the fundamentals of mental preparation can be easily forgotten.*

The benefits of repetition

BEFORE EVERY SHOT, *a golfer should perform the same pre-shot routine to prepare for it. After many years of playing, this routine becomes an automatic, almost mantra-like part of the hitting process. Without it, most good players would be lost. If you doubt this, watch a few professional tournaments and see what occurs when there's some kind of distraction while a player is going through his or her pre-shot routine. Even if the player is seconds away from swinging, he or she will stop and go back to the very beginning of the pre-shot routine and go through it all over again.*

VIP

That's because their pre-shot routines are not separate from the swing. They are part of the swing.

Programming your mind

By performing this routine religiously before every shot, good players can always clear their minds of all doubts and anger and put themselves on track to a great swing. The key to an effective pre-shot routine is to do the same things every time. Eventually, your mind and muscle memory will be programmed to execute a perfect swing automatically. It will be simple.

■ **Mental preparation** *is essential in every golfer's pre-shot routine since it focuses the mind and leads to fewer wayward shots. Here, Nick Faldo takes the time to rid himself of any distractions before taking his shot.*

Visualize to realize

MOST PROFESSIONAL PLAYERS STAND *behind the ball before making a swing and actually visualize the shot happening. They see the ball leave the club head, see it arc out over the fairway, notice which way the ball bends, and watch it land and roll exactly where they intended it to go. Pretty neat, huh? It's a great way to preprogram your mind and body to hit a good shot, and it really works if you do it regularly.*

Positive thinking

Visualization also helps you to block out any negative feelings about the success of the shot; after all, you just saw it and know that what you want is possible. Compare that with what most amateurs think before making a shot: "I hope I don't duff it." "I hope I don't hit the ball into that lake." "Oh, darn, I wish I didn't have to hit the ball over that mess of bushes." Sound familiar? That's visualization too. Negative visualization. And it works the same way as positive visualization, usually causing you to hit the ball right where you feared it would go!

Simply visualize the shot

VIP

When you are ready to hit a shot on the course, you should first visualize a perfect shot in your mind.

Stand a few feet behind the ball and imagine hitting it. You swing fluidly, with great timing and tempo. You make perfect contact. You hear the ring of the club. You see the ball's path of flight. It reaches its apex, drops gently to the green, rolls a few feet, and then stops suddenly (due to the backspin) ten feet from the flagstick. Do this every time for every shot – even putts or sand shots. Eventually you'll see that it really works!

■ **Before play**, *stand behind the ball and get a good look at the target; this will help you visualize the ball's flight path and focus your mind totally on the shot in hand.*

Waggle that club

WHEN YOU ARE UP at bat in a baseball game, your job is to hit the ball thrown to you. In other words, you have to react to something that someone else is doing. You can't do a thing until the pitcher throws that baseball at you.

Coping under pressure

In golf, you are in charge of the entire act. The ball sits there passively, daring you to hit it. Everything that happens depends on you. That's one of the reasons hitting a golf ball is so hard. All the responsibility is heaped on your shoulders. You have to stand there beside that little egg of a ball for what seems like an eternity, hoping you'll remember what to do and wishing the ball would magically get up into the air and go where you want it to. To make matters worse, several people are usually watching you.

Focus, concentrate, be positive

Golf requires you to stand there and think a lot, too. Baseball players certainly do think about hitting mechanics and wonder what kind of pitch the next ball will be, but they cannot stand there and focus on themselves. They must be focused on the pitcher and the ball, ready to react to whatever comes. Little premeditated or prolonged thought (or worry) comes into the picture. Golf, on the other hand, requires you to stand there and think about what you are going to do. This can let doubt and worry seep into your head, especially if you've just begun to play. This, in turn, causes your muscles to tense up, sometimes to the point where you can't move. You get what amounts to stage fright.

What's the cure for golfing stage fright? The answer is simple: Don't give your mind the opportunity to begin generating negative thoughts.

Focus on simple, repetitive movements. Try to keep your body loose and moving during your pre-shot routine. When you are setting up, shift your weight back and forth from foot to foot. Look at your target then at your ball. But most of all, *waggle* your club head back and forth.

DEFINITION

*A **waggle** is a short, back-and-forth motion of the club head controlled by your wrists. It moves the club head about a foot or two in each direction as a prelude to the real swing.*

Loosening up

Waggling the club head back and forth several times accomplishes several things. First, it relaxes your arm muscles, helping to prevent excess tension from ruining the swing to come. Second, it gives your body a dynamic act to perform instead of just standing there frozen in fear. Keeping some part of your body moving helps prevent your mind from generating negative thoughts. The waggle actually makes the golf swing more like a reactive baseball swing. Instead of being static and fearful, you are looser and more reactive, almost as if you were waiting for a pitch. The waggle also helps you practice the first part of the backswing.

Watch the pros rehearse

Right before you are ready to pull the trigger, so to speak, make sure you waggle the club. It can be a short little back-and-forth motion or a longer, slower technique, similar to what LPGA star Karrie Webb does before every shot. She sets up to the ball, then brings her club head back to almost a horizontal position behind her. Then she brings the club head slowly back to the ball. This move is a definite back swing rehearsal for her; a rehearsal that also doubles as a tension-freeing waggle.

■ **Gently waggling** *the club head back and forth will help introduce movement to your setup as well as ease any pre-shot tension you may be feeling.*

Whatever type of waggle you decide on, use it every time right before your swing begins.

It will keep you loose and promote the feeling of being, as the great Sam Snead once said, "oily."

■ **Like all successful golfers,** *Karrie Webb has learned to adapt the waggle to suit her game: rather than make a series of short movements she takes a slow, practice backswing.*

A typical pre-shot routine

NOW LET'S TIE ALL *of these components together into*
one seamless, workable pre-shot routine.

Step 1: Take a practice swing

Don't overdo this; just one decent swing is all you need.
So keep it simple. While you're doing it, try to think
about the swing as little as possible. Maybe just "good
tempo" or "full turn." Think about the beat of a waltz:
"one-two-three, one-two-three." Think about brushing
the turf with your practice swing, just as you would
during the real thing (unless, of course, you are using
your driver, which shouldn't brush the turf at all but
should be swung about an inch or so above it,
depending on how high you tee up your ball).

INTERNET

www.golfball.com

*You'll find tips on golfing
fundamentals, information on
new equipment, and articles
on virtually every aspect of
the game at this site.*

Step 2: Visualize the shot

Stand five feet or so behind the ball and visualize the shot to come. Picture it leaving
the club head, arcing out perfectly, then coming down right where you want it to. Doing
so will help put you in the right frame of mind to make a great shot. Stand there and
"watch" the shot happen for the same amount of time it would take in real life,
probably around six to eight seconds.

Step 3: Take aim

After visualizing the shot, continue to stand behind the ball and identify the proper line
to your target. At this point, you should simply follow the steps you learned in Chapter
8 for aligning yourself and your club head and aiming the ball; I've summarized them
here to keep things really simple. Choose an intermediate target no more than a few feet
in front of you, one that is right on line with your real target. It can be a patch of brown
grass, a divot, or even a worm poking its head out to have a look.

*Aim the bottom edge of your club face so that it is perpendicular to
the line leading to the secondary target (you remember, that cute
little worm). Next, set your grip and address the ball. Arrange your
feet so that they are parallel to the target line, then do the same
with your hips and shoulders.*

Step 4: Waggle the club head

Once you're aimed properly, it's vital that you not remain motionless or you'll invite stress and negative thoughts to seep in and ruin your shot. Instead, waggle the club a few times. Try to feel that all your joints are well-oiled and that you are relaxed and happy. After waggling, re-align the bottom of the club head so that it's perpendicular to the target line. All the while, think very little. Concentrate only on the immediate tasks at hand. Watch the club head waggling back and forth. Try to be a kid in your head. Simple. Happy.

Step 5: Pull the trigger

All good golfers initiate the actual swing with a little action, which acts like the wave of the starting flag at a car race. Tom Kite shifts his weight rapidly from foot to foot. Nancy Lopez bends her wrists slightly. Others flex their knees or tilt their head. This type of movement helps get the backswing going. You should have one, too. Whatever you come up with is up to you; just make sure you do it every time. In fact, that is the secret: do it exactly the same way every time. If you do, you'll program your mind and body to produce a consistently repeatable swing while eliminating as much stress as possible.

A simple summary

✓ By focusing on a pre-shot, ritualistic routine, your mind won't have the time for negative, swing-killing thoughts. Instead, it will be too busy concentrating on the mechanics of the ritual.

✓ Your pre-shot routine should eventually become part of the shot itself. Tell yourself the shot cannot be made unless the precursor to it (the pre-shot routine) is performed first.

✓ As part of the pre-shot routine, you should always visualize the shot you're about to make. In your mind, see the ball go exactly where you want it to go.

✓ In order to master a pre-shot routine, repeat it over and over again until it becomes automatic.

✓ Waggling the club before taking your swing helps relax your muscles and clear your mind.

✓ After you've developed an effective pre-shot routine, don't change it. Perform it exactly the same way every time.

Chapter 10

Swing Basics

Now for the hard part, the golf swing. A golf club is swung partly on the horizontal and partly on the vertical plane. This makes the act itself very hard to repeat reliably. Your legs, torso, arms, and hands all have to work together flawlessly if you are to have any chance of reliably hitting that tiny little ball sitting so calmly before you. So let's study the swing.

In this chapter...

✓ The elements of a good swing

✓ The swing plane

✓ The six parts of a golf swing

✓ Start off with your 7-iron

TIGER WOODS DEMONSTRATES THE PERFECT STANCE

The elements of a good swing

WHAT QUALITIES MAKE UP *a good golf swing? To try to answer that, let's first talk about one of the best swings on the PGA Tour, that of Ernie Els. Els is a large man (well over six feet tall), but he shows incredible grace and athleticism, especially with a golf club in his hands. His swing combines great power and coordination with amazing tempo and impeccable timing. His swing never appears rushed or forced, but instead has a velvety smoothness about it, almost as if he were swinging the club under water. His is a swing to appreciate and emulate.*

INTERNET

www.teachkidsgolf.com

This site shows video clips of all the basic swing elements. Although it's designed with the younger golfer in mind, it's the perfect primer for adults as well.

Don't kill the ball!

Unfortunately, the average player comes off looking much less graceful than Ernie Els. To prove it, the next time you go to a driving range, watch all the different swings. You'll see slashers, stabbers, hammerers, swipers, and choppers, but few graceful dancers like Ernie. Most amateurs seem to want to kill the golf ball, possibly because of their captivation with how far many of the professionals can hit it. In their attempts to do so, they end up hitting poorly and with much less power than the graceful easy swinger.

■ **South Africa's Ernie Els** *has one of the smoothest and most graceful swings in professional golf. See him in action and you'll notice that his swing is performed with perfect balance and poise – a lesson to all those who attempt to hit the ball too hard.*

Easy does it

Brute strength is not how the pros get all that distance. No professional player, not even Tiger Woods or John Daly, tries to hit the golf ball with all of his or her strength at the expense of grace and good tempo. The professional player's first and foremost thought when swinging a golf club is to make it smooth. When you try to murder the ball, you reduce or lose all the basic ingredients that make up an effective swing. These include: tempo, balance, unity, and swing.

Tempo

Each individual player will have his or her own unique tempo or pace when swinging a golf club. That's true for the pros as well. Ernie Els and Fred Couples both have lazy, languid, easy swings, while Nick Price and Tom Watson swing faster and more deliberately. All four players are top caliber, however, proving that swing speed alone doesn't determine success. You too will have your own unique

■ **Tiger Woods** *has one of the fastest swing speeds on record but he never compromises on grace and accuracy when hitting the ball.*

swing tempo, one that will probably match your personality and mannerisms. If you are an easy-going person, odds are your swing tempo will reflect that. Likewise, if you tend to be the quick-moving, fast-talking type, chances are good that your swing tempo will be faster. Faster is not automatically better. However, faster is not necessarily a bad thing, either, as long as certain fundamentals are followed.

Never start your backswing in a sudden, jerky manner, because this can often cause the rest of the swing to self-destruct.

Instead, make a deliberate attempt to take the club back smoothly. Think about the beat of a waltz: The club should be swung back smoothly to the count of one-two-three so that you reach the end of the backswing on the count of three. Remember, you are not chopping wood. Once you get the club all the way back, there should be a momentary pause in the beat instead of suddenly going right into the downswing. Concentrate on the smooth tempo of the act, almost as if you were conducting an orchestra.

Grace and accuracy

When the downswing finally does begin, it should be done gracefully, without undue force. Trying to whip the club through as hard as possible at the beginning of the downswing will almost always result in poor contact with the ball, as well as an improper weight shift that might cause you to lose balance and power. Again, think about that waltz on your downswing. Swing down on the count of one-two-three so that you complete your swing on three. By thinking of the entire swing in musical terms, you will be able to create a smooth, liquid action that produces power and accuracy.

Balance

Balance is everything in sports. Any athlete who comes off balance at a crucial time will not be able to perform effectively. In golf, staying balanced during the swing is vital to hitting the ball with any power or accuracy. Wild shifts in weight from one side to the other will destroy your tempo, making the club head go astray. Players who move their bodies sideways too much sometimes even fall over at the end of their swing – a sure sign of poor technique.

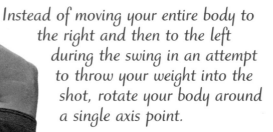

Instead of moving your entire body to the right and then to the left during the swing in an attempt to throw your weight into the shot, rotate your body around a single axis point.

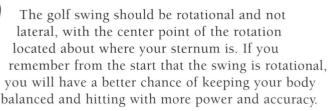

The golf swing should be rotational and not lateral, with the center point of the rotation located about where your sternum is. If you remember from the start that the swing is rotational, you will have a better chance of keeping your body balanced and hitting with more power and accuracy.

■ **To achieve a well-balanced** *and controlled golf swing your body must rotate around a central axis to allow your weight to transfer from one side to the other.*

Unity

Unity means your golf swing should be one fluid, continuous motion. Many a beginner will read books that talk about important swing keys, such as "take it inside," "release the club head," or "turn your hips" and then will try to execute all of these critical elements of the swing consecutively, as if they all happen far away from each other in time. The truth is, the golf swing is a very dynamic event that takes all of about two seconds. You can't possibly break it up into many small parts, paying attention to each one while swinging. Instead, you must think of the swing as a uniform act, one that continuously flows from one moment to the next.

Working on your swing

If your swing needs working on, do so one element at a time and don't try to concentrate on too many variables. Perhaps one day you concern yourself with slowing down your backswing and nothing else. Or another day you make an effort to keep your grip pressure light with no other thoughts in your mind. And always remember that the golf swing is one fluid act and not a series of disjointed actions.

Swing, don't hit

Perhaps as a leftover from baseball, many beginners think they need to concentrate on hitting the golf ball with the club. Of course if you don't make impact the ball isn't going anywhere, but you shouldn't think of it that way. Instead, one of the elements of a good golf swing is to swing the club and just let the ball "get in the way" of the club head. Keep it simple!

Think of it as a practice swing with no ball at all. Practice swings are nearly always smooth and well executed because there's no pressure to do well.

In order to swing well and hit the ball squarely, pretend the ball isn't there at all. You may be surprised at the positive results.

Trivia...

By the early 1980s famed European golfer Nick Faldo had already become a winner. Because his game was still unpredictable, however, he decided to call upon well-known swing guru David Leadbetter for help. The two of them proceeded to completely break down and rebuild Faldo's swing from the bottom up, essentially forcing him to relearn everything. The strategy paid off. After a year or two of diligent, hard work, Faldo began winning tournament after tournament, including several Masters and British Opens. He became known as the most mechanically minded and precise golfer since Ben Hogan.

The swing plane

THE PATHWAY YOUR CLUB *takes during the swing is known as your swing plane. Stand behind a golfer friend and watch while he or she addresses the ball and notice the angle the club shaft makes with the ground. Then have your friend swing slowly, and watch the angle of the club shaft as it goes up and behind, then back down and through. See how it remains relatively constant throughout the swing?*

At the top of the backswing the club shaft should still be on the same line, or plane, as it was at address.

That's your friend's unique swing plane, defined by his or her height, flexibility, and posture.

Steep and shallow swing planes

Generally speaking, a short person with standard-length clubs will have a flatter, or shallower, swing plane (one in which the club shaft makes a smaller angle with the ground), while a taller person using standard-length clubs will have a steeper swing plane (one in which the club shaft makes a larger angle with the ground). This can vary dramatically, however, according to the individual player's stance and physical potential. A very stiff-jointed player will tend to have a steeper swing plane than one who is very flexible, for example. There is no one correct swing plane in golf. Also, the swing plane changes according to the length of club you're using. For example, a sand wedge is a much shorter club than a driver and will therefore have a much steeper swing plane than a driver. The driver, the longest club in the bag, has the flattest swing plane.

Many different swing planes can be used with great success, but there are some things you should keep in mind. First, your swing plane should not vary tremendously during the swing. The plane of your backswing will probably be a bit steeper than that of your downswing, but that's okay as long as they don't differ wildly. Keeping them reasonably similar will help ensure good contact with the ball as well as good power in your swing.

DEFINITION

The angle your club makes with the ground at address and during your swing defines your **swing plane**. *The greater the angle, the steeper the swing plane. The smaller the angle, the flatter, or shallower, the swing plane.*

Coming over the top

A swing plane that is overly steep tends to produce poor contact and sliced shots (shots that curve wildly to the right, for a right-handed player). This is because the club head comes at the ball with a steeper trajectory and a slight right-to-left pathway (known as *coming over the top*). Having too shallow a swing plane can cause problems as well, primarily hooked shots (shots that curve wildly from right to left, for a right-handed player).

DEFINITION

A player is said to be **coming over the top** *with his or her swing when, on the downswing, the path of the club head tends to move in a right-to-left motion across the ball (for a right-handed golfer). This glancing swipe across the ball tends to produce poor shots, especially slices.*

Generally speaking, a good swing plane will be produced by a backswing that is wide and shallow. Just think of producing as large an arc as possible and you should be fine.

People with a steep swing plane usually create a very narrow arc with the club resulting in a loss of power and accuracy, especially with the longer clubs. This problem does not show up as much with the shorter clubs because their normal swing planes are much steeper.

Achieving the right swing plane

To a great extent, your swing plane will be determined by your setup, or address position. If you set up to the ball the way I described in Chapter 8, you should not have a problem. Take care not to stand too close to the ball or tilt your upper body to the left (for a right-handed player) because these can make your swing plane too steep. When you're using your driver, the club shaft should make about a 45-degree angle with the ground at address.

Driver's swing plane

6-iron's swing plane

Sand wedge's swing plane

■ **The swing plane** *varies depending on the type of golf club used; generally, the longer the club the shallower the swing plane.*

The six parts of a golf swing

I KNOW WHAT YOU'RE THINKING: "This guy just said the golf swing is not a series of individual actions performed one after another, but rather one fluid, coordinated motion." You're absolutely right. However, describing the essentials of this complicated maneuver would be almost impossible if I didn't break it down into parts. This way, I can explain how to arrive at the ideal position for each part. Once you understand just where the club should be at each important stage in the swing, you will be able to put them all together into one flowing movement. Put a ball in the way of that, and you've got yourself a game!

Step 1: The backswing: low and slow

The backswing is the first part of the whole swing picture and is possibly the most important because it sets up and defines everything to follow. If you have a lousy backswing, everything else will fall apart, causing a poor shot. Do it right, though, and you tremendously increase your chances of making a great shot. So let's get swinging.

The takeaway

From the address position (I explained that one in Chapter 8), begin to move the club back slowly, keeping the club head as low to the ground as possible. Make sure you have your left shoulder slightly higher than your right (for a right-handed player), as this will encourage a wider, more shallow swing plane. Do not pick the club head up into the air abruptly because this will create a very steep swing plane, reducing your chances of hitting with power and accuracy.

VIP

When you begin this low-and-slow move, make sure all your body parts are moving and turning in unison.

■ **The very beginning of the takeaway** *is one of the most crucial parts of the golf swing as it determines the club head's path during the swing.*

Trivia...

One of the first writings on how to play golf came from Thomas Kincaid in 1687. About the golf swing he wrote, "Stand as you do at fencing. Hold the muscles of your legs and back and armes . . . fixt or stiffe, and not at all slackening them in the time you are bringing down the stroak. Your armes must move but very little; all the motion must be performed with the turning of your body about."

Players who start their backswing with only their hands and arms rarely learn to hit with power or consistency, so be sure to move everything in one coordinated action. Arms, shoulders, and hips should all move together as you begin swinging the club head back. Think about taking the club head straight back for about a foot or so before you begin to turn. As you turn, your body will pretty much force the club head to begin its turn anyway, so don't worry too much about it.

The turn to the right

At this point in the backswing, your body should begin a rotary motion, like a spring coiling up. Your right arm will automatically begin to fold in toward your side, while your left arm should remain relatively straight (but not stiff). Try to keep your right elbow tucked in to within a few inches of your body throughout the backswing. Notice also that your shoulders are now turning, as are your hips. This will also happen naturally.

Your weight will begin to shift over to your right side (for a right-handed golfer). This weight shift is essential to a proper backswing because it helps to load up all the potential power in your body — waiting to be released onto your left side during the downswing.

The beginning of the backswing should feel as if you are turning your body and simply taking your arms and hands along with it. Try not to initiate the action with your arms and hands because they often go back on a different plane each time if you allow them to move on their own. Just let your torso control the show and you should be fine.

When your club shaft is pointing almost straight back, your wrists should begin to cock, or bend. This will happen naturally, so don't force the issue. Also, make sure not to increase your grip pressure at this point. Keep it light and in control. Now keep turning until your left shoulder (for a right-handed golfer) begins to tuck itself under your chin and your left knee bends in a bit toward your trailing knee. Your head should remain in relatively the same position it was in as you addressed the ball, although a little turning motion is acceptable.

Try not to let your body sway sideways during the backswing; it should turn on an imaginary axis.

THE BACKSWING

One of the most important things to remember is to begin the backswing as a coordinated movement of your entire body and not just your arms and hands. Doing so will help you widen your swing arc, increase power, and improve your odds of contacting the ball cleanly.

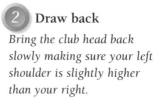

1 Setup

Set up to the ball with your left foot turned out slightly and your right foot perpendicular to the target line.

2 Draw back

Bring the club head back slowly making sure your left shoulder is slightly higher than your right.

3 Rotate

Rotate your arms, shoulders, and hips as you bring the club head back, keeping your grip light and in control.

Step 2: At the top

Swaying will reduce power and destroy consistency, so avoid doing it. As your left shoulder is tucked beneath your chin, your club shaft will be reaching the very top of the backswing, and should be pointing down your target line. Most of your weight should be on your right foot, and your left knee should be bent slightly inward. Your right knee should keep a slight bend in it throughout the backswing and should act as a brace for all the coiled power in your body. It loads up with all the power and energy of the backswing and waits to release it in the downswing. It's okay to lift your left foot a bit at the top of the backswing, but don't overdo it because this can throw off your accuracy. If possible, keep your left foot on the ground.

Everything in its place

At the very top of the backswing you should feel a tremendous amount of potential energy in your coiled body that is just waiting to spring loose and wallop the golf ball. You should feel athletic and poised to whip the club around smoothly and naturally. Your shoulders should be turned a full 90 degrees and your hips should be turned about 45 degrees. Of course, these angles will vary according to how flexible you are and are given here as benchmarks only.

Practice the backswing over and over again. Try it in front of a mirror to see if your body parts are in their proper positions along the way. Better yet, have a friend watch you and let you know if anything is out of position.

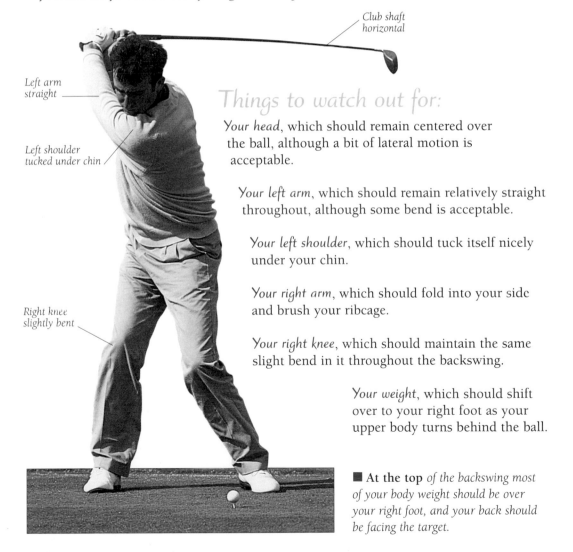

Club shaft horizontal

Left arm straight

Left shoulder tucked under chin

Right knee slightly bent

Things to watch out for:

Your head, which should remain centered over the ball, although a bit of lateral motion is acceptable.

Your left arm, which should remain relatively straight throughout, although some bend is acceptable.

Your left shoulder, which should tuck itself nicely under your chin.

Your right arm, which should fold into your side and brush your ribcage.

Your right knee, which should maintain the same slight bend in it throughout the backswing.

Your weight, which should shift over to your right foot as your upper body turns behind the ball.

■ **At the top** *of the backswing most of your body weight should be over your right foot, and your back should be facing the target.*

Step 3: The downswing: releasing all that stored energy

Now things really begin to get interesting. The downswing is the main attraction, the moment of truth. It's when all the action of the swing really starts. While the backswing should feel slow, smooth, and controlled, the downswing should convey a feeling of release and of graceful, accelerating yet unhurried power. Watch Ernie Els during his downswing, and you'll see how smooth the transition from the backswing can be. In fact, hold onto that thought:

Transitioning from the top of the backswing to the beginning of the downswing should be as seamless and graceful as possible, with no hint of yanking the club down furiously into the ball.

Unfortunately, this is exactly what many amateur golfers do. A perfect backswing and top position can be sabotaged by a poor transition down to the ball.

The worst thing to do from the top position is to initiate your downswing with your arms.

This could cause the club head to deliver a glancing, *out-to-in* (or over-the-top) blow, and can cancel out all of the stored energy in your legs, hips, and torso.

From the hip...

The first move you make from the top of the backswing should be with your hips, which should begin to turn back toward your target. In effect, your entire body is now going to uncoil itself from the hips up. Think of a twisted rubber band in a toy airplane uncoiling and releasing its energy into the propeller. Don't worry about your arms and hands; they should be the last part of you to turn. As your hips begin turning, they'll naturally pull your torso and shoulders along, which will in turn bring along your arms, hands, and club. The club head should be the very last thing to move on the downswing.

> **DEFINITION**
>
> An *out-to-in* blow, or coming over the top, happens when the club head comes at the ball from outside of the imaginary target line and hits the ball with a glancing, right-to-left blow. Imagine the target line extended behind the ball. Now visualize the club head being swung down at the ball. The proper direction from which the club head should come at the ball is inside of that target line, close to your body. Golfers who deliver an out-to-in blow come at the ball from outside that line, crossing over it as they strike the ball.

■ **The downswing** *begins from the hips, followed by the top half of the body, which uncoils in one smooth movement.*

As your body begins to uncoil, you need to make sure your weight starts to shift from your right foot to your left foot.

This weight shift plays a crucial role in hitting with power. If you fail to shift your weight (or shift it from left to right, called a reverse pivot), you will suffer a significant loss of power and accuracy. The weight shift should occur naturally, though, and should not be forced. If you shift your weight very deliberately, you could find yourself swaying laterally, a sure way to prevent solid contact with the ball.

Uncoiling your body

Once you have all your parts turning on the downswing, you should start to feel as if you are pulling the club down into the ball with your left hand. You should certainly feel this way by the time the club shaft is pointing straight back and the bottom of your grip is pointing at your target. As you uncoil, try to maintain the bend in your wrists as long as possible. They should be the very last part of you to release before hitting the ball.

Players who are able to snap their wrists open at the last moment hit with more power.

If you uncoil your body properly, this late release of the wrists will occur naturally, due to centrifugal force. Golfers who consciously try to unbend their wrists too early lose power and accuracy. A proper downswing should give the feeling of swinging the club into a narrow slot, on its way toward impact. On the way down, you should make sure that your right elbow (for right-handed golfers) remains close in to your side, almost rubbing against your rib cage. If it does not stay in close, the club head might come into the ball from the outside, causing a slice.

Cracking the whip

As your body unwinds during the downswing, the club head will be moving faster and faster toward the ball. If you have performed your backswing and initiated the downswing properly, you should have good form. Once the downswing gathers speed, you're basically just along for the ride. The centrifugal force that has built up will be too strong for your hands and arms to make any meaningful corrections to the downswing. That's why proper setup and backswing mechanics are so important. As the club head approaches the ball, your body is simply part of a golfing bull whip; the crack of that whip is impact.

Step 4: Impact

How the club head makes contact with the ball determines the flight path of the shot, plain and simple. To hit a relatively straight shot, the club head must be traveling directly down your target line, and the club face must be perpendicular to the line. If the path of the club head points to the right of the target line, your ball will go right. If it points to the left, the ball will go left. Simple physics. If the club face is open (or rotated to the right of the target line, for a right-handed golfer), the ball will spin clockwise and bend to the right of the target line. If the club face is closed (or rotated left of the target line, for a right-handed golfer), the ball will spin counterclockwise and bend to the left of the target line. Again, physics.

Weight transfer

At impact both arms should be relatively straight. Your right arm will have gradually unfolded from its tucked position and your left arm will have remained straight throughout the backswing and downswing.

VIP *At impact your body looks a lot like it did at address, except that most of your weight should now have shifted to your left foot (for a right-handed golfer).*

This weight transfer is essential to hitting the ball with power and accuracy. Failing to do so (or doing it backward – reverse pivot, remember) is one of the most common mistakes beginners make.

Practice swings

To get a real feel for proper weight transfer, take a few practice swings and intentionally shift your weight back on the backswing and forward on the downswing. Back and forth, back and forth. For a right-handed golfer it should be right foot, left foot. Ideally, you want to have your club head moving straight down the target line at impact, with the club face perpendicular to the line. Doing so will ensure a straight shot that does not hook or slice away from your target.

How do you make this happen? You guessed it: practice, practice, practice. There's no way around it. You have to experience the impact and see the results before you know if all the parts of your swing were properly dialed in. The resulting flight of the ball is the only evidence you'll have.

Step 5: Releasing the club at impact

As the club head comes into the ball during the downswing, your hands and forearms rotate counterclockwise just a bit (for a right-handed golfer). This creates what is called a *release of the club head* into the ball. The club head rotates into the ball until it is perpendicular to the target line. Without this action, the club face would stay open, or point right of the target line (for a right-handed golfer), and cause a slice.

Visualization

Visualization can help you execute the release of the club head. Simply think about your right forearm rotating over your left (for a right-handed golfer) as you swing through the ball. At the moment of impact, your right hand and forearm should be gradually turning over your left. The back of your left hand at impact should be pointing straight down the target line rather than pointing upward. After impact, the back of your right hand should begin to point skyward rather than down toward the ground.

DEFINITION

Release of the club head *occurs when your right forearm begins to cross over your left forearm at the moment of impact. When this happens, the club head is actually turning in unison with your arms and hands. This releasing of the club head ensures a straight and powerful shot.*

■ **After impact** *the hips should rotate in the direction of the club face along the target line, and the back of the right hand should rotate toward the sky.*

DOWNSWING AND IMPACT

As the quality of the impact is determined by the accuracy of your downswing, try to visualize your body's movement as you unwind into the swing. Ensure your weight shifts to the left from the hips, and that you follow through with the club after impact.

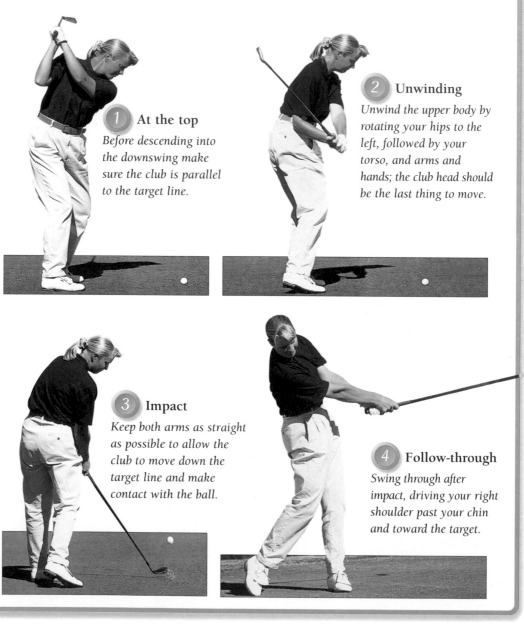

1 At the top

Before descending into the downswing make sure the club is parallel to the target line.

2 Unwinding

Unwind the upper body by rotating your hips to the left, followed by your torso, and arms and hands; the club head should be the last thing to move.

3 Impact

Keep both arms as straight as possible to allow the club to move down the target line and make contact with the ball.

4 Follow-through

Swing through after impact, driving your right shoulder past your chin and toward the target.

Step 6: Following through

The follow-through is what your body and club do after impact. Although your follow-through will not affect the ball in any way, you still need to complete your swing properly. Think about it: If you suddenly stopped swinging the club the instant you contacted the ball, you would lose club-head speed and probably hurt your wrists and arms. You would also never see exactly where the club ended up as the result of your swing, which can often tell you if you are swinging properly. So you must let the club wind back around your body after hitting the ball.

A perfectly balanced finish

When you finish your swing, your hips should be turned enough to allow your belly button to face the target. Your right foot should come up onto the toes, and most of your weight should be on your left foot. You should actually be able to lift your right foot without falling over.

The club itself should wrap around your shoulders, and your back should remain relatively straight. If your body has a "reverse C" look to it, that is, your back is bent backward, you probably left most of your weight on your right foot – a serious leak in power. If your back stays straight and your weight has shifted to your left foot, you have performed the follow-through well.

Finally, make an effort to freeze your body in the finishing position, at least for a few seconds, while you watch the flight of the ball. If you do not fall over, it means you maintained your balance well, which is crucial to good shot making.

■ **You should end** *the swing with your spine as straight as possible, and your right shoulder over your left foot. A balanced finish is a sign that your swing has been correctly executed.*

Start off with your 7-iron

AS I'VE ALREADY MENTIONED, *your golf clubs vary in many ways, including length, loft, and lie angle. The driver is your longest club, has the least amount of loft, and has the flattest (or most shallow) swing plane. Your sand or lob wedge is the shortest, with the most loft and the steepest swing plane. When you begin to work on your swing, don't practice with the longest or shortest clubs because they create swing conditions unique to their size and makeup.*

■ **Your 7-iron** *is the best club for swing practice as it allows you to see where your mistakes lie, and is your safest bet for making good, square impact with the ball.*

The best club for the job

Consider using a club that is right smack in the middle of the road, your 7-iron. The 7-iron is of average length and so will be easier to control than your driver. It also has an average swing plane and just the right degree of loft to get the ball up in the air and out a good distance. If you use a wedge to practice, the high amount of loft will create a lot of backspin, which negates sidespin, the cause of hooks and slices. Then you won't be able to tell whether there is a problem in your swing. Hooks or slices really won't show up because the sidespin that creates them is canceled out by the tremendous amount of backspin.

Practicing with a 7-iron will enable you to see if the ball is hooking, slicing, or going straight. Use it in the beginning when you're learning to swing. It will inspire more confidence because it's easier to hit with than the long clubs. The 7-iron will also reveal your true ball flight more readily than your shorter clubs.

Your 7-iron is the perfect compromise for when you're learning or whenever you need to work on improving or changing your swing.

A simple summary

✓ The golf swing involves both the vertical and the horizontal planes, while the baseball swing involves only the horizontal. That's why the golf swing is harder to perfect.

✓ The perfect golf swing is not forced or violent; it should be smooth, rhythmic, and balanced.

✓ When swinging, you should not think about hitting the golf ball. Instead, think about just swinging through the ball as if the ball weren't there.

✓ The perfect swing plane should tend toward being flatter and not overly steep.

✓ The backswing should begin slowly, with the club head moving back low to the ground. Your entire body should begin rotating back as one unit.

✓ At the top of your swing, your right arm (for a right-handed golfer) should be folded in to your side, while your left arm should be relatively straight but not stiff. Your hips should turn about 45 degrees, while your shoulders should turn about 90 degrees. Your weight should be on your right foot.

✓ Think of the downswing as your body uncoiling. First your hips turn, then your shoulders, then your arms and hands, followed finally by the club head. The feeling should be one of snapping a whip. During the downswing, your weight should transfer from the right foot to the left foot.

✓ After impact, always finish your swing. Not following through can result in injury to your wrists and will also cause a deceleration of the club head, resulting in decreased distance and poor form.

✓ When first learning your swing, use your 7-iron, the perfect middle-of-the-road club.

PART THREE

PRECISE PUTTING IS AN ESSENTIAL SHORT GAME SKILL

THE SHORT GAME

THE MAJORITY OF YOUR shots on the course will be made from within 50 yards of the green. As *exciting* as a long drive is, it's the shorter shots that set you up for good scores. The pros have known this for decades. Good putting, chipping, and pitching will  always put you one up over any *competitor* regardless of his or her distance off the tee. In other words, to lower your scores you must have a stellar short game.

In this part I'll explain how to play the *best game possible* from inside of 50 yards of the green. Although these short shots may not have the drama of a smoked drive or a long, high-flying 3-iron, they will save you from bad situations and give you the opportunity to go low on every hole.

Chapter 11

Mastering the Basics of Putting

To SAY THAT PUTTING is an important part of the game of golf is an understatement. Learning to putt consistently, particularly for the beginner, is essential. Putting well can mean the difference between a good round and one that makes you want to give up and try tennis. First I'll explain why this is so, and then I'll get into the mechanics and strategy of putting together a great putt.

In this chapter...

✓ Half your strokes means half your game

✓ Choose your weapon

✓ The putting stance

✓ The putting grip

✓ The elements of putting style

✓ What stroke is right for you?

AT WORK ON THE PRACTICE PUTTING GREEN

Half your strokes means half your game

PUTTING ISN'T just one last thing you do to finish up a hole. Believe it or not, those little strokes can have a big impact on your total score. Just do the math: If you take two putts per hole over an 18-hole course, that adds up to 36 shots, or about half of par. Half of all the shots on the course! And if you take three putts per hole (as many average golfers often do), that's 54 shots.

Putting precision

The best professional golfers average about 30 putts per round, or about 1.7 putts per hole. This means they rarely need three putts on any green and will sometimes need only one. The reason they do so well with the "flat stick" is simple: they work at it, constantly.

■ **Many professional golfers** *have developed their own successful style of putting. Ben Crenshaw (above) is well known for his long, lazy putting stroke.*

An essential skill

Professionals devote at least half of their practice time to the short game, with putting receiving the most focus. That's because they know that putting is the most fickle part of the game, and also one that can win or lose a tournament. Consider David Duval, one of the best golfers today. It is no coincidence that he won four tournaments in less than four months in 1999, while also leading the PGA Tour in putting statistics. For the pros, putting well means winning. Most of them can compensate somewhat for a swing that isn't quite up to par through good chipping, pitching, and bunker play.

Take away good putting, though, and the game is over.

Putting in the time

For most amateur golfers, two putts per hole is a great average to strive for. That's half a normal par score.

You should therefore devote half your practice time to putting if you want to have any hope of scoring well.

This is a difficult concept for most rookie golfers, who derive the most pleasure from seeing the ball go a long way off the tee. The average beginner will hit bucket after bucket of golf balls at the range, often focusing on the distance clubs. Then, after working up a good sweat, he or she might go over to the practice putting green and slap the ball around for a few minutes, just to cool down. If that's your plan for improvement, you won't be seeing lower scores any time soon.

Trivia...

The condition of putting greens back in the old days didn't come close to approaching the pristine greens of today. Until the late 1950s, players had to use a very wristy putting stroke in order to get the ball up and moving on the irregular and often long grass surfaces. Today's near-perfect greens allow players to use the more effective pendulum stroke, which doesn't use wrist break at all.

The practice green

Take some good advice and spend half of your available practice time on the putting green. It takes awhile to develop and maintain a sensitive touch with the putter, especially for getting long putts close to the hole and for learning to read the greens properly. It also takes constant practice to maintain these skills, which seem to vanish unless they're used every day. You won't regret it, especially when you start draining those long, breaking putts, to the amazement of your golfing buddies.

■ **Putting represents** *close to half of the strokes played during a round of golf, so it is important to spend time at the practice green honing your skills.*

Choose your weapon

YOU ARE GOING TO *use your putter more than any other club in your bag, so it makes sense to buy one you are comfortable with in terms of look, feel, and performance. A quick trip to the local golf store will tell you that the variety of putter styles is nearly endless. There are heel-shafted and center-shafted putters, face-balanced putters, mallet-head putters, long putters, and even wooden putters. Many models sold today have plastic, synthetic rubber, or metal alloy face inserts, which are designed to improve the feel of the golf ball's impact with the face. Some putters have distinct aiming lines applied to the top of the club head, while others have rounded outlines or unique shaft designs. Perhaps more than any other club, the putter comes in all flavors.*

INTERNET

www.npursuit.com

This is the home page of N-Pursuit, which makes George Low Silver Wiz putters with silver inserts in the face. Obviously, this is a high-ticket item.

Try before you buy

Visit a number of golf stores and try out all the putters you can. Most stores will have some type of artificial putting green set up so that you can test the club. In addition to trying out the different designs, consider experimenting with the length of the putter. Often a design you initially do not like becomes your favorite when it's shortened or lengthened by a few inches.

Make sure you are also happy with the feel of the ball coming off the putter face. This is determined by the material from which the head is constructed, and by whatever type of insert (if any) is built into the head. Even the sound of the ball being struck must appeal to you if you are to fork out upward of $100 for this club. Remember, much of golf is psychological – if you do not feel aesthetically comfortable with a club, don't buy it.

STRAIGHT-
SET TOE-
AND-HEEL

TOE-AND-
HEEL WITH
LARGE HEAD

OFFSET TOE-
AND-HEEL

CENTER-
SHAFTED
PUTTER

MALLET-
HEADED
PUTTER

ONSET-
HEADED
PUTTER

■ **Putters** *come in a wider variety of shapes and sizes than any other club in your bag.*

There's no "right way" to putt

Perhaps more than any other aspect of the game, successful putting remains an individualistic, highly subjective skill. The putting stroke is relatively simple as the club head needn't travel more than a foot or two, and the only requirement is to put the ball into the hole. That's great news for you; because putts are such simple shots, beginners have an excellent chance of doing quite well right from the start.

Consistent mechanics

What style of putting you adopt is up to you, provided you can consistently put the ball into the hole. Once you decide upon your style and it seems to work well, it's important to stay with it. Just as you need to keep your full swing mechanics relatively consistent in order to reliably hit the ball, so must you keep your putting mechanics consistent (unless of course you find yourself missing every two-foot putt that comes along).

The putting stance

JUST AS WITH THE FULL SWING, how you address the ball when you're preparing to putt is an important key to success. Even though stance is largely a matter of style, which is entirely up to you, I can give you some basic guidelines to put you on the right track for success.

Different stances

The first thing to consider is foot placement. Some players putt with an *open stance*, while others use a *closed stance*. To make things simple, consider starting out with a *neutral stance*, with your feet on a line that is parallel to the target line. You should line yourself up with your left side facing the hole, if you are a right-handed golfer, so you are putting from right to left.

> **DEFINITION**
>
> *In an open stance your feet should be placed along a line that points left of the target. In a closed stance your feet should be placed on a line pointing to the right of the target. In a neutral stance your feet should be on a line parallel to the target line.*

Adopting a neutral stance

Your feet should be about a shoulder-width apart with your weight evenly distributed between them. You should be looking straight down at the ball so that you can properly see the path the ball should take. This means you'll need to bend over enough for your head to be over the ball. Also, make sure your knees are bent slightly. The basic putting stance looks almost as if the player is crouching slightly, with arms hanging down loosely in front and face turned to the ground. You should be bent a bit at the hips, with your rear end sticking out slightly. Above all, let your arms hang down relaxed and tension-free with your elbows in close to your sides. When you're putting, it is best to avoid putting any backspin on the ball. The ball should never become airborne and should ideally begin rolling end-over-end as soon as it impacts with the putter.

Finding the ideal ball position

To get the ball rolling right away, you'll need to strike it with an ever-so-slight upward motion, catching the ball on its equator. To make sure this happens, the ball must be positioned properly. A ball that is too far over to the right (for a right-handed golfer) when hit will bounce, jump, or slide, reducing the odds of a successful outcome. To determine the best ball position for a putt, take your putting stance, hold a golf ball directly below your left eye, and drop the ball straight down to the grass. Watch exactly where it hits (never mind where it rolls off to), then simply place the ball on the grass about one inch to the left of that point. That will be the best position for the ball when you're putting.

SETTING UP TO PUTT

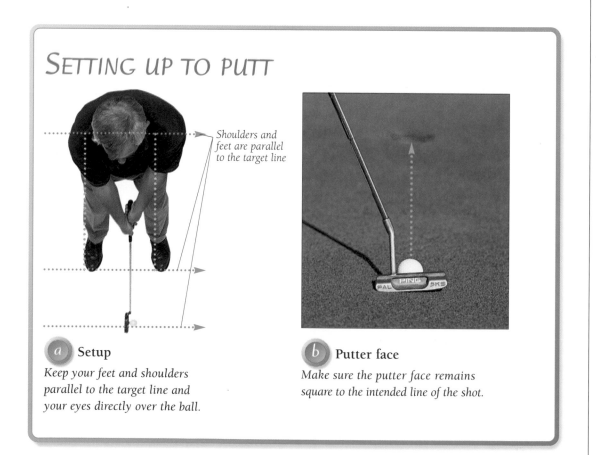

Shoulders and feet are parallel to the target line

a Setup

Keep your feet and shoulders parallel to the target line and your eyes directly over the ball.

b Putter face

Make sure the putter face remains square to the intended line of the shot.

The putting grip

THE POWER OF A GOOD PUTT lies in the grip. Although the style of your grip is up to you, whichever one you choose should help you minimize wrist action, which will give you more control.

Minimizing wrist action

Years ago greens used to be less uniform than they are now, requiring players to use some wrist action to get the ball rolling properly. With today's greens, however, this is usually not necessary.

The best strategy for today's more uniform, well-maintained greens is to remove as much wrist action from the putting stroke as possible, and instead use a pendulum-like stroke in which your arms and shoulders move in unison, creating a smooth, repeatable action.

To minimize wrist action, you'll need to hold your putter differently than other clubs.

Reverse-overlap grip

Consider trying the reverse-overlap grip to start with. The most popular putting grip, it does a good job of joining your two hands into one working unit and eliminating wrist action. In this grip, the left index finger (for a right-handed golfer) is draped over the fingers of the right hand, often fitting into the groove made by the pinky and the ring finger of the right hand.

To form this grip, place your right hand onto the grip of the putter, leaving room at the top for your left hand. The right palm should be pointing directly down the target line. Next, slide your left hand into place above the right, with its palm facing the right palm. Now drape the index finger of your left hand over your right fingers, letting it either fit into the pinky-ring finger groove or to simply sit atop all the fingers of the right hand. The thumbs of both hands should rest directly on top of the putter grip. Try forming this grip right now if you have a putter handy. Take a few strokes and try to feel how the hands work together as one, with little or no wrist action.

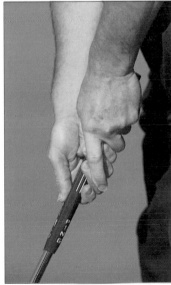

■ **The reverse-overlap grip**, *favored by pros such as Jack Nicklaus, keeps the wrist locked in position through the hitting zone.*

Cross-handed grip

Another putting grip that seems to have become more and more popular lately is the cross-handed style, in which the left hand (for a right-handed golfer) is placed below the right. Used by professionals such as Fred Couples and Vijay Singh, this style tends to do an even better job of preventing the left wrist from bending, or breaking down, than does the standard reverse-overlap grip. To form the cross-handed grip, place your right hand (for right-handed golfers) onto the top of the putter grip, with your thumb on top. Then, simply place your left hand below your right so that its heel rests atop the thumb of your right hand. Make sure that both thumbs are on top of the putter grip.

Try forming this grip now, then take a few strokes with it. Notice how it keeps the left wrist frozen? That's the advantage of the cross-handed grip.

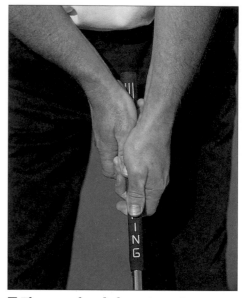

■ **The cross-handed putting grip** *ensures a pendulum-like action on the back and through strokes. It has been used by players such as Fred Couples and Bernhard Langer.*

Lighten up

The cross-handed grip will work well for some golfers, while others will feel more comfortable using the reverse-overlap grip. Try both, and go with whatever feels the best to you. Whichever grip you use, though, the most important thing to remember (besides avoiding a *wristy stroke*) is to keep your grip pressure as light as possible, to prevent muscle tension from creeping into the picture.

DEFINITION

When your wrist bends during a putt, in golf lingo it is breaking down. A wristy stroke is one in which the wrists break down, and that wrist action contributes greatly to the path of the shot (definitely not for the better).

Do not grip the putter too firmly or your accuracy will suffer.

Instead, as with the other clubs, hold the putter softly, almost as if you were holding an egg. Keeping this soft, delicate feel in your grip will improve your results tremendously, so remember to keep it simple and lighten up!

The elements of putting style

AT ADDRESS, YOUR ARMS and shoulders should appear to form a triangle, with your two shoulders and your hands (as one unit, remember) being the three points. When you make your putting stroke, this triangle should remain the same size and simply swing back and forth slightly. This way your wrists will remain as still as possible, and all the action will come from your arms and shoulders.

If you try to swing only with your arms or wrists, the triangle will change shape. Keep it the same throughout the stroke and you'll have more success on the greens. This method will deliver the putter face to the ball consistently and reproduce the same force more readily, helping you to predict distance and speed more reliably. When you're putting, don't let the putter head get ahead of your hands at any time. If this happens, it means you are using too much arm and wrist in your stroke. Make sure your hands and the putter head pass the ball at the same moment to guarantee that your wrists are not flipping at the ball.

THE PUTT SWING PATH

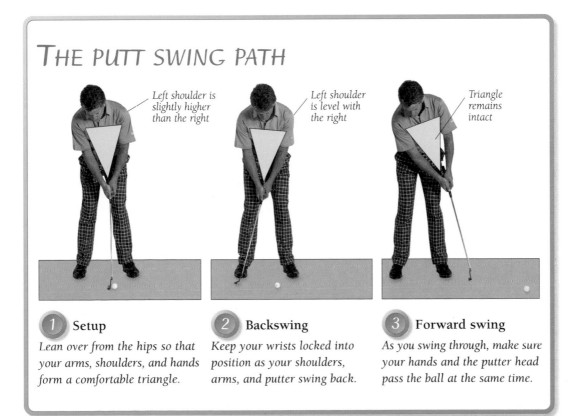

Left shoulder is slightly higher than the right

Left shoulder is level with the right

Triangle remains intact

1 Setup
Lean over from the hips so that your arms, shoulders, and hands form a comfortable triangle.

2 Backswing
Keep your wrists locked into position as your shoulders, arms, and putter swing back.

3 Forward swing
As you swing through, make sure your hands and the putter head pass the ball at the same time.

Committing to your stroke

Another important point to consider when putting is the acceleration of the putter head through the hitting zone. Simply put, this means that you must avoid at all cost slowing down the stroke. Doing so will result in poor distance control and unreliable accuracy. To prevent this from happening, make sure to commit to your stroke and then putt through the ball with a confident move. Think of the full swing: the backswing is slow and deliberate, while the downswing is much faster in comparison. Let your putting stroke mirror your full swing and you won't go wrong.

Simple symmetry

How far a putt will travel depends on the length of your backswing, once you adjust for the speed of the green you are putting on. Only practice will clue you in to what length of a backswing will produce a what-length putt. However, one general rule when putting is that your backswing should be as long as your follow-through. This will add a sense of balance to your stroke, helping you better judge distance and direction. Golfers who have a short backswing followed by a jabbing, jerky follow-through often suffer in the distance and accuracy departments, as will golfers who take a long backswing and follow it up with an abbreviated, decelerated follow-through.

Be as smooth and symmetrical as possible with your stroke, and you should do just fine.

Eyes over the ball

One last point on the fundamentals: Try to keep your head as still as possible. Keep your eyes on the ball, and then make your stroke. Then, even as your ball begins to run toward the hole, keep looking at where the ball had been. Keeping your head still through the putting stroke will help reduce the chances of your turning the club head inside of the target line and therefore missing the putt, which would go left of the hole. Keeping your head still helps keep your lower body still as well. Only your arms and shoulders should move during the putting stroke.

What stroke is right for you?

FOR MOST OF GOLF'S HISTORY, *the putting stroke has been a small-scale version of the full swing, mirroring the opening of the club face on the backswing and the closing of it on the downswing and follow-through. The putter blade is taken back a foot or two on a slight arc, then returned into the back of the ball on that same arc, the entire movement resembling a gentle curve. This is known as an inside-to-inside stroke.*

The target line

For some time now, however, many instructors have been advocating a straight-back-and-through putting stroke, in which the putter blade travels only along the line of the putt, with no arc at all. The idea behind this stroke is that it greatly reduces the chances of the ball being hit off of the target line.

Although both types of stroke seem to work well when performed properly, both can also present problems. With the inside-to-inside stroke, putts can miss the target line if the putter face does not contact the ball at the precise moment at which the face is traveling straight down the path to the hole.

Straight-back-and-through stroke

The straight-back-and-through stroke goes against the body's natural arcing geometry and requires the golfer to actually manipulate the putter head slightly on the backswing and the follow-through. In order to take the putter head back a foot or two along a perfectly straight line, you must cancel out your physical tendency to follow an arc. This is done by rotating the head of the putter slightly to the left on the backswing, and rotating it slightly to the right during the follow-through. Without manipulating the putter head in this way, it would be impossible to move it back and through on a straight path. Your arms just wouldn't allow it. The wrist manipulations needed to accomplish this straight-line club path do exactly what basic putting mechanics tell you not to do: introduce wrist action into the stroke.

STRAIGHT-BACK-AND-THROUGH PUTTING

Use this stroke for putts of less than eight feet. The putter head moves less than a foot in either direction and remains on the target line throughout the shot. Using this stroke on short putts will result in fewer misses left or right.

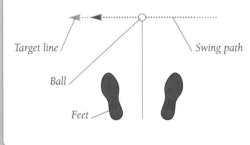

Target line
Swing path
Ball
Feet

Thumb points down shaft

Relaxed stance

Putter face is square to target line of shot

1 **Setup**

Lean over from the hips, letting your shoulders, arms, and hands form a triangle. Keep your eyes over the ball.

INSIDE-TO-INSIDE PUTTING

Use this stroke for putts of more than eight feet. The putter head follows a gentle, curving arc through the backswing and follow-through, striking the ball at the center of the arc.

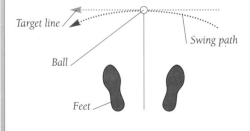

Target line
Swing path
Ball
Feet

1 **Setup**

Let your shoulders, arms, and hands form a triangle, and keep your eyes over the ball.

2 **Backswing**

Take the putter blade back several feet on a slight arc away from the target line.

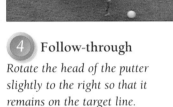

2 Backswing

Rotate the putter slightly to the left as it moves back so that it travels only along the line of the putt.

3 Forward swing

Keep the putter head on a straight path as you swing through to strike the ball.

4 Follow-through

Rotate the head of the putter slightly to the right so that it remains on the target line.

3 Forward swing

Return the putter blade to the back of the ball on that same arc, resembling a gentle curve.

4 Impact

Strike the ball at the center of the arc, keeping your wrists locked in position throughout the stroke.

5 Follow-through

Ensure the follow-though is a smooth, continuous action and the same length as your backswing.

Short putting

Which stroke is the right one to use? Good question. The answer is probably a compromise of the two. On putts of less than eight feet, using the straight-back-and-through stroke makes sense because the putter head needs to move less than a foot in either direction. Keeping the putter head on a straight path will be easy because of the short stroke, making the minute wrist rotations almost imperceptible. Using this stroke on short putts will result in fewer misses left or right.

Long putting

On putts of more than eight feet, however, the straight-back-and-through stroke becomes harder to execute. The laws of physics will force the putter to travel in an arc once you begin to take it back more than a few inches. A putt of 35 feet, for instance, might require you to bring the putter head back and through as much as two to three feet in each direction. Under these circumstances the putter head should be allowed to follow a gentle, curving arc. The ball should be struck at the very center of the arc. To make sure this happens, your backswing and follow-through must be equal in length.

Use the straight-back-and-through stroke on putts of less than eight feet, and the inside-to-inside stroke on any putt that's longer. This compromise will result in better distance and accuracy control.

■ **There's nothing** *like the sound of the ball plunking into the hole, so head for the practice green to improve your chance of making that putt!*

Getting a feel for your putter

Go out and practice both styles to get a feel for the dynamics of each. Place a yardstick down on the ground and, directly over it, make some practice strokes with your putter to get a feel for the natural arc the head wants to follow. Then try the straight-back-and-through stroke over the yardstick and notice how much wrist rotation is needed to keep the putter head running along a straight line. Eventually you will get a feel for both and understand why the inside-to-inside stroke is better-suited to longer putts.

A simple summary

✓ There is no right way to putt. All that matters is that you feel comfortable in your address position, and can hit the ball consistently and with success.

✓ One key to good putting is to find a putter that you feel comfortable with.

✓ Which putting stance you adopt is up to you, although it might be a good idea to start off with one that is neutral, with the line of your feet parallel to the target line. Generally the ball should be positioned closer to your left foot than your right foot, if you're a right-handed golfer.

✓ A light grip and a pendulum motion of the arms and shoulders are essential to a good putting stroke. Don't move your wrists through the stroke – let your arms and shoulders do the work.

✓ The length of your backswing should equal the length of your follow-through.

✓ Always keep your head down during your stroke.

✓ Whether you choose the straight-back-and-through stroke or the inside-to-inside stroke, make sure you are as consistent as possible.

Chapter 12

Simple Putting Strategies

There's more to a putt than your stroke. Putting requires a very different technique than any other kind of shot. You putt the ball over short distances, but your aim must be extremely precise. You must control speed, distance, and accuracy to an extremely exacting level. And the line of your shot must be dead-on. In this chapter I'll explain the finer points of putting, from controlling the speed of the ball to the all-important pre-shot routine.

In this chapter...

✓ A feel for speed and distance

✓ Reading the break

✓ Making short putts

✓ Lagging long putts

✓ Your pre-shot routine

JACK NICKLAUS, MASTER STRATEGIST

A feel for speed and distance

MUCH OF WHAT THE BALL DOES *while it's heading toward the hole is determined by its speed. Hit it too hard and the ball will fly past the hole, leaving you with a long recovery shot. Hit it too gently and the ball will end up short of the hole (and you will end up groaning).*

Hitting the ball

Also, the harder you hit the ball, the less it will curve, or *break*. If you plan for six or seven inches of break but hit the ball too hard, it will break only two or three inches and miss the hole. Hit it too softly and the ball will break more than you planned, again missing the target. Even a two-foot putt hit too hard can miss the cup completely and scoot right over it, or *lip out*.

Clearly, the speed of a putt is crucial to its ultimate success. Speed and distance are intimately tied together on the putting green — one defines and determines the other.

So how can you decide how hard to hit the ball? You need to get the ball to the hole, right? No ball that ends up two feet short of the hole has any chance of dropping in. Not ever. So the first requirement when putting is to hit the ball hard enough so that, if it does miss, it will not roll more than two feet past the hole. At least then the follow-up putt will be easy.

> **DEFINITION**
>
> *The break of a putt is the amount the ball curves left or right, according to the slope of the green. Lip out means the ball enters the hole on the very edge and, instead of dropping in, swirls around the circumference of the cup and pops back out due to excess centrifugal force. That will really make you groan!*

■ **Jack Nicklaus** *is an expert putter who knows just how hard to hit the ball. As a result, he has spent many years at the top of world golf.*

How hard is hard enough?

How do you learn to do this? It's simple. You go out onto the practice putting green and hit putts of various lengths until you begin to get a feel for how much force a 20-foot putt requires, and a nine-footer, and a 40-footer. You hit balls from different positions and begin learning how a certain length putt feels in your hands and arms.

After enough practice, your mind will begin to develop a certain sense of how hard is hard enough. Muscle memory will kick in and enable you to dial in just the right amount of force needed to hit the putt with just the force you need. (If you're like me, you were hoping there was some quicker way to learn this, or maybe a basic formula. Sorry, but there isn't.)

Simple practice drills

When you're working on developing distance control, don't hit putt after putt from the same location and distance.

This does nothing to improve your putting skills. Anyone can eventually make a 15-foot putt if he or she tries it enough times from the same spot. Real golf isn't like that; no two putts are ever the same. Your practice should therefore mimic the real thing if you really want to improve.

You need to putt every ball from a different distance and angle. Or putt several balls from the same spot but to different locations on the green. Pace off 10 , 20-, and 30-foot distances and try to putt a ball to each spot in succession. Drills like these will greatly improve your feel for distance and for what speed you need to hit any given putt. Learning to gauge speed and distance on the greens is perhaps the best way to lower your golf score – short of taking lessons from Jack Nicklaus.

■ **Putting** *can be the cause of more frustration in golf than almost anything else. To develop a sense of how hard to hit the ball, practice making shots from different positions around the hole.*

183

Reading the break

ONCE YOU'VE BEGUN TO *understand and master how to putt the ball specific distances, you can begin to learn how to analyze other conditions of a putt. You will then be able to tell how much the ball will break during its short trip across the green, and what you need to do to compensate for those conditions so you can sink the ball. The break of a putt is determined by a number of factors, including the slope of the green itself, the direction the grass is growing (known as the grain), the speed of the green, and the wind direction and speed. Reading the break is very important, because if you know your ball is not going to travel in a straight line, you can aim your shot accordingly.*

The slope of the green

Figuring out the *slope* of the green is the first part of reading the break. Look at the green and imagine a small stream of water flowing out from a hose. If the nozzle were placed right where your ball is, which way do you think the water would flow? That's the course your putt will take. To get a good view of the slope, look at the line of the putt from behind the ball and from behind the hole. This is the best way to see the break.

DEFINITION

The various contours of a putting green are referred to collectively as the slope. Reading the slope can only be learned through experience.

Judging the slope

Often the slope will be very obvious to the eye: The putt will be uphill or downhill, and you won't have much problem seeing how the ball will break. Other times a green may appear to be relatively flat, making your job of judging the slope a little harder.

■ **Bernhard Langer** *often blinkers his eyes for total concentration when reading a break. This "tunnel vision" technique enables him to visualize the shot more clearly.*

Surveying the lie of the land

There may be so little slope that, to your eyes, it looks as though your putt will travel dead straight. Then, after putting, you watch your ball break three or four inches to one side, not understanding why you couldn't detect that small slope differential. To pick up on subtle slope changes, learn to mentally survey the lie of the surrounding land.

For instance, if there is a body of water on the left side of the green, odds are the green slopes off slightly toward it. If there is a series of hills off to one side of the green, chances are the green slopes away from them.

Watching for these topographical clues will help you decide how your putt will break. Reading the break is not an exact science. It is, in fact, an exercise in feel, and although most greens tend to slope more one way than another, only with practice and experience will you master the art of reading the subtleties.

■ **Watch your** *playing partner and observe how his ball behaves as it approaches the hole. This will help you predict how your putt will break.*

Check the grain of the grass

Take an overall view of the green

Observe the slope

■ **Reading the green** *is something that can only be done successfully with experience. Study the green upon approach, looking in particular at the general slope and the direction in which the grass is growing.*

Aim for the break point

Let's say you've decided your putt is going to break to the right about four or five inches, provided that you hit it with enough force to stop the ball about a foot or two past the hole (remember, the harder you hit it, the less it will break). Your next step is to aim the ball at the spot where you believe the ball will begin turning. Make that spot your target, not the hole itself.

Visualize the ball traveling to that spot and then curling in toward the hole. By doing this you are actually treating the putt as if it were a straight one and not one that curves – and what could be simpler than a plain old straight putt? Decide at what point the ball will begin to break and simply aim for it, using enough force to send the ball just past the hole.

The effects of grain

Grain, the direction the grass is growing, can have a substantial effect on which way a putt breaks on the green. Blades of grass tend to grow in a certain direction, and which direction depends on the type of grass and the conditions on the course.

Trivia...

The two most common types of grass used on putting greens today are bent grass and Bermuda grass. Bent grass greens, found primarily in milder, more seasonal regions, have very little grain to them and will barely affect the roll of your ball. Bermuda grass, found in warmer regions, has a more noticeable grain that can affect the break of your putt substantially. Bent grass usually grows in the direction of the nearest body of water, while Bermuda grass grows in the direction of the setting sun.

If the grass is growing directly away from you, your putt will travel slightly faster than you think it should. If the grain is toward you, your putt will be slower. If the grass is growing across your line, the ball will have a tendency to turn slightly with the grain.

Determining the grain

There are several ways to determine the grain of the green. If the grass in front of you looks shiny and lighter green, it probably means the grain is pointing away from you and toward the hole. If the grass appears duller, it probably means the grain is pointing toward you. Another way to check the grain is to look at the grass around the circumference of the hole itself. One side of it will appear sharply cut, while the other will appear shaggier. The grain will be growing in the direction of the shaggy blades of grass.

WHAT THE HECK IS PLUMB-BOBBING?

Sometimes you see a player standing five or ten feet behind a ball dangling a putter by the grip in front of his or her face while facing the hole. That person is plumb-bobbing to read the slope of the green, in hopes of predicting how a putt will break.

Does plumb-bobbing work?

Although it seems a bit strange, plumb-bobbing can work – if it is done correctly and only one break is involved in the putt. It won't tell you anything about grain or irregularities on the putting line or around the hole, and it won't tell you anything about the wind or the speed of the green. It can be helpful in reinforcing your ideas about the slope of the green, though.

Using your dominant eye

Before you try plumb-bobbing, you must figure out which is your dominant eye. To do this, place your index finger in front of your face and use it to cover up an object 20 or 30 feet away, keeping both eyes open. Now close your right eye. If the object you covered with your finger is still covered, your left eye is dominant. If the object moves, your right eye is dominant. When plumb-bobbing, use only your dominant eye.

■ **Laura Davies** *plumb-bobs with her putter to read the slope of the green.*

Reading the slope

While standing about five to ten feet behind your ball, dangle your putter by the very end of the grip so that the shaft falls through the center of the cup and your ball.

Now, using only your dominant eye, note which way the cup seems to be slanting. If it slants down to the left, the putt will break left. If it slants down to the right, the putt will break right. Remember that this is not an extremely reliable method of determining break, but a way to support your initial conclusion. Also remember that speed, weather, regional topography and grain will all affect break. Plumb-bobbing is just a fun way to confirm your feelings.

Making short putts

WHEN YOU FIND YOUR *ball within a few feet of the hole, the only thought in your mind should be to sink that putt. Watch a professional tournament, and you will see very few missed short putts. The pros cannot afford to give these* gimmes *away. They're just too valuable.*

DEFINITION

A **gimme** *is a putt that is so short and so easy that your opponent concedes it to you without your having to take the shot. Perhaps the most famous gimme is the three-foot putt Jack Nicklaus conceded to Tony Jacklin in the 1969 Ryder Cup, thereby allowing his opponents to tie the match.*

You should always think you can make any putt inside of six feet, and be absolutely sure of making one inside three feet. How do you make that happen? First, believe it; you will make that putt! Second, be sure to use a short, straight back-and-through stroke (you remember those from Chapter 11, right?) to reduce the chances of the putt going off-line.

Hitting with confidence

Read the break carefully on every shot, but realize that the break on short putts can be reduced substantially by hitting the ball firmly, with good speed. This tactic takes confidence, because if you miss that firmly hit three-footer, the ball is going to go at least three feet past the hole, and maybe more. You could be left with a longer putt than you started with.

Even so, hitting a short putt with a little extra oomph will take out most of the break. All you need to do is aim at the center of the hole and stroke it.

With all your short putts, make sure to keep the putter head low to the grass on the backswing and the follow-through. This will keep you from coming down too steeply into the ball, which would cause it to hop and bounce off target. Your tempo and balance should be smooth and controlled, just as it is with the full swing. Think of that waltz (one-two-three) and you won't go wrong.

■ **At the height** *of his career, Tom Watson was one of the finest putters in the world. He always struck the ball positively and with confidence.*

Short putts

To master short putts, go out onto the putting green and practice as many three-foot putts in a row as you can. Measure out one club-length from the hole, and place a ring of ten balls around it. Take your time and try to sink all of them. Keep practicing this until you can make all ten. Always include this drill in your putting practices. It will pay off whenever your ball ends up a few feet from the hole during a round of golf. You'll make every short putt and eliminate the dreaded *three-putt* from your vocabulary.

■ **Your putting practice** *should include a number of three-foot putts, one after another. You'll then feel more relaxed and confident when making this shot on the course.*

> **DEFINITION**
>
> *A* **three-putt** *is when you take three putts to get your ball into the hole. Amateurs should work toward a two-putt average. The pros will need one-putt games.*

Longer putts

When you've mastered the three-foot putt, try the same drill with six-foot putts. You may not be able to make ten in a row, but you should be able to drop at least two or three out of ten. Eventually you'll develop a real feel for putts of this length. Take this feeling out onto the course and put it to good use.

■ **Spending time at** *the practice green helps you develop a feel for making putts of different lengths. Focus on developing a smooth, controlled stroke until you are consistently striking the ball straight and true.*

Lagging long putts

ALL GOLFERS WHO *are good putters have one thing in common: They have a great feel for speed and distance. This feel cannot be taught. It is learned over time and with lots of practice.*

VIP

When you're practicing putts longer than ten feet, a feel for proper speed is essential.

Your goal with these longer putts is to lag them; that is, not to sink them, but to get the ball as close to the hole as possible, leaving yourself an easy two- or three-foot putt to clean up. Being able to lag a 30-foot putt to within two or three feet of the hole will help drastically reduce the chance of making a dreaded three-putt – one reason why amateurs score such high numbers on the course. Too many times a golfer will make a good approach shot to the green, leaving a 20-footer for a birdie. He or she then powers the next putt six feet past the hole, and the comeback putt is missed by a few inches, giving up a par for a bogey. This frustrating scenario happens all the time to golfers who don't practice long lag putts consistently.

Mastering long putts

Mastering long lag putts means developing a good feel for distance. Which way the putt will break is less important for long putts than getting the right distance. Even if the ball breaks more or less than expected, with the right speed and distance it won't veer more than a few feet left or right of the hole. The putts that are six feet short or long will destroy your score, so practice those lags.

INTERNET

www.pelzgolf.com

You'll find great advice and instruction on putting, as well as all other aspects of the short game, at this site.

■ **The aim of** *lagging a long putt is not to sink the ball but to get it as close to the hole as possible, leaving yourself an easy two- or three-foot putt to finish.*

Improving your skills

One exercise to help you develop a good feel for lag putting is to place four balls at ten-foot increments away from the hole, so that the farthest one is out at the 40-foot mark and the closest is only ten feet away. Start with the shortest one, and work your way out to the longest. Another exercise you can do is to place balls down randomly on the practice green and putt them all to the nearest fringe – the edge of the green. Don't worry about hitting to an exact spot, just try to get each ball as close to the edge as possible. You'll be surprised at how close you can get them with a little practice.

■ **Develop your feel** *for distance by putting balls to the edge of the green, trying to get them as close to the fringe as possible. Competition with a friend will add a little edge to the exercise and help to focus your mind.*

Pretend it's for real!

After practicing these two exercises, place one ball about 30 feet from the hole and set up as if it were a putt in a tournament. Pretend that all you need to do is lag this one to within two or three feet, then make that easy short one. Do it and you win half a million dollars. Hunker down and think about the exact amount of force needed to roll the ball close. Use a smooth backswing and follow-through, making sure they balance each other out. Stroke the putt and watch it home in on the hole. Then tap the short putt in for the win!

Never hit the same shot twice

During your putting practice, try this drill at random times during the session. Try to mimic real-life conditions, hitting those long putts from different spots and different distances.

Also, never hit two in a row from the same spot. That's just not real golf, and it won't teach you to lag putt under pressure.

Your pre-shot routine

IN BOTH PUTTING AND making a full swing, you are hitting the ball toward the hole with a golf club. The only difference is that when you're putting, the ball never leaves the grass and travels a relatively short distance. Because the principle is the same, you should go through the same kind of pre-shot ritual you use for your full swing.

Simple steps for success

First, read the break by standing about five to ten feet behind your ball. Then confirm that impression by reading the break from behind the hole, looking toward your ball. Next, take a few practice strokes and try to imagine how hard you need to hit the ball. While you're busy imagining, visualize hitting the ball and seeing it take the right course toward the hole. Doing so will help you determine the right speed. Then place your putter head behind the ball, and aim the face directly on the line you have chosen. Remember to aim at the spot where you believe the ball will begin to turn toward the hole. If you feel that the putt is dead straight, then aim right for the center of the cup.

Trivia...

Back in the 1960s, Arnold Palmer started a trend by carefully peeling off his glove before putting. He'd neatly fold it and slip it into his back pocket with the fingers hanging down. It quickly caught on. Most players take off their gloves when they're on the putting green to increase their sense of touch. They often do it when they chip, too.

■ **Trish Johnson** *visualizes the ball traveling into the hole before making a shot. She knows that the best putting stroke in the world won't be successful without an established pre-shot routine.*

Taking the shot

After aiming the putter head, take your stance. Play the ball an inch or so to the left of the spot that your left eye looks down to on the turf. Aim your feet, hips, and shoulders along the target line, then putt the ball, trusting your feel for the line and speed. Be careful not to decelerate the putter head, and always use good tempo. The last step is to watch the ball drop into the cup!

A simple summary

✓ Your strategy on the putting green will depend on several factors, including reading the break and grain properly. You'll also need to develop a good feel for speed and distance if you want your golf score to drop.

✓ The only way to develop a feel for speed and distance is to practice and practice at the putting green, and then practice some more!

✓ Reading the break is crucial to sinking your putt. Once you have decided where the ball will break toward the hole, aim for that spot as you take your shot.

✓ Plumb-bobbing is a way to use your putter to determine the slope, by seeing how far the hole is off from the true vertical. Although it doesn't work for everyone, it might for you – at least as a way to confirm your original read of the slope.

✓ When you're in putting practice, don't hit every putt from the same spot. That's not real golf. Mix up your shots so you get a feel for a variety of angles and distances.

✓ Just as you use a pre-shot routine for full swing shots, so should you use one for all your putts.

Chapter 13

Chipping and Pitching

CHIPPING AND PITCHING can make or break your golf game. If you know how to get the ball close to the hole from various lies off the green, you will score well. If you don't, your scores will soar. It's that simple. So let's learn how to make perfect chip and pitch shots.

In this chapter...

✓ The most valuable game

✓ What's the difference between a chip and a pitch?

✓ When to chip

✓ How to chip

✓ Using different clubs to chip

✓ When to pitch

✓ How to pitch

A GOOD CHIP SHOT CAN BE YOUR BEST FRIEND

The most valuable game

ALL GOLFERS, ESPECIALLY BEGINNERS, *must learn to chip and pitch well to make up for not hitting accurate shots off the tee and onto the green. In the beginning, much of your game will be dominated by off-target shots followed by recovery shots. If you are to shoot a respectable score, you must be able to regularly recover from trouble.*

Chips and pitches are the bread-and-butter recovery shots that will help you salvage a decent score on those less-than-perfect holes.

Short game skills

Not having a strong short game takes away any advantage you might gain from a good long game. Chipping and pitching well, though, will enable you to take advantage of a good long game or to compensate for any inadequacies, such as shots that are not long or accurate enough, causing you to miss the green. In a nutshell, your short game is your ace in the hole.

That's because a good chip or pitch ideally puts you inside the scoring zone – an invisible six-foot circle drawn around the flagstick. Get your chip or pitch close, and you'll be able to sink that three-foot putt easily.

■ **The hallmark of** *Seve Ballesteros' game is his genius around the green. This outstanding chip shot onto the 18th green at Royal Lytham secured victory at the 1988 British Open Championship.*

What's the difference between a chip and a pitch?

DURING A TYPICAL ROUND *of golf, you won't always hit your ball onto the green in the normal number of shots, but you might leave it somewhere within a short-iron shot from the green. When this happens, you have to decide whether your next shot needs to be a chip or a pitch.*

The chip

When your ball is within five or ten feet of the putting surface, it's a good time to use a *chip*, which is basically any shot hit from fairly close to the green. The objective of a chip shot is to cozy your ball up as close to the hole as possible, leaving a short putt for par. A properly executed chip will travel for a short time in the air, then land and roll on the green to the hole. The distance it rolls is always farther than the distance it travels aloft.

DEFINITION

A chip is a low-running shot typically played from near the edge of the green toward the hole. A pitch is a lofted short shot to the green with a little run at the end of its flight.

The pitch

A *pitch*, on the other hand, is usually hit from farther off the green than a chip. The objective of a pitch is the same as that of a chip: to hit your ball as close to the hole as possible, leaving only one short putt. A pitch comes in especially handy when you've missed the green by a good margin, and you need to save par. A pitch is also the preferred shot when you need to loft your ball over a hazard or some other obstacle, or if the flagstick is located very close to the edge of the green with your ball sitting less than 40 or 50 yards away. A properly executed pitch will travel higher and farther in the air than a chip, and it also has more backspin on it, which enables the ball to stop more quickly once it lands on the green.

Techniques for chipping and pitching

The technique you use for a chip is different from the one you use for a pitch. A chip shot requires a shorter, less wristy stroke than a regular swing, while the pitch calls for a longer, wristier movement, which is almost a miniature version of the full swing. The chip stroke resembles the putting stroke, which attempts to put little or no spin on the ball so that it rolls end over end to the hole with no unpredictable backspin. The pitch needs to have backspin on it, which explains the need for a longer swing and more wrist action.

Choosing your shot

VIP

A chip is always preferable to a pitch, because it gets the golf ball down onto the putting surface quickly.

Distance control is always better when the ball is rolling on the green instead of flying through the air. Also, a chip imparts very little backspin on the ball, making it easier for you to predict how far it will roll. A chip is quite similar to a putt, apart from the time the ball spends in the air. Usually, a chip is hit from a good lie in fairly short grass.

You can use almost any club in the bag for a chip, although most players opt for anything from a 6-iron through a sand wedge, depending on how far away the green is and how far the ball needs to travel once it's on the green. If there is only ten or 15 feet of green before the ball rolls into the hole, you'll need to use a more lofted club such as a sand wedge. If you have lots of green to work with, you might opt for a less-lofted club like a 6- or 7-iron, which would get the ball up in the air to clear the fringe, then let it land and roll on the green.

■ **The majority of** *chip shots are hit from a good lie in fairly short grass.*

When to chip

LET'S SAY YOU'VE HIT YOUR approach shot to the green, only to come up a bit short. Your ball lies in the fairway with nothing in the way of the hole except grass. The flag is set in the back of the green, a good 40 feet from the front. Your ball lies only six feet short of the front of the green, but the fairway grass is just a bit too long for you to use a putter.

Question: What do you do?

Answer: You make a textbook chip to the hole, choosing a 6-iron or 7-iron and hitting the ball just hard enough to carry it the necessary distance to the green, where it should then begin to roll nicely toward the hole. You choose a chip in this situation because the distance from the ball to the front of the green is much shorter than the distance from the front of the green to the flagstick.

6-IRON 9-IRON SAND WEDGE

■ **When making a chip,** *most players choose a club between the 6-iron and the sand wedge, depending on the distance to the green and the hole.*

Playing it safe

You could choose to pitch the ball way up into the air, land it close to the flag, and hope it will stop close by, but that would be a silly risk to take. You don't need to do that. Remember, golf is a game of percentages. To score well you must choose the shot that has the best odds of succeeding, and in this case the chip is it. Jack Nicklaus swore by the best-odds method and became the greatest golfer of all time.

Selecting a club

You can also choose to chip when the flag is closer to the same side of the green as your ball, provided that the distance from your ball to the green is proportionally shorter as well. For instance, let's say the flagstick is in front of you about eight feet onto the green. Your ball is in the fringe, no more than two feet away from the beginning of the green. You need a club that will successfully loft the ball onto the green and let it roll the rest of the way. In this case, you might want to select a slightly more lofted club to chip with, perhaps a pitching wedge or even a sand wedge, which will

■ **Choose to chip** *if you need to clear a low hazard or if the flagstick is located farther from your side of the green.*

ensure that the ball will have less forward momentum than if you use a 6-iron or 7-iron. Just as with the longer chip, the ball will be lofted into the air no more than a foot or so, then come down onto the green and roll toward the hole – just the way a putt would.

Choose to chip whenever possible. Even when you are 30 feet away from the green, if there's enough green to work with, it will be the better percentage shot than the pitch.

Chip the ball if you need to loft it high enough to clear some broken ground or a few old divots are in the way. Also choose to chip if it is a very windy day, because the wind will play havoc with a high-flying pitch. The low chip won't be affected by the wind nearly as much.

Bump-and-run shots

You can even choose to chip if you are as far away as 30 or 40 yards from the green to avoid the affects of wind. Called a bump-and-run shot, this is really a chip that lands before the ball reaches the green, rolls through the fairway and fringe, hops up onto the green, and then rolls toward the hole. The bump-and-run, used more in Europe than in the United States, can be a very effective way of cheating the wind, provided no hazards or large obstructions lie between the ball and the green. If the flagstick is located back far enough on the green, the chip is still a preferable shot to the pitch.

How to chip

LET'S LOOK AT A TYPICAL *situation in which a standard chip shot is called for. Your ball is lying on the fairway about ten or 15 feet from the putting green. The lie is good, but the grass is too long to consider using your putter to simply roll the ball all the way to the hole. The flagstick is located about 40 feet away from the front of the green, leaving you plenty of space for the chip shot to roll.*

Choosing the right club

Because most fairway grass is cut fairly short, you will probably want to choose a 7- or 8-iron for the chip. Either club will get the ball up in the air just enough to clear the fairway and fringe, land the ball nicely on the green, and enable it to roll most of the way to the hole. If the flagstick were positioned closer to you, you would need to use a more lofted chipping club, say a pitching or sand wedge, which would loft the ball higher and impart less roll. A more lofted club would also be needed if your ball were lying in one- or two-inch rough as opposed to on the fairway.

THE CHIP SHOT

To make the chip shot, use a pendulum-like movement, just as you would when putting. Don't use any wrist action; simply rock your arms and shoulders back and through. The length of the backswing determines the length of the shot, so to hit a longer chip shot, simply use a longer backswing and follow-through.

1 **Setup**

Take a narrow stance with the ball positioned inside your right heel and aim the club head at the intermediate target.

2 **Takeaway**

Place about 75 percent of your weight onto the left leg and keep your eye on the ball as you take the club back.

The landing spot

Next, you need to decide on a landing spot for the chip. This should ideally be on the green, not the fringe or fairway, because the green is usually a much more consistent, flat surface, reducing the chance the ball will take a bad first bounce. Focus on a spot about two or three feet onto the green, one that is in line with the flagstick. Remember, with a chip shot you want the ball to be in the air just long enough to clear the fairway and fringe, and then touch down onto the green and roll as far as possible to the hole.

Visualizing the shot

Stand behind the ball and visualize the target line. Now, just as you would with a regular shot, choose an intermediate target that is in line with the flagstick – a blemish in the grass two feet in front of the ball will do. Next, you need to set up to the shot. Take a narrow stance with your feet positioned no more than 16 inches apart. Position your feet on a line that angles slightly left of the target line (for a right-handed golfer). This will enable you to clearly see the intended path of the shot. Don't worry; you won't hit the ball hard enough for it to travel left of the target. Make sure your shoulders are aligned to the target line.

3 Backswing

Take the club back with a pendulum-like movement, keeping your wrists locked into position throughout.

4 Downswing

Keep your hands ahead of the club head, and ensure that the club face stays open as it impacts with the ball.

5 Impact

Make sure your right hand stays ahead of your left and clip the ball off the turf with a crisp, descending blow.

6 Follow-through

Make sure the follow-through is the same length as the backswing. Your weight should remain on the left side.

Making the shot

Set up so that the ball is positioned just inside of your right heel (for a right-handed golfer), a position well to the right of where you would typically place the ball for a full swing. Having the ball this far back in your stance will ensure that the club face contacts the ball first, with the sharply descending blow that's necessary to hitting a good chip. Next, grip your club using your putting grip instead of your full-swing grip. Holding it this way will help keep your left wrist from bending during the stroke. With chips and putts, you want as little wrist action as possible. Aim your club head directly at the intermediate target, then place about 75 percent of your weight onto your left leg (for a right-handed golfer) to help remove any lower-body movement from the shot. To ensure the accuracy of a chip shot (as well as a putt), you should not move your lower body at all. The last thing to do before hitting the ball is move your hands into a position slightly ahead of the club head, which will further ensure crisp, downward contact.

Using different clubs to chip

ONCE YOU DEVELOP A GOOD feel for chipping, you should experiment with different clubs for different shots to get a feel for ball trajectories and lengths

of roll. Chipping with a 6-iron, for instance, will impart less air time and more roll than chipping with a 9-iron. With experience, you'll learn how each club performs. In the beginning, consider using only three clubs to chip with, perhaps a 6-iron, a 9-iron, and a sand wedge, and alternate between these three clubs to help develop a real feel for each one.

■ **Practice your** *chip shots with different clubs to determine which club works best in a particular situation.*

The Texas wedge

After you've gotten a feel for your three basic chipping clubs, you can experiment with other clubs in your bag. For instance, when your ball is lying on the close-cut fringe grass just short of the green, often the best choice of club to chip with is your putter. Yes, you heard right: the putter, sometimes called the Texas wedge. Basic chipping strategy, which is to get the ball down and rolling as soon as possible, can be easily executed with the putter. It rolls the ball from the very start, enabling you to predict more effectively just where the ball will go. If the grass that the ball is sitting on (the fringe or even the fairway) is closely cropped and free of irregularities, your choice should be the putter.

It's an old golf axiom that your best chip won't get the ball as close as your worst putt; this saying has more truth to it than you might think.

A putt is more controllable and predictable than a chip or a pitch because the ball is rolling on the ground. So, whenever possible, choose the Texas wedge for chipping.

For this type of chip, you need to hit the ball slightly harder than a putt of the same length on the green, because the ball must roll through the longer grass of the fringe or fairway before it gets onto the putting surface. Mastering the Texas wedge shot takes practice, so you should work on it during every practice session.

■ **Tiger Woods** *often makes a chip shot using a fairway wood.*

The fairway wood

You can also chip with a fairway wood, as do Tiger Woods and a number of other professionals today. When would you use a fairway wood instead of a lofted iron or a putter? The best times are when your ball is on the fringe but resting right up against the higher cut of fairway grass, and when your ball is on the fairway but resting up against some light rough. In these situations, it can often be difficult to make solid contact with a putter or an iron because the higher grass behind the ball slows the club head down, causing short shots, a loss of accuracy, or even a missed swing. The large, wide head of a fairway wood, however, will glide right through the high grass so you can make solid contact. The loft of a 5-wood or a 7-wood will be just enough to pop the ball up into the air and onto the green, sending it rolling nicely toward the hole.

Move your grip down

To be successful at this technique, you should move your grip down all the way to the shaft of the wood and then set up to the ball as if you were attempting a normal chip shot. Instead of playing the ball off your right foot, though, try moving your ball a few inches to the left. Then simply take a normal chipping stroke, contacting the ball with a slightly descending blow. Use a bit less force than a normal chip, however, because the head of the fairway wood will impart more energy to the ball than an iron would. Don't try this shot during a game unless you've practiced it beforehand, because it takes some time to perfect.

■ **When using a** *fairway wood to make a chip shot, place your hands farther down the shaft of the club than usual.*

The sand wedge

Another interesting shot often used by professionals is the sand wedge putt. When a player's ball is on the putting surface but is resting up against the higher fringe grass, the putter blade often won't be able to make solid contact with the ball. Although a fairway wood can be used in this instance, many players choose a sand wedge instead. They simply make a putting stroke with a wedge gripped way down on the shaft, striking the ball with the blade, or leading edge, of the iron at the equator of the ball rather than below it.

Preparing to make the shot

One important key to successfully making this shot is to set up with the ball even with your right heel, ensuring that you hit with a descending blow.

The blade of the iron passes over the higher fringe grass and imparts no loft because it strikes the ball at its equator. The ball simply rolls toward the hole like a normal putt. The advantage of a sand wedge over a putter is that you eliminate the chance of the putter blade being slowed down by the fringe grass, which might cause the shot to come up short of the hole.

Some players prefer this method over the fairway wood technique because of the shorter length of the club. Again, don't try this shot during a round until you have practiced it a number of times.

Trivia...

A good chip shot is one of the simplest shots to learn. Larry Nelson, who has a great short game, didn't pick up a golf club until he was 21, and he learned how to play from a book!

When to pitch

WHEN THERE IS NO WAY TO *put your ball onto the putting surface with a well-struck chip, you will need to pitch the ball. Typically played only with wedges, pitches are higher and longer shots than chips, requiring you to use a longer swing with more wrist action. You should use a pitch shot when some hazard or other obstruction stands between your ball and the green, or when the hole is located very close to the edge of the green, giving you very little if any room to roll the ball.*

Avoiding obstructions

Also, use a pitch when your ball lies in deep rough, which requires a longer, more forceful swing to get the ball up and out. The pitch shot, if properly hit, will spin enough to stop quickly, keeping it close to the flagstick. If you tried to hit a chip shot over a bunker, for instance, the ball would possibly bounce into the sand and get stuck there, missing the green entirely. Or if you tried to hit a chip from the rough eight feet away from the green to a hole located three feet back from the fringe, the ball would just roll by the hole and leave you with a long comeback putt. The pitch shot allows you to avoid obstructions, escape rough, and stop the ball quickly as close to the hole as possible.

■ **A pitch shot** *is played when a hazard, such as this bunker, lies between the ball and the green.*

Mastering the pitch

Pitches are harder to master than chips, which is one reason why you should choose a chip over a pitch if at all possible. Pitches are difficult to perfect because the swing is longer – often one-half or one-third of a normal swing.

When making this long partial swing, many players decelerate on the downswing, causing poor contact and bad results.

A tremendous amount of "feel" is involved, something that takes time to master. Chipping uses a much shorter, more mechanical stroke that can easily be mastered, even by a beginner.

Spin control

Pitches are also useful when your ball lies 30 to 60 yards short of the green. This distance means you can't take a full swing with any club, making a pitch necessary. The partial swing of this shorter finesse shot will impart less spin on the ball than it would if you shot it 80 or 90 yards, because the club-head speed is much slower.

The perfect escape shot

All cautions aside, the pitch, when properly struck, is a fun, effective shot to have in your arsenal. It can get you out of some sticky situations, particularly when sand or water hazards stand between you and the green. And it can help set you up for a good scoring attempt by gently dropping your ball onto the green from 20 to 60 yards away.

How to pitch

A GOOD STROKE ON *a pitch shot evolves out of the longer chip shot stroke and setup, with some added wrist action thrown into the equation. You could also almost see it as an abbreviated version of a full swing. First, let's look at a typical pitch shot situation. Your ball is located in some very light rough ten yards behind a greenside bunker, with the putting surface directly on the other side. The flagstick is located in the middle of the relatively flat green about 25 yards from your ball. You have to somehow loft your ball over the bunker and onto the green, stopping it as close to the hole as possible.*

■ **The pitch shot** *requires a crisp downward swing to achieve backspin on the ball so that it lands on the green with the minimum of roll.*

A chip shot won't make it over the bunker, and a full swing will send the ball flying over the green. The right strategy is to pull out a wedge (probably a sand wedge or a lob wedge) and pitch the ball high into the air, allowing the ball to come down softly onto the green and roll the few remaining yards to the hole.

THE PITCH SHOT

Unlike the chip shot, the swing for the pitch shot involves some leg action and a lot of wrist break in order to put as much backspin as possible on the ball. Do not overdo your leg action, though, because this could throw the pitch off the target line.

1 **Setup**
Aim the club face at the target and align your feet, knees, and hips to the left of the target line.

2 **Takeaway**
Keep your weight on the left side and move your club, hands, arms, and shoulders in unison.

Choosing the right club

Let's go through the steps needed to hit the perfect pitch shot in this situation. First, choose the right club, usually a sand or lob wedge, both of which will create a high shot with as much backspin as possible. You'll need this spin to stop the ball quickly once it touches down. Unlike the chip, a pitch flies most of the way there and then rolls a short distance. The roll of a pitch shot is hard to predict, due to the increased backspin. The only aspect of the shot that you can (with practice) predict is the distance it flies through the air.

The landing spot

Next, you must decide on a landing spot for the pitch. If you're making a shot of 20 to 30 yards, you'll probably want to land the ball about 15 feet short of the hole and let it bounce and roll the rest of the way. The ideal landing spot will depend on many factors, including the slope and speed of the green, and the amount of backspin you are able to generate. Only experience and practice will help you to decide the best spot to land your ball.

Setting up

Next, visualize the flight of the ball and your intended target line. Now you're ready to set up to the ball. Aim the club face directly at the target, but (unlike for the chip or full swing) align your feet, knees, hips, and shoulders to the left of the target line, at least 15 degrees open. This will make the club head cut across the ball at impact, sending

3 Backswing

Bend your wrists as the club moves back. Your hands should not pass shoulder height.

4 Downswing

Use light grip pressure through the downswing, and keep the club face square to the swing path.

5 Impact

Strike the ball squarely and on the correct path. Don't decelerate the club head just before impact.

6 Follow-through

As your body weight flows to the left, the club should be carried up to a perfectly balanced finish.

it well up into the air. This setup position increases the loft of the club as well as the amount of spin. Because you won't be swinging as hard, the ball will not travel left of the target or slice. Instead, it will go wherever the club face was aimed.

The stance

Take a stance that is slightly wider than the one you used for the chip shot but narrower than a full-swing stance. Place about 60 percent of your weight on your left leg (for a right-handed golfer), and position the ball centrally between your feet. Make sure you use very light grip pressure to ensure a relaxed, almost lazy swing.

Making the shot

When you are ready, take the club back behind you until it is a bit past horizontal to the ground, making sure to begin bending your wrists as soon as the club starts back. Then go directly into the downswing, keeping it as rhythmic as possible. Your wrists should feel as if they are hinging and unhinging lazily, right up until impact. Take care not to decelerate the club head as it gets closer to impact because this will give you a much shorter shot than you intended. Pitching properly absolutely requires acceleration at impact.

You vary the distance of a pitch not by changing swing speed, but by changing the length of your backswing and follow-through.

With practice, you will be able to feel what length swing will pitch the ball 20, 30, 40, or even 50 yards. Just remember that the longer the swing, the more backspin will be imparted to the ball, causing it to stop sooner once it touches down. Unlike a chip shot, in which you should feel as if you are definitely hitting down on the ball, a properly executed pitch shot should feel as if you are quickly sliding the club head under the ball and then popping it up out of the grass and into the air. You should not try to help it up at all, however – the club's loft will do that for you.

■ **This long pitch shot** *requires almost a full swing to get the ball onto the green.*

Longer pitch shots

As the distance of the pitch increases, so must the length of your backswing and follow-through. Once the pitch distance approaches 60 yards, your swing will be almost full, especially if you are using a lob wedge with at least 58 degrees of loft. As you approach this length pitch, consider setting up with your feet and body nearly parallel to the target line, instead of open, to ensure accuracy.

Perfecting the "feel factor"

You'll need to practice pitches more than chips, because they involve more of that intangible "feel factor." You need to learn to feel the difference between a 30-yard pitch and a 60-yard pitch, and you should also experiment with hitting them as high and as short as possible. Phil Mickelson, one of the best players in the world, can take his lob wedge and pitch a ball almost directly up into the air, landing it only a few yards away. As in all other aspects of golf, perfection takes practice – so get out there!

INTERNET

www.golfacademy.com

Golf Academy has plenty of instructional information on chips, pitches, and all other areas of the game.

A simple summary

✓ A chip is a low-flying shot that rolls most of the way to the hole.

✓ A pitch is a high-flying shot that is airborne most of the way to the hole.

✓ All golfers, especially beginners, must learn to chip and pitch well to make up for not hitting accurate shots off the tees and into the greens. Accurate chipping and pitching will give you a reliable way to recover from trouble.

✓ When you're faced with the choice between a chip and a pitch, always choose the chip if you can. It's an easier shot to make, and its longer roll means you have more control over where it lands.

✓ A chip shot requires a shorter, less wristy stroke than a regular swing, while the pitch calls for a longer, wristier movement, almost a miniature version of the full swing.

✓ Use a chip when you have plenty of green between you and the hole. Use a pitch when your ball is as far or farther from the fringe as the fringe is from the hole.

✓ Learn to use as many clubs as possible to chip and pitch with. Practicing with these clubs will give you a real feel for how high and how far they will hit your ball.

Chapter 14

The Bunker Mentality

THE MERE THOUGHT of being in a sand bunker strikes fear into the hearts of most amateur golfers, but it needn't be this way. Believe it or not, professional golfers prefer to be in a bunker rather than in the rough for two reasons. First, the lie is almost always better. Second, they have perfected the technique needed to easily hit the ball out. It's really quite simple.

In this chapter...

✓ It's not the beach

✓ It's not as hard as you think

✓ The bouncing sand wedge

✓ The basic bunker shots

EXPLOSION SHOT FROM A BUNKER

It's not the beach

A BUNKER (OR SAND TRAP) is an oblong depression lined with a layer of sand, designed to penalize a wayward shot. Located either close to the green or alongside the fairway, bunkers come in many different shapes and depths, from long and shallow to round and cavernous. Even the type of sand used in a bunker can vary from fine and powdery to coarse and gritty. A bunker can have no grassy lip at all, or it can have a high lip of sod, making the escape shot even more difficult.

Types of bunker

Course designers put a lot of thought into where to place bunkers. Most greens have at least one strategically placed bunker, often either in front of or behind the putting green. The reason is simple: The designer wants to punish you for bad distance control on your approach shot. Bunkers are often placed on the sides of greens, too, to penalize approach shots that go left or right of the green. These are known as greenside bunkers. On par-4 and par-5 holes, long, small-lipped bunkers are often placed on either side of the fairway at a point where a normal-length tee shot might land to penalize inaccuracy. These are known as fairway bunkers.

Choosing the right club

VIP

The location of bunkers is one of the key factors in deciding what strategy you will use to play a particular hole.

For example, if you know there is a fairway bunker on the left side of the fairway about 250 yards out from the tee, you should strongly consider using a club that will not hit the ball that far so the bunker won't be in play on your tee shot. That might mean using a 3-wood instead of a driver. Or, if a large, deep greenside bunker is located directly in front of the green you are hitting to, you should use a club that will definitely hit the ball past the bunker. That might mean using a 6-iron even though you think a 7-iron is the perfect club for the shot. The extra five or ten yards generated by the 6-iron might just make the difference between an easy putt and a challenging bunker shot.

■ **For each hole,** *choose your club and strategy with care to avoid playing out of a bunker.*

It's not as hard as you think

REALLY, IT ISN'T VERY HARD *to reliably and consistently hit your ball out of a bunker, provided you practice at it diligently and use the right technique every time.*

The unique thing about most shots out of the sand is that you don't actually have to hit the ball at all (except when you're hitting out of a fairway bunker). Instead, you contact the sand behind the ball, which forces the ball up and out.

The margin for error on the point of impact is therefore larger. With a normal shot from the fairway, for instance, your club face must strike the ball at a precise point, with a margin of error of less than a quarter-inch. Out of a bunker, however, you can successfully hit your ball out even if the point of contact with the sand varies by as much as an inch or two. Distance and rate of backspin might be affected, but the ball will still pop up and out. Simple physics says it has to. Here's why: When your sand wedge strikes the sand directly behind your ball, the club face glides through the sand and under the ball, causing the sand your ball is sitting on to be splashed up. The ball simply rides this magic carpet of sand out of the bunker. If you execute the shot correctly, your ball has no choice in the matter. It must go!

Challenges for the beginner

There are several reasons why beginners have a hard time hitting bunker shots. First and foremost is that the shot is totally different from any other on the course. You spend so much time learning to make clean, crisp contact with the ball that when you have to purposely hit behind it an inch or two, your mind and body resist. You have developed muscle memory that says "hit the ball here." To suddenly be asked to swing differently can be difficult at first.

Making practice shots

Beginners also rarely practice bunker shots, because they are too busy trying to learn the other fundamentals. Statistically, you won't need to make as many sand shots as you will shots from the fairway or the rough, so it's only natural that you'd tend to practice them less often. Additionally, many practice facilities don't have a practice bunker on the premises, making mastery of this shot nearly impossible. So, the average player goes to the golf course totally unprepared for bunker play.

Think positive!

The biggest reason beginners fail at bunker play is that, because of the lack of practice time, they tend to panic when they're actually faced with the task. A poorly prepared golfer either will sullenly climb down into the bunker, make a tentative, stiff-armed swipe at the ball resulting in a total miss, or will hit a *thinned* or *topped* ball that rockets out of the bunker, past the green, and over to the next tee box, where another unfortunate golfer might be standing. Or, he or she will make a half-hearted swing that doesn't even budge the ball. Clearly, attitude affects performance, and attitude can only be improved through practice and success.

■ **Your club face** *should strike the sand directly behind the ball to propel it up and out of the bunker.*

> ### DEFINITION
>
> *If the bottom of the club strikes the ball at its equator instead of its bottom portion, it's a thinned shot. This sends the ball off on a very low trajectory. A topped shot is one in which the bottom of the club head makes contact with the very top of the ball, causing the ball to roll and never get into the air at all.*

Setting up for the shot

The lack of practice causes yet another problem: ignorance of basic bunker setup mechanics. When faced with a shot from the sand, the typical beginner sets up to the ball much as he or she would for a regular shot from the grass, with the body parallel to the target line and the ball positioned in the middle of the stance. This is the kiss of death for a bunker shot, which requires the player to set up with an extremely open stance – with feet, hips, and shoulders pointed at least 20 degrees left of the target (for a right-handed golfer). This sharply open stance promotes an out-to-in swing path necessary to cut across the sand and pop the ball out of the bunker. Using a regular, parallel setup sends the club head straight into the sand, where it will just dig in. The result is a ball that stays put or moves only a few feet.

■ **When setting up** *to play from a greenside bunker, your shoulders, torso, and hips must be open to the target line.*

Open stance

Target line

The bouncing sand wedge

THE SAND WEDGE, *a marvelous tool, is designed specifically to hit a golf ball out of the sand. If you look at the head of a sand wedge, you will notice that the bottom of the blade is thicker than it is on your other clubs. When you swing correctly, this thick part, the* bounce, *contacts the sand first, before the leading edge of the blade. Look at your sand wedge from the side, and you can see how the bounce of it hangs down below the leading edge. The bounce slides across the sand and keeps the leading edge from digging in. This is what enables the sand wedge blade to slip underneath the ball and pop it out so nicely from the bunker.*

DEFINITION

The bounce of a wedge is the part of the club head that hangs down below the leading edge. The lower the bounce hangs below the leading edge, the more the club will bounce off the sand.

The bounce of a sand wedge is measured in degrees. Specifically, it is the angle between the club face and the surface of the bounce.

■ **Gene Sarazen**
designed the sand wedge in the 1930s to improve his bunker play.

You can see this angle when you're looking at the club face from the side. Most of the irons in your bag will have very little, if any, bounce. The sand wedge, however, will have anywhere from five to 15 degrees of bounce, or even more in certain clubs. Most players should use a sand wedge with at least ten degrees of bounce, which will help make sure the ball gets up and out of the bunker.

How much bounce is best?

The finer and fluffier the sand is, the more bounce you'll need. If the bunkers you typically play out of have firmer, coarser, wetter sand, however, you might want to go with slightly less bounce because lots of bounce will make the club head ricochet off this type of compacted surface, causing it to contact the ball at the equator and send it screaming across the green.

When swung properly, the sand wedge should feel like it's slipping underneath the ball, cutting its "legs" off. That's the picture you should have in your mind when you're hitting out of a greenside bunker. The ball does not need those silly legs, so cut them off! Legless, the ball can then fly up, up, and away.

The basic bunker shots

BUNKER SHOTS COME IN *three basic varieties: the splash, the explosion, and the fairway bunker shot. Let's look at them one by one.*

The splash shot

This is the basic bunker shot. It should be used when your ball has found a greenside bunker but has not buried itself and is sitting on top of the sand. The splash is the most important of the bunker shots. Mastering it will save you an untold number of strokes. The splash shot got its name because when you eject the ball from the bunker, it will exit in a splash of sand.

INTERNET

www.st-duffer.com

On this site you can learn about Saint Duffer, patron saint of frustrated golfers, who has been known to work miracles on the course.

Setting up

To make a big splash, enter the bunker and set up to the ball so that your body is at least 20 degrees open (or aimed left, for a right-handed golfer) to the target line. It will feel odd at first, but you must set up this way so that the sand wedge can slip under and across the ball. Remember not to touch the sand with your club at any time as this is a violation of the rules; you would incur a one-stroke penalty for doing so. Play the ball about even with your left instep, and then dig your feet into the sand to get a firm, balanced platform.

THE SPLASH SHOT

This is the most frequently played bunker shot, so perhaps the most important to master. It should be used when your ball has landed in a bunker and is sitting on top of the sand. Be sure to keep the club head above the sand at address, and vary the length of your backswing and follow-through for longer or shorter shots. Your body weight should remain on the left side throughout to promote a downward and through swing.

1 Setup
Adopt an open stance with firm footing and the ball even with your left instep.

2 Backswing
Let the backswing follow the line of your body, aligned left of the target.

It is important to play the ball this far up in your stance as you will be making contact at a spot well behind it, closer to a normal ball position. Make sure your stance is fairly wide, about shoulder-width or more. Place 60 percent of your weight on your left foot, then turn the club face to the right (for a right-handed golfer) until it is pointing at the target. You must open the blade this way to get the bounce of the sand wedge to work properly.

Preparing to swing

Now grip down on the club about an inch below where you'd hold a club for a normal shot, to allow for your feet digging into the sand. Then make your swing, taking care to let it follow the line of your body, which should be aimed well left of the target (for a right-handed golfer). Do not swing toward the target because this will make the club head dig into instead of slide through the sand. Also, make sure you concentrate on a spot in the sand about two inches behind your ball rather than on the ball itself. The idea is to slice out a postcard-size divot of sand from under the ball. Cut off its legs, remember?

Making the shot

When you make your swing, focus on taking a nice, lazy swing rather than a quick, hard one. Swing too fast and you might slide the club head right underneath the ball without moving it. Just make a relaxed swing with a bit more wrist action than normal and keep your lower body as still as possible. Odds are you'll need to try this a few times before understanding the basic mechanics of the splash bunker shot. Then practice, practice, practice!

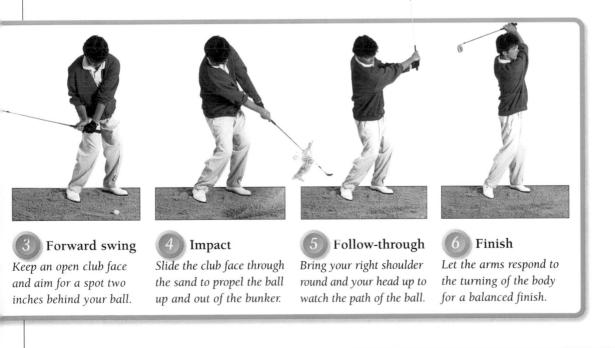

3 **Forward swing**
Keep an open club face and aim for a spot two inches behind your ball.

4 **Impact**
Slide the club face through the sand to propel the ball up and out of the bunker.

5 **Follow-through**
Bring your right shoulder round and your head up to watch the path of the ball.

6 **Finish**
Let the arms respond to the turning of the body for a balanced finish.

Distance control

To make a longer shot, simply take a longer backswing and follow-through, instead of trying to swing harder or softer.

With practice, you will begin to get a feel for varying distance. As you get better at this shot, you'll start to notice a relationship between where the club head enters the sand and how much backspin is transferred to the ball. When the flagstick is located closer to your position, more spin will help stop the ball sooner. Basically, the closer to the ball your club head enters the sand, the more the ball will spin. Getting too close can be dangerous, though, because you might actually hit the ball first and send it flying across the green.

If the flagstick is located a good distance away from the bunker, you may want to impart very little spin on the ball to ensure lots of roll. To reduce spin, enter the sand two inches or more behind the ball.

Just remember, think of the splash shot as a slicing action beneath the ball, not a digging action into it.

Trivia...

Generally considered the best bunker player of all time, golf legend Gary Player never ends a sand shot practice session until he puts one into the hole.

THE EXPLOSION SHOT

Play the explosion shot from a greenside bunker when your ball is partially buried in the sand. Also called a buried lie, this shot requires you to thump the club head into the sand to blast the ball up and out of the bunker. This technique imparts little spin on the ball, causing it to roll for some distance after landing on the green.

1 **Setup**

Take a slightly open stance with the ball positioned centrally. Align the club face slightly left of the target line.

2 **Backswing**

Use a lot of wrist break to keep the takeaway steep and promote a steeper angle of attack.

The explosion shot

Sometimes you'll approach a bunker and find that your ball has partially buried itself into the sand. That's not good. When this happens, you cannot use the splash shot. If you did, the ball would probably stay right where it was or else fly out at an altitude of about three inches. The explosion shot solves this problem nicely, though.

An explosion shot, also called a buried lie, requires the club head to dig into the bunker and eject the ball atop a large amount of sand. An explosion shot will have little spin, causing it to roll quite a ways.

■ **A half-buried ball** *requires you to play an explosion shot.*

Setting up

To perform the explosion, first take an open stance (not quite as open as for the splash). Dig your feet in, and grip down on the club to compensate for this. Put most of your weight on your left foot, and play the ball from the middle of a wide stance (instead of farther up). Then align the club face so that it points slightly left of the target line – a much more closed position than for the splash shot. The idea behind this different setup is to get the club face to dig into the sand behind the ball, the opposite of what is called for with the splash. Because the buried ball is surrounded by a crater of sand, it's necessary to dig in with the club head to cut through the ridge of the crater.

3 **Forward swing**

As you go into the forward swing, keep your body centered over the ball and maintain a tight grip.

4 **Impact**

Use a swift action to punch the club head down into the sand about two inches behind the ball.

5 **Follow-through**

There will be little or no follow-through (sometimes the club may even remain stuck in the sand).

Making the shot

Make your swing much steeper than you would for the splash shot, and feel as if you are coming straight down into the sand. Use lots of wrist break, and just punch the sand with the club head about two inches behind the ball. Because of the steep approach, you won't have much, if any, follow-through with your club. The club head sometimes just stays where you've stuck it into the sand. The ball will pop out and run toward the flagstick with no spin on it at all. Because of this, you should allow for much more roll once the ball touches down.

The fairway bunker shot

Not all bunkers are located close to the green. Some are deviously placed out on the flanks of the fairway at just the point where a nice, long tee shot might land. These fairway bunkers are different from their cousins near the green in several crucial ways. First, they are quite far from the green, often as much as 200 yards. Second, they are usually larger and longer than the typical greenside bunker. Third, the sand in them is usually a bit firmer underfoot. And finally, they usually have a lower lip than a greenside bunker.

INTERNET

www.cybergolf.com

Click on the Lessons section for information on all the basic bunker shots.

> ### Trivia...
> *Bobby Jones, one of the greatest golfers of all time, said of the bunker shot, "The difference between a bunker and a water hazard is the same as the difference between a car crash and a plane crash. You at least have a chance to recover from a car crash."*

THE FAIRWAY BUNKER SHOT

Play this shot if your ball lies atop firm sand in a low-lipped fairway bunker. Your choice of club will depend on the distance to the target and the amount of loft needed to clear the lip of the bunker. Aim to hit the ball off the sand cleanly and, unlike the splash and explosion shots, strike the ball rather than the sand to have a chance of reaching the green in one shot.

1 Setup

Take a wide stance with your body parallel to the target line. Play the ball farther to the right than usual.

2 Backswing

Move the club, arms, and shoulders back in a one-piece takeaway movement.

A different technique

How do all these differences affect your play out of a fairway bunker? In a number of ways. If your ball lies in a fairway bunker located 150 yards from the green, you obviously won't be able to reach the putting surface from there with a sand wedge unless you are Tiger Woods. That means you will need to choose one of your regular irons, say a 6-iron or 7-iron, to make the shot. These clubs don't have any bounce designed into the blade, so they cannot be used the way a sand wedge might be.

VIP *Instead, you will have to hit the ball off the sand cleanly, striking the ball first, if you are to have any hope of getting the ball to the green in one shot.*

The firmer quality of fairway bunker sand makes this clean stroke technique a bit easier, but it still remains a delicate shot.

The lie of the land

The first thing to do when you're considering a fairway bunker shot is to determine what kind of lie you have in the sand. Is the ball sitting up nicely atop firm sand, is it buried, or is it lying next to several small rocks? If the lie is poor, you will have no choice but to play it safe and hit a short recovery shot back into the fairway using a splash shot. The odds of reaching the green from a poor lie in a fairway bunker are minute, so it's best to play the percentages and just put the ball back into play.

3 At the top
Make a full-shoulder turn, keeping the club parallel to the target line.

4 Forward swing
Swing smoothly with little leg movement, and keep your eye on the ball.

5 Impact
Accelerate through impact and make clean, crisp contact with the ball.

6 Follow-through
Bring the club up to a controlled and perfectly balanced finish.

■ **If your ball** *lands in a high-lipped bunker, a safety shot is often needed to get the ball back into play.*

The next thing to determine is the height of the bunker's lip. If it is very low, chances are small that your ball will catch on it regardless of which club you select. If the lip is more than a foot or so high, however, club selection becomes an issue. Will that lip be too high for you to use the club you'll need to hit the green?

Selecting a club

Let's say your ball lies in a fairway bunker 160 yards from the flagstick, calling for the average player to use a 4-iron or a 5-iron. The ball is sitting only three or four feet from a three-foot-high sod lip. Odds are that a 4-iron or a 5-iron will not have sufficient loft to clear that lip, even though that much club is needed to hit the ball to the green. In this scenario you would need to play it safe and choose a wedge to get the ball back into play. But if the ball were located ten yards from a very low lip, you would be able to easily hit that 4-iron or 5-iron with little chance of clipping the lip on the way out.

The moral of this fairway bunker tale is to always play it safe when the lie or the lip threaten to ruin your shot.

Go for the green!

If you have ideal conditions (firm sand, good lie, low lip), you can consider going for the green. First, determine your distance to the target. Let's say you are 125 yards from the green – a perfect 9-iron shot for you. Instead of hitting that 9-iron, though, consider using an 8-iron – for an important reason. When you're hitting from a fairway bunker, you will be swinging more smoothly with very little lower body action to keep yourself from slipping in the sand. This will cause you to hit a bit shorter than you usually do, calling for a less lofted club to reach the target.

Setting up

When you're setting up to the ball in a fairway bunker, dig your feet in and grip down on the club slightly to compensate. Remember that you can't touch the sand with your club at any time, as this is a violation of the rules. Take a wide stance and play the ball about an inch farther to the right in your stance than you otherwise might. This is to ensure that you contact the ball first, before making contact with the sand – a crucial ingredient in a successful fairway bunker shot. Aim just as you would with any other shot, but do not set up with an open stance as you would when hitting from a greenside bunker. Instead, set up with your body parallel to the target line. Make sure your hands are slightly ahead of the ball at address so that you are certain to make descending contact with the ball first.

Making the shot

When you take your swing, make clean, crisp contact with the ball, taking as tiny a divot as possible. You know what it feels like to contact only the ball; it almost feels as if you have hit the ball "thin," or a bit too high up. That is how you want to hit the ball from a fairway bunker. If your club face digs into the sand before contacting the ball, the ball will only travel a few yards, possibly not even making it out of the bunker.

Swing smoothly, with little leg movement. Keep your eye on the back of the ball and make sure you do not lower your body during the swing. Finally, be sure to accelerate the club through impact to avoid coming up short. Many players fear this shot so much that they slow down when they're getting close to the ball, resulting in a poor shot. Commit to the shot, then do it!

As with greenside bunker shots, you will need to practice these fairway bunker shots regularly. To really become proficient at them, try using different clubs. Even consider using a lofted fairway wood, such as a 7-wood, because the large club head will tend to glide over the sand rather than dig in, as an iron could. Just be sure to hit the ball first!

A simple summary

✓ A bunker is a hazard filled with sand. It can be placed near a green, alongside a fairway, or anywhere else on a course.

✓ Hitting your ball out of a bunker needn't be difficult, provided you use the right technique – and practice, practice, practice!

✓ The sand wedge is the club of choice for getting out of a greenside bunker because its special design pops the ball up and out of the sand.

✓ In a greenside bunker, the basic shot is the splash. You hit the sand behind the ball, and the sand propels the ball up and out.

✓ When your ball is partially or totally buried in the sand, you must use the explosion shot. You also contact the sand behind the ball, but at a much steeper angle than for the splash.

✓ Fairway bunker shots needn't be difficult. Just be sure to make contact with the ball before hitting the sand.

PART FOUR

BEN CRENSHAW CELEBRATES A MOMENT OF VICTORY

BECOMING A BETTER GOLFER

BY NOW YOU'VE LEARNED the basics of this great game and are able to get around the course in a respectable number of strokes. Good for you! You're not *satisfied*, though, are you? You want to do better? That's the spirit!

Everyone who becomes addicted to this game has the same *desire* to improve and to one day get to the point of shooting par or better on an 18-hole course. That goal is certainly attainable if you work hard on your game, get some help from a professional, and play often enough.

My *objective* in this part is to show you how simple it can be to improve your golf skills, and take you from just getting around the course to scoring low and bringing that course to its knees.

Chapter 15

More Consistent Contact

AS YOU COME TO PLAY more consistently on the course, you will become aware of how subtle little changes in your setup position, club choice, and swing plane can substantially affect your game. In this chapter I'll share with you some fundamental swing tips that will enable you to plan better shots and lower your scores.

In this chapter...

✓ Fine-tuning your backswing

✓ Come from the inside

✓ Release the club face

✓ Get greasy!

✓ Ball position and tee height

✓ Getting a feel for your clubs

THE MOMENT OF IMPACT

Fine-tuning your backswing

IN AN ATTEMPT TO GET A BIT *more extension or turn on the backswing, many players will loosen their grip on the club, particularly with their left hand (for a right-handed player). Although loosening your grip will enable the club head to get a bit farther behind you (technically, you're increasing the arc of the club), the re-tightening of the left hand on the downswing will almost always change the alignment of the club head, causing it to be either open or closed at impact, resulting in much less accuracy.*

Make sure to maintain a light yet controlled grip on the club at all times. Never vary your grip pressure during the swing. The only way to properly increase the arc of your backswing is to increase your left shoulder turn until your left shoulder has turned over your right foot. Doing so will ensure a full turn, which will give you the fastest swing speed possible. Remember, keep a constant light grip with both hands on the club at all times!

At the top of the swing

To make sure you are achieving a full backswing and are on the proper plane, check the position of your club shaft when you reach the top of your backswing.

VIP

The club should be exactly parallel to the target line, with the club head actually pointing at the target.

Have a friend help you determine this, or videotape you while you take a few swings. If the club points directly at the target, your swing is on the correct plane. If it points left of the target (for a right-handed golfer), you have the club *laid-off* and will most likely slice the ball. If the club points to the right of the target, you have *crossed over* and may very well hook the ball. Work on getting your club head pointing directly at the target, and you should then hit the ball straight and true.

DEFINITION

When the shaft of your club points to the left of the target at the top of your backswing, it's known as being laid-off *(for a right-handed golfer). When the shaft points to the right of the target, it's known as being* crossed over.

Come from the inside

TO HIT THE BALL WITH POWER *and accuracy, you must be able to avoid what is commonly known as coming over the top, a swing flaw that causes the club head to stray outside the target line on the downswing and results in the ball slicing horrendously.*

To avoid coming over the top, you must learn how to keep your club head from straying outside the target line. This can be done by working on the opposite of coming over the top – coming at the ball from the inside. Most powerful, accurate players are able to do this time after time. Making impact with a downswing that comes from slightly inside the target line will help rid you of a nasty slice and will even get you *drawing* the ball slightly. To train yourself to come from the inside try these two drills.

DEFINITION

The draw, a gentle right-to-left curve of the ball (for right-handed players) travels farther than a slice, partly due to a lower trajectory and partly due to less backspin.

SWING PATH DRILL

Inside-to-outside swing plane

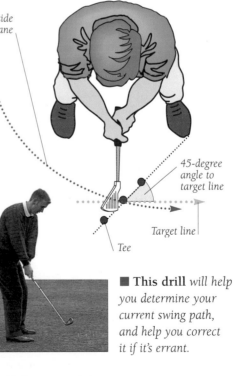

1 Line up three tees

Stick three tees into the turf about three inches apart so they form a line that makes a 45-degree angle with your target line. The line should point to your left foot (for a right-handed golfer). Make sure there is enough space between the tees to swing the club head through.

2 Find your swing path

Take some swings with a 5-iron, trying to clip the top of the middle tee only. The club head will have to pass between the outside tees at a slight in-to-out pathway to avoid hitting them. If you can do this consistently, you know your club head is correctly traveling from the inside and not the out-side. Hitting the outside tees means you're coming over the top and need to work on your swing.

45-degree angle to target line

Target line

Tee

■ **This drill** *will help you determine your current swing path, and help you correct it if it's errant.*

INSIDE PATHWAY DRILL

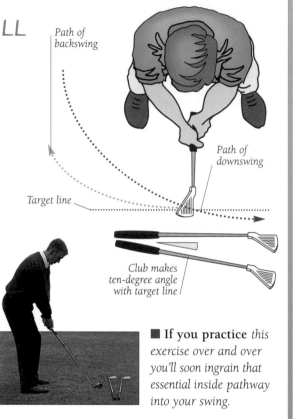

Path of backswing

Path of downswing

Target line

Club makes ten-degree angle with target line

1 Set up your clubs

Place a ball on the ground, and lay a yardstick or a club down eight inches beyond the ball and parallel to your target line. Lay a yardstick or another club outside and in front of the first one, with it pointing about ten or 20 yards to the right of the intended target (for a right-handed golfer). The second club should make an angle of about ten degrees with the target line. Make sure both clubs are far enough away so you don't hit them when you swing.

2 Swing inside to out

Practice taking your club back along the club that is parallel to your target line and then forward along the path that the angled club makes – hitting the ball with an inside-to-out swing.

■ **If you practice** *this exercise over and over you'll soon ingrain that essential inside pathway into your swing.*

Release the club face

WHEN YOU BEGIN YOUR DOWNSWING, *your body begins to uncoil and release all of its pent-up energy. First your hips turn, then your shoulders, then your arms and wrists. The whole action is like a bull whip snapping. The very last thing that should happen before impact is that your forearms and hands turn over, or release.*

As the club face approaches the impact zone, it is quickly moving from an open position to a closed one, like a shutting door. This releasing movement is caused by the turning of your forearms and hands. Without this release, the club face would remain open, resulting in a bad slice.

At the exact moment of impact, the club face should be pointing straight down the target line but on its way to closing, or pointing well left of the target line (for a right-handed golfer).

Bad golfers (you, of course, are not among them) do not release the club face in this way, resulting in poor accuracy and distance.

CLUB FACE OUT OF POSITION

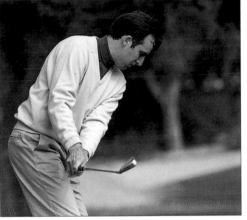

a **Open club face**

If the club face is fanned into an excessively open position on the downswing the likely result will be a bad slice.

b **Closed club face**

A closed club face occurs when the forearm and hand are not rotated properly and so the club face is not square to the target at impact.

Relax and aim

To make sure you release properly, the first thing to do is work on maintaining light grip pressure throughout your swing. Nothing jams up the works like tension in the hands and arms, so grip lightly. Second, make an effort to swing with good tempo. Golfers who swing as fast and as hard as possible almost always leave the club face open at impact – and also come over the top more often than not. Third, make an effort to keep the back of your left hand (for a right-handed golfer) pointing straight down the target line at impact. Players with a poor release move usually have their left hand pointing upward at the sky rather than down the line.

Getting the impact right

Fourth and finally, you should have the feeling that your right forearm (for a right-handed golfer) is turning over your left at impact. Try practicing this regularly in slow motion: Swing the club up and through, paying attention to the movement of your forearms. Make a conscious effort to turn the right one over the left. At the point of impact, freeze and check the position of the club face. Is it open, square, or closed? If it is square to the target line, you know you are doing it right.

■ **To achieve good impact,** *rotate your right forearm over your left hand so that the club face is square to the target when it hits the ball.*

Get greasy!

SAM SNEAD, ONE OF GOLF'S GREATS, *always used to say that in order to swing properly he had to feel as if his body were filled with hot oil, making his swing feel greasy. He had what was perhaps the most beautiful, languid, smooth swing of all time, so there must be something to this.*

What Snead is saying is that to swing well and hit with accuracy and power, you need to feel as loose and limber as possible.

■ **Sam Snead,** *famed for having one of the smoothest swings in golf history.*

You must never try to muscle the ball out there. That may work for Ken Griffey, Jr., but it won't bring success to any golfer. Even Tiger Woods, who hits the ball a mile (well, figuratively), swings the club with grace and fluidity. In other words, keep it simple.

To achieve consistency in your shots, let your swing get greasy. Swing with an almost lazy, graceful timing. Feel your body wind and unwind at a leisurely pace. Never try to whip the club through the ball with all your might. Remember, distance comes from good contact and club-head speed, both of which are produced by a swing with a wide, shallow arc. Hard swingers fail to hit for distance or accuracy because their swings are far too tense and their arcs are narrow and steep. Be like Sam: get greasy.

Ball position and tee height

USUALLY, WHERE YOU PLACE the ball in your stance depends mostly on the club you're using. When you're shooting with a driver, you normally play the ball off of your left heel. Fairway woods require the ball to be moved to the right about an inch, with long irons a hair behind that. With middle irons you normally have the ball an inch or two left of midstance, while the short irons and wedges are played from the center of your stance.

Knowing where to place the ball

Once you are able to make consistent contact, however, you can begin to experiment a bit. Varying these positions will change the flight of the ball, which is often necessary when you're faced with unusual circumstances. For example, moving the ball to the right an inch or two when you're using a middle or short iron will require you to come into the impact zone on a slightly steeper angle. This will produce a lower shot – a necessity when you're playing into a strong wind. Moving the ball to the left in your address position will tend to produce a higher shot – needed when you must get over a tall tree. Teeing the ball up higher when you're preparing to drive the ball will also tend to produce a higher ball flight, while teeing it lower will cause the ball to stay closer to the ground.

INTERNET

www.cegolf.com

Check out this site for great information on all aspects of the game, including ways to improve your swing.

Inside information

Experiment with ball position when you're on the practice range. Learn how small adjustments can produce significant changes in ball flight. The best players use this knowledge to tailor their games to the current conditions. You should too. Just remember to work on these exercises on the practice range and not the course, where any shot you use should be well rehearsed and ready to go.

■ **Tee the ball up** *(above left) if you want to generate a higher ball-flight, essential for playing downwind or for getting the ball over high bushes or trees. Tee down (above right) if you're playing into the wind, as this will keep the ball's trajectory low and under the wind.*

Getting a feel for your clubs

THE BEST WAY TO DO WELL *on the course is to be able to hit a variety of shots. Adaptability will help you deal with unexpected circumstances, which no golfer can avoid. Let's say you have hit your tee shot to within 150 yards of the green, but a low tree branch is threatening to deflect your approach shot, normally a 7-iron for you. What do you do? The answer is to hit a shot of the same distance but with less height so that the ball will pass under the tree branch. Instead of using the 7-iron, you should grab your 5-iron, grip down about two inches, and move the ball to the right in your stance about an inch.*

Gripping down on the club is necessary to reduce the distance your 5-iron will hit the ball. Playing the ball back in your stance will generate a lower shot, guaranteeing that the ball will clear the tree branch.

The resulting shot will travel those 150 yards, albeit with a lower trajectory and more roll. In other words, there's more than one way to skin a cat! Practice making shots of the same length with different clubs. Try to hit your 3-wood lower and shorter. Work on hitting a 4-iron with a three-quarter swing to get your ball out of trouble and back into play. Hit your 8-iron the same distance you would your pitching wedge – a great shot when you're hitting into a strong wind. By developing this adaptability in your game, you will be creating valuable shots for your arsenal and increasing that immeasurable, invaluable factor called feel, which is so crucial to playing the game well.

Understanding your swing plane

Because each club is a different length, each one will have its own unique swing plane. Your driver, the longest club, will have a very shallow swing plane, while your sand wedge, possibly the shortest club in your bag, will have a much steeper swing plane. Try to swing the driver on the same plane as your wedge and you won't fare very well. Likewise, swinging the wedge on the same plane as a driver will result in a "whiff" (the noise made by your club swiping at but missing the ball). To establish the correct plane for each club, make sure that at the top of the backswing your left hand is sitting above your right shoulder (for a right-handed player).

The different swing planes are necessary for each club to work properly. A wedge must make contact with the ball at a steep angle to loft the ball high and impart enough backspin to stop it on the green quickly. A driver must make contact with the ball at a shallow angle to achieve maximum distance and to impart as little backspin as possible so the ball will roll on the fairway after touching down.

A little insight

Understanding how the swing planes change with different clubs will help you get a better feel for how each club works. It will also help you to understand why the shorter clubs are usually easier to hit than the longer ones. A sand wedge has a short, steep arc, making it easy to control. A driver or a long iron has a long, shallow, sweeping arc, often more difficult to control. That's why beginners always have an easier time with the shorter clubs, and also why it's crucial to swing the longer clubs with a smooth, languid grace, instead of a fast, choppy rhythm.

A simple summary

✓ Make sure to maintain a light yet controlled grip on the club at all times. Never vary your grip pressure during a swing.

✓ Making impact with a downswing that comes from slightly inside the target line will greatly improve your accuracy.

✓ At the moment of impact, the club face should be pointing straight down the target line but on its way to closing. The movement that makes this happen is the release.

✓ To achieve consistency in your shots, swing with an almost lazy, graceful timing. Never try to whip through your shot with all your might.

✓ Practice variations in ball position and tee height to prepare yourself for unexpected shots on the course.

✓ By developing adaptability, you will be creating valuable shots for your arsenal. Practice making the same length shots using different clubs, and you will be prepared to make the right shot under any circumstances.

✓ Understanding how the swing planes change with different clubs will help you get a better feel for how each club works.

Chapter 16

Fixing Common Flaws

As you play the game of golf more and more frequently, you will undoubtedly begin to run into a few snags. Golf is simple, but it's not always easy. You might have trouble with direction or with distance, or you might have trouble consistently making good contact with the ball. Whatever the problem, rest assured there is a solution – as long as you're prepared to work at it. In this chapter I'll point you toward simple solutions to all your golfing woes.

In this chapter...

✓ Where did it go?

✓ Poor contact

✓ Poor results with longer clubs

SEVE BALLESTEROS AGONIZES OVER A SHOT

Where did it go?

BY FAR THE MOST *common problem beginners struggle with is accuracy, particularly with the longer clubs. Balls go left, balls go right; will they ever go straight? Yes! Here's how to make it happen.*

The beginner's bane

Every beginner's bane, the slice is perhaps the most frequent and annoying problem in all of golf. There is absolutely nothing good about a slice. You make what feels like a good swing and watch the ball start off straight, only to have it begin curving off to the right (for a right-handed golfer). It sails almost as far right as it does out and away from you, nearly always ending up in big trouble. Out-of-bounds, water hazard, trees, rough – you name it and your slice will find it.

■ **Shots that veer off** *to the left or the right of your intended target can often result in a frustrated rummage among the trees and bushes.*

The banana ball

A sliced golf ball doesn't go very far, either. It carries up into the air, making it susceptible to the wind. It loses golf balls. It humbles. It enrages. It makes you want to throw your longer clubs in the lake. Yet, the majority of golfers slice the ball. For proof, just go to your local driving range, sit down, and watch. You will see banana ball after banana ball soaring up and over, balls that wouldn't stand a chance of staying in the fairway on a real course. So if you are one of the millions who do slice the ball, realize at least that you have some company. Realize also that there is light at the end of the fairway. You can stop that nasty slice, with work and the proper technique.

INTERNET

www.golfdigest.com

Check out Golf Digest for great information on how to cure common faults.

Are you a slicer?

Most golfers slice for a very simple reason: Their club face is open in relation to their swing path.

When the club face is turned open (to the right of square, for a right-handed golfer) at impact, the golf ball will have a lot of clockwise sidespin on it, causing it to slice.

If a golfer's swing is severely outside-in, which means the club face will strike across the ball with a glancing right-to-left action, the ball will also spin clockwise and slice. Combine the two swing errors, and you get the mother of all slices: a ball that has no chance of staying in play.

On impact the ball will spin in a clockwise direction

OPEN CLUB FACE

Slicers tend to swing more with their bodies than their hands and arms. They also tend to have much more tension in their muscles, usually because they're afraid of hitting another slice. Additionally, most slicers try to swing the club too fast. You'll rarely see a lazy, languid swing produce a slice. It is nearly always the players trying to kill the ball who suffer from the banana ball. Another problem some slicers have is using a grip that is too weak. This can turn the club face slightly open at impact, causing a slice.

Stopping the slice

The first step in ridding yourself of a slice is to relax those arms and hands, and take a smooth, lazy swing. Don't worry about distance; that will come. Besides, you will actually hit the ball farther with a long, lazy swing than with a fast, tense one. Next, you need to strengthen your grip a bit. Address the ball, then look at how many knuckles are visible on your left hand. If you see only one knuckle plus a bit of the second, your grip is too weak.

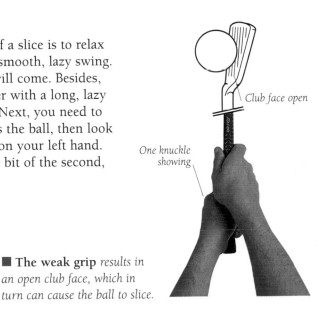

Club face open

One knuckle showing

■ **The weak grip** *results in an open club face, which in turn can cause the ball to slice.*

Grip the club so that you can see two to three knuckles of your left hand, then place your other hand on the grip so that both palms are facing one another. Using this new grip should help close the club face more at impact and reduce your chances of slicing. Now make sure you are not swinging outside-in. First, try setting up with a slightly closed stance, with your feet on a line pointing a few degrees to the right of the target line (for a right-handed golfer). Doing so will help you have a longer backswing and get the club inside the target line.

More practice drills

Try the two drills I described in Chapter 15, in the section called "Come from the inside." For the first drill, really make an effort to take the club straight back along the target line and then swing at the ball from an inside path. Swing the club head through the two outside tees and only hit the middle one. For the second drill, make sure your downswing follows the line of the outside club or yardstick, the one pointing ten degrees right of the target. Keep it straight and simple. Now here's another good drill to practice.

PENCIL DRILL

1 **Insert the pencil**

Stick a pencil into the ground about two feet outside your right foot, right in between the target line and your stance line.

2 **Make an in-to-out swing**

Swing your club straight back along your target line, making sure it stays outside the pencil. Then, on your downswing, let the club pass inside the pencil, so that the club head makes an inside-to-outside swing path.

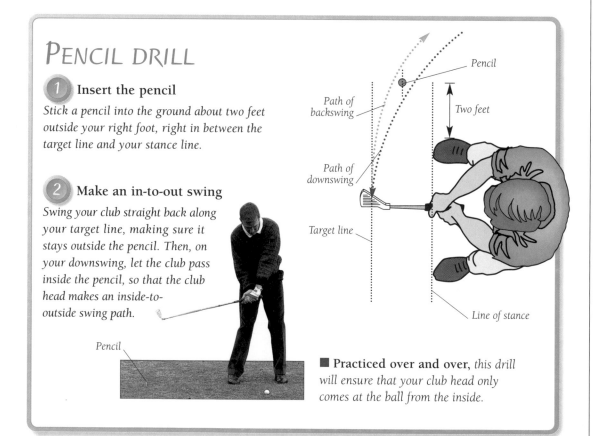

Pencil

Path of backswing

Two feet

Path of downswing

Target line

Line of stance

Pencil

■ **Practiced over and over,** *this drill will ensure that your club head only comes at the ball from the inside.*

Check the club face at impact

Practice all three of these drills religiously and you should be able to eliminate an outside-in swing path. Try them first with a 6-iron and then slowly move up through the longer clubs until you are using a driver. Try moving the ball back in your stance about an inch. This will cause the club face to make impact with the ball sooner, while it is still coming at the ball from inside the target line. Doing so will help reduce the amount of clockwise spin on the ball and cut down on that slicing action. Now you need to make sure your club face is not open to the target line at impact – which can happen even if your club head is coming from the inside.

An open face is nice for a sandwich, but not for a golf stroke. The face must be perpendicular to the target line, or even slightly closed, to prevent a slice.

Using your 6-iron again, take a normal stance and begin making three-quarter swings, concentrating on rotating your right forearm over your left (for a right-handed golfer). Try to get the back of your left hand pointing at the target at the point of impact, then turning downward immediately after. The back of your right hand should be rotating into the upward position immediately after impact. Working on becoming aware of your hand and forearm position in this manner will help you close that club face properly, thereby avoiding the dreaded open face and the resulting slice. After practicing with a three-quarter swing, move on to a full swing. Then graduate to the longer clubs until you can reliably rotate your hands and forearms through impact for all the clubs. Try hitting a few balls and see what happens.

The hook

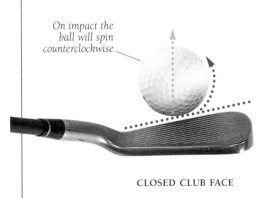

On impact the ball will spin counterclockwise

CLOSED CLUB FACE

Players who hook the ball suffer the exact opposite fate of the slicers. They hit a low tee shot that goes straight for a little bit but then makes a quick left turn and buries itself into the woods or dives into water or rough. A golfer prone to hooks has the club face closed in relation to his or her swing path, causing counterclockwise sidespin (for a right-handed golfer) and a resulting hook to the left. In most cases the problem is simple physics: The club face is closing too soon so that it points to the left of the target at impact.

If you're hooking the ball, you may discover that you are swinging with too much hand and arm action and not enough body movement – the opposite of a slicer. Your club head gets manipulated into the closed position by all that upper body movement, while your hips never really get to open up fully.

Closed hips and overactive arms and hands at impact will almost always produce a hook.

You may also be using too strong a grip, with three or more knuckles showing on your left hand at address, causing the club face to be closed at impact.

Stopping the hook

To prevent a hook, you must first make sure your hips are turning properly through the downswing. At impact, your belt buckle should be just about pointing at your target, and your weight should have shifted almost entirely to your left foot. You should think of your arms and hands as just being along for the ride, not controlling the swing. They should be as passive as possible, like the tip of a bull whip that gets snapped through the air by the action of the longer, thicker parts of the whip. Videotape your swing (or ask an experienced golfer to watch it) to confirm that you are getting your hips turned properly and that your weight is being transferred to your left foot.

Club face square to the ball

Two knuckles showing

■ **Setting up with a neutral grip,** *where two knuckles are showing, is one step toward ridding yourself of those unintentional hooks.*

Next, try weakening your grip so that at address you see a maximum of two knuckles on your left hand. This will help open the club face up a bit at impact, lessening the chances of counterclockwise spin (for a right-handed golfer). Involving your body more (and your hands and arms less) will help rid you of that hook. Also, try moving the ball up in your stance about an inch so that the club head will have an instant more travel time before making impact. Giving the club head that extra time to travel through its arc will enable it to leave its inside path and begin traveling in a straight or outside-in direction, helping to prevent the hook spin.

The shank

The only shot worse than a slice is a shank. Caused by hitting the ball with the *hosel* of the club instead of the face, the ball bounces off the thin, round surface and scoots off to the left or right, barely leaving the ground and traveling in most cases only 20 or 30 yards. Hitting a shank is the most embarrassment you will ever experience on the course, worse even than missing a two-foot putt. Shanks must be avoided at all costs!

DEFINITION

The hosel is the curved part of the club head into which the shaft is fitted.

When you shank the ball too often, odds are that you are either pushing the club out and away from your body during the downswing, or you are approaching the ball on an extreme outside-in pathway, causing the hosel to lead and deliver a glancing blow before the face ever gets there. To cure this problem, first make sure your swing path is coming from the inside. When the toe of the club leads the hosel, as is the case with an inside-out swing and a properly released club head, you can't shank. To train yourself to avoid the shank, try this drill.

STOP THE SHANK

1 Insert two tees into the ground

Place a tee in the ground where the ball would normally be, and then place another tee about two inches outside of the first one.

2 Aim for the first tee

Make an easy swing, trying to hit the first tee squarely while missing the outside tee. If you consistently hit both tees, you know you are pushing the club out away from you. Once you are hitting only the first tee you will be making the correct in-to-out swing path and won't be able to shank.

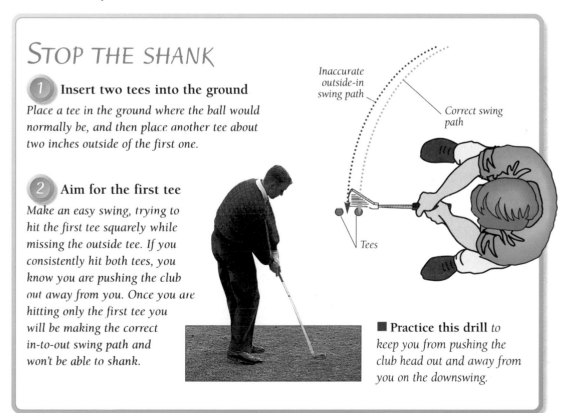

Inaccurate outside-in swing path

Correct swing path

Tees

■ **Practice this drill** *to keep you from pushing the club head out and away from you on the downswing.*

Another trick you can use to see if your club head is straying off the target line is to powder the ball with some talc. After hitting it, check the face of the club to see where contact was made.

If you see a ball mark on the center of the face, you are okay. But if you routinely see the mark close to the heel, you know you need to work on reducing that outside push of the club.

■ **Hitting the ball** *with a powdered club head will show you exactly where your club face is making contact with the ball.*

The pull

A pulled shot starts out going left and continues left (for a right-handed golfer). It travels perfectly straight but off target. This happens when the club head approaches the ball from outside of the target line with the face pointing the same way, instead of at the intended target. When you pull the ball, the club gets out ahead of you too soon because your shoulders are turning too early. At impact, your shoulders have already opened up. Another cause of a pulled ball is having the ball positioned too far left in your stance. By the time the club face gets to the ball, it has already begun to close and move left of the target line (for a right-handed golfer).

Solving the pull

To solve the pull problem, you must have your shoulders in line with the target line at impact. Make sure you are properly aimed and aligned at address, with your feet, knees, hips, and shoulders all parallel to the target line. Pay close attention to your shoulders, making sure they aren't aimed left or right. You must also be sure to shift your weight properly to your left side (for a right-handed golfer). Not shifting your weight properly to your left foot will open your hips and shoulders prematurely, encouraging the pull.

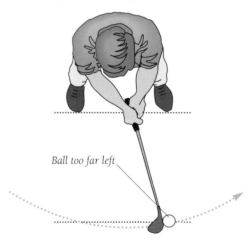

Ball too far left

■ **A pulled shot** *can be caused by the ball being positioned too far left in your stance, resulting in a closed face and an outside-in swing.*

Work on the weight shift, aim and alignment, and swinging smoothly. Don't hit at the ball; swing through it instead, and that pull should disappear. You might also try moving the ball back slightly in your stance, which will cause the club face to make impact a moment sooner, while it is still pointing at the target and not traveling to the left. Do so in half-inch increments and see if this solves the problem.

The push

A push starts out to the right and stays right (for a right-handed golfer) without curving at all. This happens when the club head approaches the ball from an inside path, with the face open relative to the target line. If you push the ball, most likely you are not rotating your body fully on the downswing, which is causing your arms to lag behind. It is a late hit, where the club head does not get into the hitting zone on time.

If you do not properly release the club head, you are likely to push shots even if you are coming at the ball from the inside.

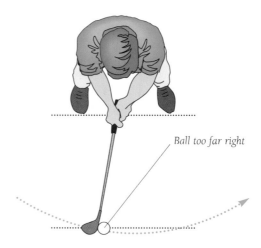

Ball too far right

■ **If the ball is too far right** *in your stance the club head will be on an in-to-out path at point of impact, resulting in a push shot.*

The club face points in the same direction as the swing plane itself, causing the ball to travel straight and to the right of the target (for a right-handed golfer).

Yet another reason you might push the ball is if the ball is positioned too far back in your stance, causing the club head to make impact with the ball too soon. The face meets the ball before it has a chance to point straight down the target line.

INTERNET

www.xgolf.com

Chat with fellow golfers; sound off about the rules, equipment, and what ticks you off; learn the lingo and more on this somewhat unorthodox site.

Solving the push

To solve a push problem, you first need to practice getting your hips turning fully on the downswing so that your belt buckle points at the target by the time you have finished the swing. To achieve this, you need to make sure you are shifting your weight completely from your right foot to your left foot. Practice the weight shift at first without a club. Bring your arms back and through repeatedly, while consciously shifting your weight from back to front.

Your body should not move backward and forward during the swing. Just rotate back and through.

■ **To prevent the push** *make sure your belt buckle is pointing toward the target at the end of the swing, as this will ensure that you turn your hips fully, shift your weight correctly, and make good square impact.*

Once you get the weight shift down, pick up a club and practice again, taking note of the position of your belt buckle at the end of your swing. Your hips should whip open, with your shoulders and arms following a split second after. Opening your hips enough will make room for your arms, which need somewhere to go in order to come around properly. Also, make sure you are releasing the club head properly, by practicing turning your right forearm over the left as you enter the impact zone (for a right-handed golfer). You should feel as if the back of your right hand is beginning to point upward just after impact. This subtle rolling feeling in the hands will help close the club face and get the ball traveling straight instead of to the right of the target. Finally, check to see that your ball is not positioned too far back in your stance. Try moving it up a half-inch at a time and see if that solves the problem.

Reasons for unpredictable distance or direction

If the distance and direction you hit your ball varies tremendously from shot to shot, it probably means two things. First, you may not be consistently striking the ball on the sweet spot of the club, causing a substantial loss in distance. Tests show that balls hit off of the toe or heel of irons or woods can lose as much as 20 to 30 percent of their distance. If you aren't making square contact, odds are that you may be hitting some of these heel-toe shots.

The other reason distance control can be erratic is that you are varying the length of your backswing too much. Instead, try to take the club back the same distance each time for a reliable, predictable swing speed, which will help you hit the ball the same distance each time. If you find yourself hitting the ball all over the place with no predictability whatsoever, you may be getting lazy with your alignment and aiming techniques. Be sure to have your feet, knees, hips, and shoulders parallel to the target line, and make sure to aim the club face right down the target line every time before you swing away.

Poor contact

IN THE BEGINNING of your golfing career, you will hit your share of poor shots. That's okay. You just need to get your timing down as well as the fundamental mechanics of the swing and of impact. While you're learning, you will undoubtedly experience the frustration of poor contact with the ball. You make a great, smooth, well-timed swing only to have your club face hit the turf behind the ball or barely tip the top of it. Your smooth swing results not in a pretty shot, but in a shot that travels only a few miserable yards, leaving you muttering and angry. The good news is that the reasons for poor contact are often easily identified and corrected. Here are the most common, easily remedied contact errors you might be making, complete with solutions.

The fat shot

Hitting the ball fat simply means your club head strikes the ground first, before making contact with the ball. Fat shots are embarrassing, maddening, and often painful to your wrists because the ground is quite a bit less yielding than a golf ball. A fat shot will often travel less than half the desired distance, sending an immense divot up into the air in the process. Hit enough of them and your wrists will feel as if you've been using them for sledge hammers all day.

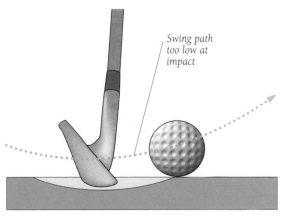

Swing path too low at impact

■ **The fat shot** *results from the club head hitting the ground before making impact, sending the ball sky high.*

VIP

Most of the time when you hit a fat shot, the bottom of your swing arc is too far behind the ball.

This can be caused by bending too much at the waist or knees during the downswing, or by an improper weight shift in which most of your body weight is left on your right foot instead of shifting to the left during the downswing. It can also be caused by a swing plane that is too steep. Still another cause of fat shots is simply playing the ball too far forward in your stance.

Preventing the fat shot

To reduce the chances of hitting a fat shot, try these adjustments. First, make sure you don't bend into the ball during the downswing. You should try to maintain the same amount of bend in your knees, waist, and hips throughout the downswing. Keep your spine straight. Try watching your shadow during a swing. Have the sun directly behind you, and watch your head during the backswing and downswing. If it bobs up and down, you know you must be bending somewhere. Practice until the shadow of your head remains at the same level throughout your swing.

Keep your weight evenly balanced between your heels and the balls of your feet at address. By all means keep it off of your toes. Next, be sure to properly transfer your weight from the right foot to the left foot on the downswing, because this will help keep the club head from bottoming out too soon. Try to make as full a backswing as possible, taking care not to take the club back on too steep a plane because that will almost guarantee a fat shot. Finally, try moving the ball back about an inch in your stance so that the bottom of your swing matches up with the ball position.

The thin shot

Hitting a shot thin means your club head made contact with the ball at or slightly above the equator of the ball, sending it zooming out at no more than two or three feet off the ground. A thin shot hit with a middle iron, long iron, or wood will typically travel much less than a well-hit ball, while a thin shot hit with a wedge or short iron will travel farther than normal. Thin shots usually have very little if any backspin on them, causing the shot to roll quite a distance after touching down.

Trivia...

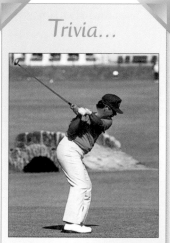

Lee Trevino, one of the finest U.S. golfers ever, hit most of his shots with a pronounced left-to-right curve. It was such a predictable shot shape for him that he learned to use it masterfully during competitions. Trevino won many tournaments on the strength of this curvy shot.

When thin is a good thing

Hitting a thin shot isn't always a disaster, especially when you're hitting off the tee or from the fairway. The ball won't go as far, but at least you will advance it toward the hole. If you're trying to clear a body of water or a bunker, however, the thin shot just won't cut it. Your ball will drop right into the hazard and ruin your day. Thin shots can also hurt because they make your club vibrate, especially if the shaft is made of steel instead of graphite. Your hands will feel as if they have just received a mild electrical shock. Basically you will want to avoid hitting the ball thin. But how?

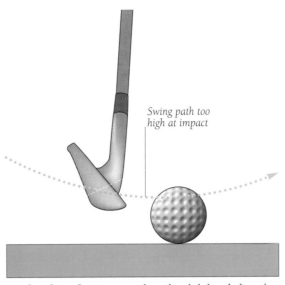

Swing path too high at impact

■ **The thin shot** *occurs when the club head clips the top of the ball, resulting in little backspin and much roll.*

Thin shots are the opposite of fat shots (of course!), which means most happen when the bottom of your swing is too far forward. Others are caused by raising up your body just before impact. Still others are caused by your trying to lift or scoop the ball up into the air with an iron. Incorrect ball position at address can also cause thin shots.

Preventing the thin shot

To avoid hitting thin, keep your spine as straight as possible during the swing, but avoid any straightening of the knees or torso on the downswing. Next, try experimenting with ball position at address. If you are thinning shots with your driver, try teeing the ball up an inch farther back in your stance, enabling the club head to contact the ball a bit sooner. Move the ball back an inch or so with your irons, too; to make sure you contact the ball while the club head is still descending.

Remember, a good iron shot always makes impact with a slightly descending blow. Once the club head begins to ascend, it's too late. Moving the ball back a bit will help ensure proper contact.

Skying a tee shot

One of the most annoying mistakes you can make on the tee is hitting a skied shot, in which the ball goes almost straight up into the air and not very far forward. This happens because the head of the driver slips underneath the ball, with only the very top of it making contact. Not only does the ball go almost nowhere, but a nasty ball mark is left on the top of your nice, shiny driver.

If you hit skied tee shots, you're either swinging your driver into the ball at much too steep an arc or are teeing the ball up too high. If the driver makes impact at too steep an angle, a pop-up is the inevitable result. If it slides beneath the ball under too high a tee, only the very top will connect, sending the ball almost straight up.

To solve the problem, first make sure your swing arc is as shallow as possible with your driver. Take the club back low and slow, attempting to keep the club head close to the ground for as long as possible.

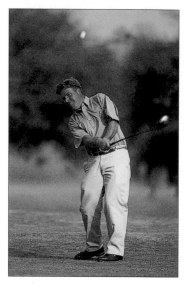

■ **The skied tee shot** *is usually a result of too steep a downswing, which causes the club head to impact the ball below the equator.*

When you reach the top of your backswing, your hands should be about a foot above your right shoulder (for a right-handed golfer) instead of way up over your head.

Making sure of this will help shallow out your swing arc and prevent too steep an entry into the ball. Additionally, try teeing up the ball a bit lower. Adjust the height of the tee so that no more than half of the ball sticks up over the head of the driver. This should help minimize the chances of a skied tee shot.

Topping your tee shot

Worse than a thinned shot, a topped shot is what you get when the club head just barely grazes the top of the ball. The resulting shot dribbles away a few yards at best. Very embarrassing and exasperating, to say the least. A player will top a ball when he or she has a lot of up-and-down body movement during the swing, causing the club head to rise up. If you tend to lift up your body during the downswing, chances are you may top your share of balls.

To avoid topped shots, you must keep your head as level as possible during the swing. Try turning away from the sun until your shadow is directly in front of you, and then take some practice swings. Watch for lots of up-and-down motion of your head.

If you see your noggin bouncing up and down, you know the cause of your topped shots.

Work on keeping the top of your shadow as still as possible during the swing; try to maintain the same amount of bend in your knees and torso, and don't try to uppercut the ball in an attempt to get it airborne. Simply trust in the loft of the club face to do that for you.

Self-analysis

Another great way to determine whether or not your swing has too much up-and-down movement is to videotape yourself swinging. Have a friend set up a camcorder on a tripod and tape your swing from the front, side, and rear. You will undoubtedly see lots of unusual movement, including back-and-forth swaying as well as up-and-down bobbing. After viewing the tape, take a deep breath and begin to work on keeping as level as possible during subsequent swings. After a day or two, tape your swing again to see if you have improved. Then hit a few balls with your new, more level swing and see what happens.

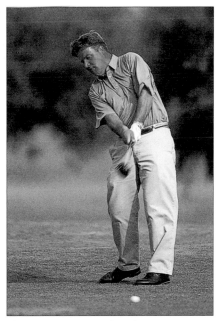

■ **No matter how hard** *you swipe at the ball, a topped shot (hitting it above the equator) will cause it to roll or hop only a few feet in front of you.*

Poor results with longer clubs

MOST BEGINNERS HAVE little problem learning to hit with the shorter clubs, but they tend to have a harder time mastering shots with the longer irons and fairway woods. The reason for this is simple: The shorter the club, the easier it is to control. When you swing an 8-iron or a wedge, you can sense more easily where the club head is and what it is doing. Also, the swing arc is much tighter and steeper, adding to the feeling of control. The long irons (1 through 5) require a longer, more sweeping arc and, being several inches longer, are harder to control than the shorter clubs. Fairway woods are often harder to hit cleanly than the driver because the ball lies flush with the turf instead of up on a nice tee.

If you want to hit the longer clubs well, you must forget about swinging hard and fast.

Instead, you must swing smoothly and with a sweet tempo, like Ernie Els or Fred Couples. Your swing arc must be long and shallow; as with the driver, take the long iron or fairway wood back low and slow. Unlike with the short irons and wedges, you should try not to hit down too aggressively into the ball. Instead, sweep the ball off the grass. Also, make sure to play the ball farther up in your stance than you would with a middle or short iron. Instead of positioning the ball in the middle, try moving it up an inch or two from that point. Doing so will allow for the club's longer shaft and wider swing arc.

Keep life simple: use the easy clubs

Even for good players, long irons tend to be difficult to master. The small club head, long shaft, and paltry amount of loft all combine to make hitting these clubs a real art. Beginners should not even consider carrying a 1-iron, a 2-iron, or even a 3-iron; and they might even be better off leaving the 4-iron home for awhile. Instead, many players are now replacing these hard-to-hit clubs with low-profile, low-center-of-gravity fairway woods, which tend to be much easier to hit than long irons. The larger, heavier head of the fairway wood tends to glide through the grass better and also has a larger sweet spot than a long iron, which enables you to hit a decent shot even if the club face makes contact with the ball off center.

Trivia...

Different players have different swing speeds, but all the greats swing at a speed that allows them to control the club. One way to discover your ideal tempo is to go to the practice range and hit ten balls at 50 percent power, then ten balls at 60 percent power, and so on. Which swing gives you the greatest level of consistency in terms of both accuracy and distance? That's your ideal swing speed.

Beginners should consider dropping the 1-, 2-, 3-, and 4-irons completely and replacing them with 5-, 7-, and 9-woods, which will hit the ball just as far and with a higher trajectory that allows the ball to land more softly onto the green.

Although fairway woods remain more difficult to hit than middle or short irons, they are much easier to master than the long irons will ever be.

A simple summary

✓ A slice veers off to the right because the club face is open at impact, because you're making an outside-in swing, or both. Relaxing your arms and strengthening your grip will help.

✓ A hook takes a turn to the left because the club face is closed at impact, because you're making an exaggerated inside-out swing, or both.

✓ A shank is a short, unpredictable shot that results from hitting the ball with the hosel of your club.

✓ A pulled ball travels left in a straight line. It happens when you hit the ball with a closed face and an outside-in swing.

✓ A push travels to the right in a straight line. It results from hitting the ball with an open face and an inside-out swing.

✓ Unpredictable trajectory or distance results from poor contact on the club face, poor alignment technique, and inconsistency in the length of your backswing.

✓ A fat shot is caused by poor ball position and vertical body movement during the swing.

✓ A thin shot is caused by upward motion on the downswing, as well as poor ball position.

✓ A skied tee shot flies straight up off the tee and does not travel very far.

✓ A topped shot is what happens when the club face barely makes contact with the top of the ball.

✓ Long clubs are more difficult to control and master than shorter ones. Beginners should consider avoiding the long irons entirely.

✓ All problems are solvable. With practice, patience, and persistence you will be able to put your game on the right track.

Chapter 17

When the Going Gets Tough

CONDITIONS ON THE GOLF COURSE change from shot to shot. That's what makes golf so challenging. If you hit every shot from a perfect lie with no wind and no obstructions, the game would be much easier but way less enjoyable. Part of the fun is overcoming golf's ever-changing character and succeeding in the face of adversity. In this chapter I'll explain how to handle some of the more common challenges you'll confront on the course.

In this chapter...

✓ Stormy weather

✓ The hills are alive

✓ Tricky lies

✓ Timber!

Stormy weather

GOLF ISN'T PLAYED INDOORS. *It's played outside under the big sky, on acres of rolling grass. Because of this, the flight of every shot you take will be affected by the prevailing weather conditions. The best players learn to adapt to the weather. The ones who don't really enjoy playing will grumble and complain.*

It's not such a bad thing

Many professionals actually prefer less-than-perfect weather conditions, for one simple reason. When the weather is perfect, most of the players in a tournament will be able to score well, making the competition fierce. When the weather takes a turn for the worse, though, only those capable of managing their games under difficult conditions will be able to survive the round. Fair-weather competitors get weeded out, leaving only the most experienced players to compete for the prize money. Players who know how to use the wind to their advantage or who can adapt well to extremes in temperature or precipitation will dominate the less capable or less experienced.

■ **If grey skies loom** *make sure you're suitably equipped for wet play, and be prepared for higher scores and a longer game.*

■ **Use the wind** *to your advantage by adjusting your aim to let the wind take the ball.*

Wind

When the wind begins to blow on the course, your score on each hole is likely to be higher. That is an inescapable truth.

Once you accept this, wind play will become less stressful and could even get interesting. The wind is a bully of sorts. It will shorten great drives or lengthen perfect approach shots, making them fly right on past the green. The wind will grab your perfect shot and force it left or right into all manner of trouble. It will make a long hole longer and will cost you dozens of golf balls, blown helplessly into lakes, woods, and rough.

As with any big, strong adversary, the best way to deal with the wind is not to resist it, but to use it to your advantage. For instance, if a strong left-to-right wind is blowing while you are on the tee, hit your tee shot well left of your intended target in the fairway, knowing that the wind will push the ball to the right. If a strong wind is blowing down the fairway, use it to add a few extra yards onto your tee shot.

Simple guidelines for playing in the wind

1. Grip down on your club for more control.

2. Choose a club with less loft than you think you need, to lower the trajectory of the shot. Don't worry; if you grip down on the club an inch or so, the ball won't go any farther than the more-lofted club you would otherwise have used. Lowering the height of the shot will help minimize the effects of the wind on the ball. Remember that the higher the shot, the more the wind will affect it.

3. Don't fight the wind. Instead, use it to your advantage. Determine which way the wind is blowing. If there is a left-to-right wind, aim your shot left of the target and vice versa.

4. If you're hitting into the wind, keep your shot as low as possible by using a less-lofted club, and expect the ball not to go as far.

5. If you're hitting with the wind, expect the ball to go farther than normal. This means you may need to use a more-lofted club to allow for the added distance that the wind will give you.

6. Make a steady, smooth swing, using about three-quarters of your strength, to ensure that your shot is as accurate as possible. The wind will amplify any mistakes you make, so concentrate on accuracy, not distance.

Don't try to play your regular game in the wind. Hitting the ball high in the air will wreak havoc on your accuracy and distance control. Get the ball down, and try to use the wind whenever possible.

Trivia...

Conditions at the 1992 U.S. Open at Pebble Beach started out calm enough. By the weekend, though, the wind had begun to pick up, eventually increasing to near gale force. Most of the competitors had no idea how to play under such extreme conditions. Not so Tom Kite, however, who had grown up playing golf in the windy state of Texas. Using his expert wind management skills, Kite was able to win the U.S. Open, his first major tournament.

Rain

When you're playing in the rain, several things happen that make the game more difficult. First, you're not as comfortable, especially because rain often comes with wind and cold. Second, your hands and grips get wet, making it more difficult to control the club. Third, the course actually begins to play longer than if conditions were drier. Why? Good question. Because when the fairway gets wet, your tee shots won't roll nearly as far as they do when it's dry. This creates a longer second or third shot for each hole. Also, when the grass and the ball become wet, the ball won't spin as much. This may cause an approach shot to the green to fly farther than you expected.

INTERNET

www.golftipsmag.com

For great advice on how to play golf under less than ideal weather conditions, log on to Golf Tips, click on the search link, type in "weather," then hit "search."

One plus about playing in the rain is how quickly the ball stops on the green. It's almost like playing darts: Wherever the ball hits, it stays. An approach shot that might ordinarily scoot through the green and into trouble will stay put on the rain-soaked putting surface. Putts will also roll more slowly when the green is soaked.

Simple guidelines for playing in the rain

1. Have several dry towels in your golf bag to keep your hands and grips as dry as possible during the round.

2. Bring along a few extra golf gloves as they tend to get rather wet on a rainy day.

3. Carry a good umbrella with you.

4. Make sure to have a cover for your golf bag to keep the rain from dripping in and soaking your clubs. Most golf bags come with a decent cover. If yours didn't, you can buy one.

GOLF BAG WITH
COVER AND UMBRELLA

5. Use a smooth swing, and don't swing hard because the club could fly right out of your hands. Make up for the easier swing by using a less-lofted club for each shot.

6. Buy and use a quality rain suit if you intend to play in the rain. Available at all good golf stores, they will make the experience much more tolerable.

If there is any chance of lightning, end your round and find the nearest shelter. Do not stand underneath a tree or hold a golf club in your hands! Most courses will give you a rain check anyway, so go home!

WATERPROOF RAIN SUIT

Temperature extremes

Although most players prefer to play when the weather is temperate and calm, you will undoubtedly find yourself playing golf in the spring, fall, and even early winter. Golf can be played in nearly all conditions, provided there is no frost or snow. Sometimes playing on a crisp autumn day can be a real treat, especially since fewer players will be out on the course. Cooler weather is a great time for a beginner to play golf, for that very reason. You will feel less rushed with no one behind or in front of you. You might even be able to take a few practice shots from each position, to help perfect your game. Just make sure there is no one behind you if you do this!

Simple guidelines for playing in cold weather

1. Dress for the weather. Wear layers of lighter clothes, which can be easily shed if necessary. Turtlenecks work well on the golf course. Consider wearing a quality pair of thermal underwear, too, if temperatures drop below 45°F.

2. Make sure your golf shoes are waterproof and that you have on a warm, comfortable pair of socks.

3. A hat is a must. On a very cold day consider wearing a hat with ear flaps. You might look silly, but you'll stay warmer.

4. Don't expect the ball to travel as far in the colder, denser air. A shot that normally calls for a 7-iron will most likely require a 6-iron instead.

WET-WEATHER BOOTS

5 Consider bringing along a pair of mittens or winter gloves to wear between shots. Warm hands are a must for making a decent shot.

6 Keep a ball or two in an inside pocket, to warm it up. When teeing off, always use a ball that has been warmed this way. The warmer the ball, the farther it will go.

7 Take along a thermos of hot tea, coffee, or broth. Stay away from alcohol because it will actually cool your body down over time.

Don't expect to score as well on a cold day, either. The extra clothes will hinder your swing somewhat thereby cutting down on your distance and control.

MITTENS

Simple guidelines for playing in warm weather

1 Wear light-colored, loose-fitting clothes.

2 Drink more fluids than you think you need. Always carry a large water bottle with you.

3 Always take sunscreen along with you, with an SPF rating of at least 15. Apply it to all exposed skin before you head for the first tee, and reapply it before you start the back nine.

4 Take a wide-brimmed hat to protect your face and neck.

5 Consider playing early or late in the day, when the sun and heat are not as intense.

6 Expect the ball to travel farther on a hot day than it would otherwise, because of the warmer, less-dense air. A shot that normally calls for a 7-iron may require you to use an 8-iron instead.

SUN VISOR

7 Consider using a golf cart to minimize your exposure to the sun and help prevent dehydration.

Extremely warm weather can be fun, but you must be prepared for it. Summer in many areas can bring with it brutally hot temperatures and the threat of heat stroke and sunburn. Golf courses in the south and the southwest of the United States can be especially hot during the summer months, with temperatures regularly reaching well above 100°F. This kind of weather tends to keep many golfers home so that you get to play on a less busy (and less stressful) course.

The hills are alive

FEW GOLF COURSES ARE designed to be flat. That would be too easy. Rolling hills, steep embankments, and deep hollows all make the golf course more beautiful and the game more challenging. You will often find yourself having to hit your ball off of a slope. With a sidehill lie, the ball may be above or below your feet. With an uphill or downhill lie, your feet will be on different levels. Those beautiful strokes you've been working hard to master will require some adjustment. Don't worry! You can do it.

Uphill lie

When you're hitting a ball from an uphill lie, you will be creating more loft in the shot than usual because the hill acts like a launching ramp. This added loft will reduce the distance that your club will hit the ball, so you need to select a less-lofted club for the shot. Play the ball about an inch farther forward in your stance because the bottom of your swing arc will be farther forward due to the slope of the hill.

Your weight will tend to shift onto your back foot with this type of shot. That's okay, as long as you:

Make sure the line of your shoulders matches the slope of the hill.

As the ball will tend to veer to the left, aim a little to your right when making your swing. Keep the swing smooth, using as little lower-body action as possible to prevent any up-and-down or lateral motion. Just keep it simple.

■ **An uphill shot requires** *a club with less loft than usual because of the ball's higher trajectory. In addition, when addressing the ball be sure to shift your weight to the right to counteract the slope.*

Downhill lie

When you're hitting a shot from a downhill lie (taking a swing with your front foot lower than your back foot), you will be taking away loft from the shot due to the downward slope of the hill. Because of this, you need to choose a more-lofted club for the shot. You should play the ball about an inch farther back in your stance than you normally would because the bottom of your swing arc will be farther back due to the slope of the hill. Your weight will shift to your front foot on this shot. That's okay, as long as the line of your shoulders matches the slope of the hill. Make a smooth swing, using very little lower-body action to prevent any unnecessary motion, and aim a little to your left as the ball will tend to veer to the right.

■ **A downhill shot** *requires a club with greater loft since the ball's trajectory is much lower from this angle.*

Sidehill lie

Sometimes you will be hitting sideways off a hill, rather than up or down. When you set up to the ball, it will either be above or below your feet, depending on which way the slope goes. The difficulty with this type of shot is that the ball lies either above or below your normal swing arc. If it's below, you won't make contact with the ball at all using a normal swing. If it's above, you'll hit the ground several inches behind the ball. The slant of the hill will also have an effect on the direction the ball travels. Basically, the ball will always curve in the direction of the downward slope. For instance, if the ball is above your feet at address, it will curve to the left (for a right-handed golfer).

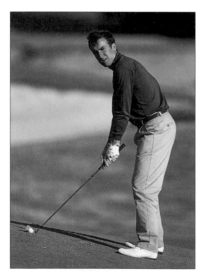

■ **To play a ball** *above your feet, grip farther up the club and position your weight more on your toes to counteract the destabilizing effect of the slope.*

Above and below your feet

To hit a ball lying above your feet, aim slightly to the right (for a right-handed golfer). Grip down on the club about an inch or two to compensate for the ball being higher up. Then make a smooth swing, keeping your lower body as still as possible. Hitting a ball lying below your feet, first aim slightly left (for a right-handed golfer) to compensate for the curve that the hill will put on the ball. Make sure you grip the club as far up as possible. Then bend your knees more than you normally would and make a smooth swing, keeping your lower body as still as possible.

Elevation changes from tee to green

Any differences in elevation between you and your target will affect how far the ball will travel. If your 7-iron usually hits a ball 150 yards along a flat fairway, it will hit the ball farther if your target is below you. For instance, you might come to a 170-yard, par-3 hole and find that the green lies at least 50 feet lower than the tee box. Normally you might use a 4-iron for that distance. Choose a 4-iron now, though, and you will most likely fly a good 20 yards past the green.

You need a more-lofted club for this job. Generally speaking, for every ten to 15 feet of elevation change between you and your target, you need to change your club selection to the next club up.

This works whether the elevation goes up or down. On the par-3 hole I just described, you would probably need to hit a 7-iron instead of the 4-iron. If the green had been higher than the tee box by about 50 feet, you would probably have to go to a fairway wood to make the shot, most likely a 4-wood or a 5-wood. With experience, you'll know exactly which club to choose when you're facing a change in elevation. Start with the formula I just gave you, but remember that the prevailing winds will affect your choice, as will the temperature. You will need to experiment and see what works for you.

Changes in altitude

The higher up in elevation you are, the thinner the air becomes. A ball hit 240 yards at sea level will travel about 15 percent farther at 5,000 feet above sea level, or about 276 yards! Makes you want to move to Colorado, doesn't it?

Basically, for every 1,000 feet higher in altitude, your shots will travel about three percent farther than they would at sea level.

The reverse holds true as well; if you are used to playing on a high altitude course and go to play on one at sea level, your shots will travel three percent less per 1,000-foot drop than you are used to.

Trivia...

Keeping your balance while standing on sand is not always easy. Bernhard Langer has compared it to riding the moguls of a ski slope. When you're moving that fast, weight shifts must become instinctive or you're going to fall down. Good skiers naturally transfer their weight to their lower leg. Good golfers in a bunker do too. Shifting your weight to your lower leg gives you a stable platform to balance on. It also helps bring your shoulders in line with the angle of the slope, so that you can swing at the correct angle.

Tricky lies

IF YOUR BALL *always lands on the fairway or the putting green, just skip this section. But if you are like the rest of us, you will often find your ball lying in something you would prefer to have avoided. Part of the challenge of the game, then, is to successfully hit your ball off of a less-than-perfect lie, suffering as little as possible along the way. That's really what golf is all about: You don't hit great shots as much as you hit great recovery shots. Simple, right?*

Rough play

Rough, or tall grass, can be very difficult to hit out of. Your ball can sink to the bottom so that you can barely see it. The thick, tangled grass can catch your club head as you swing and cause your shot to veer off to the left or right, or hold it back to just a few yards. Land in the rough and you'll probably score high on that hole.

■ **If your ball lands in the rough** *try to focus solely on getting it back into play by using a higher lofted club and a steeper swing plane.*

The fairways on each hole are usually bordered by varying lengths of rough. When you try to hit a ball out of it, the grass grabs the club's hosel, often causing it to turn in. This makes the ball go to the left of the target (for a right-handed golfer). Also, the tall blades of grass get in between the ball and the club face, minimizing the amount of backspin on the ball. This makes the shot fly and roll farther than normal. Are you beginning to understand how the rough got its name?

Hitting out of short rough

If your ball lands in relatively short rough (one to two inches long), you should be able to make decent contact. Use a more-lofted club to allow for the extra carry and roll and to ensure that you can get it up and out successfully.

Always go for more loft when you're coming out of the rough.

Your primary goal should be to get out of it and back into play. Even if you end up short of the hole on the fairway, you will then be able to successfully shoot for the green.

VIP

Hitting out of medium rough

Too many beginners try to make miraculous shots from the rough, only to find themselves in deeper trouble than when they started. When you're hitting out of medium-length rough, play the ball farther back in your stance and use a slightly steeper swing arc so that you come into the ball with a descending blow instead of a sweeping action. This will help keep the club head from whacking into too many blades of grass along the way, which could deflect it and cause an offline shot. Also, grip the club a bit tighter than usual to minimize club-head deflection as much as possible.

Pitching out of long rough

If you find your ball in rough that is deeper than two or three inches, you should give up any ideas of going for the green and try to pitch the ball out into a more favorable position. Just keep it simple.

To pitch the ball out of the rough, choose a sand wedge and hit the ball the way you would an explosion shot out of a bunker.

Address the ball in the middle of your stance, aim your body to the left of the target (for a right-handed golfer), turn the club face slightly clockwise, and then take a three-quarter-strength swing, slipping the club head under the ball. Make sure to grip the club more firmly than usual, and use a steep, descending blow to minimize the amount of grass encountered by the club head. The ball should pop out nicely and end up in a much more favorable lie, from which you can then go for the green.

■ **Divots can be easy traps** *for your ball. If you are faced with this situation, remember to use an iron with more loft than usual and to hit down on the ball (like chopping wood).*

Hitting from an old divot

As you know, most iron shots leave a divot in the grass. As I'm sure you recall, a divot is a small patch of grass and dirt that was scooped out by the blade of an iron in front of the ball during a normal swing. Most courteous players retrieve the piece of sod and replace it. A divot will then re-root within a few days, and the course maintains its appearance and playability. Unfortunately, many golfers do not take the time to replace divots. What is left instead is a rectangular hole in the ground, just waiting for your perfect tee shot to roll in. When this happens, your ball ends up sitting atop sandy soil instead of grass, making the next shot a perilous one, to say the least.

VIP

Hitting a golf ball from an old divot hole is similar to hitting from a fairway bunker: You have to make contact with the ball first, not the ground.

If you hit the shot even a tiny bit fat (that is, behind the ball), the ball won't go very far. To hit a ball out of an old divot hole, first set up so that the ball is back in your stance, about an inch behind the midpoint between your feet. Set up with your hands slightly ahead of the ball, which will encourage a steep, downward pathway into the impact zone. Take the club back steeper than usual, and hit down firmly, making sure to catch the ball first.

Delofting the club face

When you're faced with this tricky shot, it's best to use an iron with a good amount of loft, even if you can't reach the green with it. The extra loft will help get the ball out of the divot, which is the most important thing. By moving your hands ahead of the ball, you will be *delofting* the club face anyway, effectively increasing the distance that particular club can hit the ball.

Hitting off hard pan

Hitting your ball off a hard-pan lie is also tricky. Solidly packed dirt with no grass whatsoever doesn't make the best platform from which to hit a golf ball, but it's usually easier to deal with than hitting from a divot. At least the ball is not below ground level!

■ **Hitting off hard pan** *requires a steep swing to ensure the club makes contact with the ball. Be aware that the ball will produce a lower flight than normal.*

The problem with hard pan is that the club head tends to bounce off the solid earth. If you hit behind the ball at all, the club head will bounce up and catch the ball thin, causing it to whiz down the course at about two feet off the ground. To successfully hit a ball out of a hard-pan lie, simply set up the same way you would for hitting from an old divot hole. Play the ball back in your stance, move your hands ahead of the ball, and make a steep swing, catching the ball first. It's not a good idea to use a sand wedge for this shot because the bounce on the bottom of this club will increase your chances of hitting the shot thin.

Hitting off a cart path

A cart path is considered an immovable obstruction, according to the rules of golf. This means you are entitled to a free drop of the ball, without penalty, off the path and onto the surrounding grass. However, sometimes the area available to drop the ball in will give you a worse shot than you had from the path itself. A tree or bush might then be in the way, for example. In this situation, it can make better sense to hit the ball off of the cart path than to move the ball. Remember to keep it simple: Play the shot that has the best chance of succeeding.

Unlike hitting out of an old divot or from hard pan, you do not want to hit this shot with a steep, descending blow.

The dangers of a paved path

The paved path will not give at all, and hitting down steeply would injure your wrists and probably damage your club head. Instead, you should hit the ball with a sweeping blow so that contact is made while the club head is at the very bottom of its arc. To do this, play the ball from the middle of your stance, and try not to use your lower body at all during the swing. Take a much wider-than-normal stance to help minimize leg movement and keep your spikes from slipping on the hard surface. Also, consider gripping down some on the club to increase your control. Try to make contact just below the equator of the ball – not at its bottom – to be sure you don't slam the club head into the path. And don't worry about getting the ball to the green. Just get it back in play.

What about that wet bunker?

When a bunker gets wet, the sand in it becomes packed down, making the surface firmer than usual. This can cause the blade of your sand wedge to bounce too much and contact the ball at its equator, resulting in a low screamer that goes 50 yards or more. Very embarrassing – and preventable. If the bunker you are playing from is wet, you can make adjustments to your setup to compensate.

■ **When playing a wet bunker shot,** *keep the club face slightly square and your stance square at address. You may prefer to use a pitching wedge, as its sharper edge will allow you to get under the ball more easily.*

Getting out of a wet bunker

Instead of setting up open (or aimed to the left of the target, for a right-handed golfer), set up so that your feet, knees, and shoulders are aimed at the flagstick. Instead of playing the ball off your front heel, play it about an inch in front of the midpoint of your stance. Also, don't open the blade of the sand wedge as much as you would with a regular splash shot. Just open it a few degrees. This setup should allow the blade of the wedge to dig into the wet sand and get underneath the ball, popping it out nicely.

If you do this, allow for a bit more roll on the green because the ball will come out with very little backspin.

Playing out of water

Impossible you say? Not entirely. If your ball ends up in a water hazard, most of the time you'll have to swallow your pride, take the penalty, and drop the ball back into play. If more than half of the ball is above the surface of the water, though, you can attempt to hit it out. If most of the ball is dry, you will have a good chance of hitting it out and advancing the ball. The advantage of taking the shot is that you will not incur the penalty. The disadvantage is that you might not get the ball out at all.

Prepare to get wet

To hit the ball out of the water, make sure that more than half of it is above the surface of the water. Then put on your rain suit because you will get wet! At least take off your shoes and socks, and roll up your pant legs too if you have to actually stand in the water to address the ball.

Next, set up to the ball as if you were going to hit a regular bunker shot. The ball should be forward in your stance, and your body should be aimed to the left of the target. Choose a wedge for the shot, and open the blade up by turning it clockwise (for a right-handed golfer). Then, make a relatively steep swing, making sure to contact the water about an inch behind the ball. If you do this correctly, the displaced water will lift the ball right out, just as the sand would on a typical bunker shot.

Remember, though, that you should not attempt this unless more than half of the ball is above the surface of the water.

A submerged ball probably won't pop out but probably will leave you wet and grumbling. If you have any doubts at all, take the penalty and drop your ball onto dry land.

■ **Attempting to play a ball out of a water hazard** *is very risky, but can be done. Here, South African David Frost hits into the water in a brave attempt to propel the ball into the air.*

Timber!

TREES AND BUSHES *on the golf course are beautiful to look at, but they can be a terror to play through. They seem to have the ability to attract your golf ball. Nothing will depress you more than seeing your tee shot bury itself in a tangle of branches and tree trunks or a thick, thorny bush. Don't panic! You can learn to extricate yourself from the gnarly grasps of those pretty but pesky plantings. As long as your ball sits atop a decent lie, you should be able to advance it.*

Tucked in the trunk

Depending on how close the ball is to the tree trunk, you may or may not have a chance to hit it. If the ball lies at least three or four inches away, on turf or rootless earth, you might be able to hit it out. If the ball lies any closer than that, though, don't take the chance of hurting yourself and breaking your club. Declare an unplayable lie, take the penalty, and drop the ball into a better position.

Attempting the shot

If you're presented with a decent lie and at least three or four inches of space, the next question is, do you have a shot toward your target or at least a line back onto the fairway? Often a ball will rest near a tree in such a way that the trunk prevents you from setting up to the ball properly. But if you can set up to the ball properly and the lie is good, the next thing to check is possible interference from tree branches. If any branches threaten to block the flight of the ball, choose a less-lofted club (say a 4-iron or a 5-iron) and simply pop the ball out and back into play. If no branches threaten the shot, though, choose whatever club you need to reach your target, then set up with the ball an inch or two behind the midpoint of your stance. Make a smooth, full swing, and try to contact the ball first.

■ **If the ball** *lies within four inches of the trunk, you should be able to hit it successfully away from the tree and back into play; if not, drop it two club lengths from the tree and take the penalty.*

Try the other hand

If the ball has stopped near a tree trunk in a position that makes swinging impossible, you might consider turning around and hitting the ball from the opposite side. In other words, a right-hander would hit left-handed, and a lefty would hit right-handed. To do this, reverse your grip on the club, turn the iron on to its toe, and play the ball back in your stance. You will actually be striking the ball with the broad toe of the club, swinging with an abbreviated, punchy swing. You will have to aim the club face so that the flat of the blade is perpendicular to the intended target line. I know this sounds hard, but if you practice this shot it will work for you. Sure, the ball won't go very far and you won't hit it with much accuracy, but at least you'll be able to get it away from the tree and back in play.

Beneath the branches

Sometimes your shot will end up under a tree with a good lie but with several low-hanging branches blocking your ability to hit a shot of normal height. To hit the ball out of there without striking the branches, choose a low-lofted iron – probably a 4-iron or a 5-iron – grip down on it, and make a punchy, three-quarter swing. Play the ball about two inches behind the midpoint of your stance. Your downswing will have to be steep, and your follow-through should be restricted. The shot should feel more like a slap shot with a hockey stick.

Be sure to hit down on the ball, making contact with it first, then the ground. The ball should come buzzing out from under the branches with a very low, running trajectory.

■ **If your ball lands** *beneath a low-hanging tree, play the shot with a lesser-lofted iron. This will keep the ball's trajectory low, and you should be able to sneak the ball out from under the branches.*

The hazard beneath the trees

Those same evergreen trees that can make a course so beautiful well past summer can also pose a hazard any time of the year. Sometimes you'll have to hit a shot from under a grove of them, and a thin layer of pine needles on the ground creates a less-desirable lie, as well as questionable footing. And don't forget the challenge of dealing with overhanging branches.

Hitting off pine needles

To hit your ball off of pine needles, first take a wider-than-normal stance to make sure you keep your balance. Then simply play the shot as if you were hitting off of hard pan. Set up with the ball an inch or so behind the midpoint of your stance. Move your hands slightly ahead of the ball position, then make a steep swing, delivering a descending blow into the ball. Try to hit the ball first, before you hit the ground.

If there are tree roots lurking beneath the needles, you should either chip the ball out a few yards to the fairway or declare an unplayable lie, take the penalty, and drop the ball into more favorable surroundings.

Striking your club head into a big tree root can injure your wrists and damage your club, so don't take the chance.

In the bushes

If your ball ends up inside a thick, gnarly bush, odds are you won't be able to get a club on it. You will just have to declare an unplayable lie, take the penalty, and drop the ball into a more favorable spot. If, however, the bush is small and thin and it looks like you might be able to make contact with a club, you might consider trying to make a shot.

■ **Trying to hit your ball** *out of the bushes requires much patience and sometimes a touch of ingenuity. If you can reach the ball, attempt a shot: you only have to make contact with the ball and you'll avoid a penalty drop.*

First, choose your sand wedge, not only for its loft but because it is the heaviest club in your bag and will be able to swish through the spindly little branches of the bush better than any other club. Set up with the ball well back in your stance, and grip the club firmly. Then deliver a very steep, descending blow right at the back of the ball.

Your angle of attack should be so steep that no follow-through will be possible, almost as if you were hacking at the bush with an axe.

With some luck, the ball should be blasted free. If you have any doubts about trying this, however, or if the course has a rule prohibiting the destruction of any plants, take the penalty and drop, then move on.

A simple summary

✔ Golf is not just a fair-weather game, so prepare yourself for all the types of weather conditions you might run into on the course. Taking the time to do so will make your round much more productive and enjoyable.

✔ Don't try to play your regular game in the wind. Hitting the ball high in the air will wreak havoc on your accuracy and distance control. Get the ball down, and try to use the wind to your advantage.

✔ Don't panic if you find your ball resting on a slope. By using the proper setup techniques, these shots shouldn't be any harder to hit than ones from a flat lie.

✔ Remember to take into account how elevation changes can profoundly affect how far you will hit your shots. You will hit the ball farther if the target is below you, and less far if it is above you.

✔ Altitude also affects how far your ball will fly. For every 1,000 feet of rise in altitude, your shots will travel about three percent farther than they would at sea level.

✔ Don't panic if the lie of your ball is less than perfect. Remember that golf is a game of recovery, not perfection. Proper setup and technique will almost always enable you to hit the ball well.

✔ Trees and bushes are not always ball-eating monsters. With some ingenuity and patience, you should be able to free your ball from their clutches and get on with your round.

Chapter 18

Strategy Session

SUCCEEDING AT GOLF REQUIRES you to think ahead. For each hole you play, you should have a plan of attack to get your ball into the hole in as few shots as possible. Strategy is more important than brute strength, finesse, and even luck. In this chapter, I'll discuss the strategies you'll need to do well on the course and give you some tips on how to implement them.

In this chapter...

✓ Golf is like a game of chess

✓ Play the percentages

✓ Enhancing your accuracy

✓ Use the entire tee box

✓ Analyze your lie

✓ Shaping the shot

✓ Measuring up

THE 10TH HOLE AT VALDERRAMA, SPAIN

Golf is like a game of chess

IN CHESS, THE PLAYER *who plans ahead and understands what he or she is up against will almost always succeed over the player who plays only from move to move with no foresight or strategy. The golf course is very much like a chessboard, with an abundance of choices available to each player at any given moment. Some moves will work out better than others, and golfers who choose the best strategies will score lower than those who simply get up to the ball and swing away without planning where they want to end up.*

CHESS: A GAME OF STRATEGY

■ **At the 9th hole** *at Turnberry, Scotland, the player has to hit the ball safely across the water so that it lands on the fairway on the other side of the small bay.*

A game plan for every hole

Each hole on the course is different in many ways. Some holes are longer or have a different par. Some play uphill, while others play downhill. A few play into the wind, while some always play with the wind. Some dogleg right, while others turn left or play dead straight. One hole may have many bunkers, while another has water along one side. Golf holes, in other words, are like fingerprints. No two are alike, even on the same course. When you play a course, you have to learn as much as you can about each hole in advance so you can be prepared for what lies ahead.

How to get a feel for the hole

It's not easy to learn about each hole in advance, but you can get a real feel by doing several things. First, see if there is a yardage book available in the pro shop. The yardage book will show you the design of each hole, point out all of its hazards, and give you yardages to hazards, ideal landing areas, and important parts of the green. Try speaking to the resident golf professional at the course. He or she might offer you some valuable information about special features on the course, especially areas to avoid, such as water hazards or out-of-bounds. Talk to other golfers at the course who might have played there before. They will be able to give you choice inside information not necessarily available in the yardage book.

Once you have a general idea of the structure of each hole, you can go ahead and begin reasoning out what your game plan for each should be. Generally speaking, when you step onto the tee of any hole, you need to decide quickly on the best, safest landing area for your tee shot. Look for trouble (such as out-of-bounds, hazards, rough, or severely sloping lies), and try your best to avoid it. Choose a specific spot as a target instead of just hitting away and hoping the ball will find the fairway. Remember, golf is a tactical game; position is everything.

The par-3 hole

Par-3 holes usually measure anywhere from 80 to 235 yards. When you're playing a par-3 hole, you will ideally be hitting your ball directly onto the green from the tee box. When you step up to the tee, you should already have a picture in your mind of the shape of the green and exactly where the flagstick is located. If the flagstick is in the middle of a fairly large, flat green, you can safely aim for it. If it is tucked away in a corner, however, or protected by several bunkers or a water hazard, you shouldn't even think about aiming for the flag. The risk is simply too great. Instead, play the safer shot to the widest part of the green, leaving you two putts for par. Know the distance to the part of the green you intend to hit your ball to.

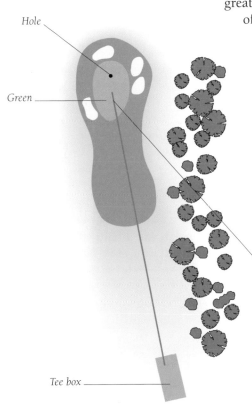

Hole

Green

Tee box

Simply aim for the green rather than trying to get close to the hole on your tee shot.

Usually, your scorecard or yardage book will give you the distance from the tee box to the middle of the green. As a beginner, that's where you should be aiming.

■ **As a beginner on a par-3,** *tee off from the front of the tee box and aim for the green. By playing a safe shot you should avoid the dangers of bunkers and trees.*

Hitting to a protected flagstick (also called a sucker pin, for good reason) is a low-percentage shot that rarely works out well, so don't be a hero! Keep it simple and aim for the middle.

Playing a par-3 hole

You know the yardage, so choose a club you know you can hit that distance (something you should already have determined at the driving range), and then hit the shot with confidence. Remember to focus on a small area of the green as your target zone. Even if you are hitting for the middle of the

■ **Valderrama is Spain's** *most challenging course, with few straightforward holes. Many of its par-3 holes are lined with trees that can threaten players' chances of making par.*

green, choose a section of it as your target and shoot for that. Don't let the bunkers or other hazards psyche you out. Visualize the perfect shot, fill your mind with positive thoughts, and swing away.

If your ball misses the green, odds are a simple chip or pitch shot will get you onto it, leaving you a putt for par. If your ball gets on the green in one shot, the next step is to analyze the putt before you. If you are more than ten feet away from the hole, you should attempt to lag the putt as close as possible to the hole, leaving yourself an easy tap-in for par. If it's closer than ten feet, consider going for it. You might score a birdie. If you do go for it, make sure to hit the ball at a speed that allows the ball to stop no farther than two feet past the hole so that the return putt will be an easy matter.

Playing a par-4 hole

Most par-4 holes measure anywhere from 250 to 450 yards. When you're playing a par-4, you need to think backwards. That's right, backwards. First, make sure you know what part of the green you want your ball to end up on by locating the flagstick and seeing what hazards (if any) protect it. Then determine the best spot on the fairway from which to get your ball onto the green. For instance, if the best part of the green to land your ball on is left of center, then your best approach shot would be from the middle-right portion of the fairway, ideally no farther than 125 yards from the green.

Hitting from there will give you the best angle of attack into the green and will enable you to use a short iron or wedge, which are the most accurate clubs in the bag. Once you decide where you want to end up on the fairway, you know where to hit your tee shot. Placing your tee shot as close as possible to that ideal spot in the fairway will give you the best possible angle of attack into the green. The pros use this backward tactic all the time. You should too because it works.

Many par-4 holes will be too long for a beginner to be able to reach the green in two shots. That's okay; simply think of the hole as a par-5 instead.

When you first start playing the game, bogey is a very good score on any hole. Simply hit your second shot to a spot on the fairway that gives you an easy shot to the green. This might be an 85-yard wedge shot or a short little chip or pitch. It all depends on what you feel most comfortable with.

Choose the appropriate club

Your main aim is to keep the ball in play. Sometimes this will mean leaving your driver in the bag and hitting a fairway wood or even an iron off the tee to ensure the most accurate shot possible. Remember, the more loft a club has, the more accurate your stroke will tend to be. The ball may end up farther from the green than you want, but at least it will be on the fairway.

VIP

Don't always reach for your driver; it can often add points to your score because it just doesn't hit the ball with as much precision as the more-lofted clubs.

Even the pros can't keep the driver on the fairway all the time. Most have a success rate of about 70 percent. So when you're on the tee, seriously consider throttling back to a more-lofted club if your ideal target area in the fairway looks like it might be hard to hit.

■ **On a par-4 hole,** *the most important thing to remember is to keep the ball in play, preferably on the short grass of the fairway.*

Hole

Try to get your second shot onto the green, avoiding the bunkers.

Play the ball to the middle of the fairway on your tee shot.

Choose the amateur's tee box closest to the fairway.

Playing a par-5 hole

A par-5 hole usually measures anywhere from 450 to 600 yards long. These long holes can be challenging to play, but they offer even the beginner the chance to make par or, at the worst, bogey. That's because you have three shots to get the ball to the green instead of just two. Use the same backward strategy on a par-5 hole as you do on a par-4. The only difference is that you must include one extra backward step.

After deciding where your approach shot to the green should come from, you must then decide how to get there with your second shot. For instance, the ideal approach shot to the green might be from the right side of the fairway, from 100 yards out. So how can you best get your ball to that spot? With a properly hit second shot, which should come from the middle-left section of the fairway. That middle-left area of the fairway, then, is exactly where you want to hit your tee shot.

Get the distance

As on a par-4, you must try to keep the ball on the fairway grass at all times. Although distance is a bit more crucial on a par-5, you should still consider throttling back to a fairway wood or iron off the tee if the ideal landing zone seems narrow. Only on a wide-open fairway should you consider using the driver.

Try to reach the green with your third shot, avoiding the bunkers.

Hole

Your second shot should give you a perfect approach to the green.

Aim your tee-shot for the middle-left of the fairway.

■ **Playing on a par-5 hole** *can almost be easier for the beginner because the distance allows for a greater chance of making par.*

Tee box

VIP *The most important point to remember is to make good contact on each shot on a par-5, to eat up as much distance as possible while maintaining accuracy.*

Don't just try to hit your second shot as far as possible. Instead, hit it to the ideal spot that will give you a perfect approach to the green. Your plan on a par-5 should be to give yourself an approach shot to the green of no more than 125 yards and no less than 70 or 80. Any more than that and accuracy will suffer; any less and you might not be able to spin the ball enough to stay on the green. Your second shot, then, needs to be not only directionally accurate, but also of the right length. By knowing how far you hit each club, you should be able to accomplish this.

Play the percentages

GOLF IS TRULY *a risk-reward type of game. On each shot you must decide on how much risk to take. Are the chances of successfully pulling off a tough shot too high to warrant the risk? Or are the potential rewards worth it?*

Weighing up your shot

For example, you might come to a par-4 hole that has a lake bordering the right side of the fairway. Toward the end of the fairway the lake bends to the left and borders much of the right side of the green. The pin is tucked in safely to the right, behind the water. The safest way to play the hole is to hit your second shot to the far-left side of the green, avoiding any air time over the water and leaving you with a long putt for birdie. The risky way to play the shot is to aim your second shot right at the flagstick, requiring the ball to fly over nearly 150 yards of lake. The reward awaiting you for taking that chance is a short birdie putt. The peril awaiting you is that big, ball-swallowing lake. If you miss-hit the ball, choose the wrong club, or misjudge the wind, your ball is going in the water and you'll end up making a double-bogey – or worse. Still think it's worth it?

Should you risk it?

It might be worth it if you were down a shot on the 18th hole of a tournament – maybe. But not under any other circumstances. The better strategy would be to play the percentages and hit your second shot to the far-left portion of the green, avoiding the water entirely. By doing so, you know that if the shot falls short, you won't be in the lake. You will simply have to chip or pitch the ball onto the green, at worst making a bogey.

Most of the time, you should play the safest shot available to you instead of going for the heroic play. Your score will thank you for it.

Examine the hole carefully, and choose the safest areas to hit to that will head off disasters and lower your stress level. If you don't have at least a 75-percent chance of pulling off a shot, don't do it. Play the safer shot instead, even if it means a longer putt or approach shot.

The short stuff is the right stuff

The easiest way to lower your score is to keep your ball on the short grass as often as possible. That means keeping tee shots (and second shots on a par-5) on the closely cropped grass of the fairway and hitting your approach shots onto the finely manicured putting surface. By doing so, you will avoid all the pitfalls that await you, including rough, trees, and other hazards. To accomplish this, you must strive to hit the ball with as much accuracy as possible as often as possible. It sounds simple, but most golfers have trouble heeding this advice. They get up on the tee and automatically pull out their driver, thinking that distance is the key to good scoring.

Hitting the ball far enough is an important ingredient, but it's not nearly as vital as keeping the ball in play.

■ **Sometimes the risky shot** *is not always your best bet as the ball is likely to end up in the rough, and jeopardize your chances of scoring low.*

Choose the safe shot

If given the choice of hitting a tee shot either 180 yards right down the middle of the fairway or 250 yards into a right-side fairway bunker, I'd choose the shorter, safer shot every time. On the fairway you will have a perfect lie, enabling you to make clean, crisp contact with the ball and put enough backspin on it to hold the green nicely. A longer tee shot that lands in a bunker or the deep rough practically guarantees that you won't score well. You have to get out of trouble first, then make a near-miraculous recovery to avoid a bogey, or worse. In the meantime your shorter-hitting but more-accurate playing partner puts his approach shot on the green and makes a sweet par.

Enhancing your accuracy

ACCURACY IS THE KEY to keeping your ball on the fairway and giving yourself the best opportunity to hit those greens. You can enhance your accuracy by remembering a few simple points.

a Always aim for a target. It is important to choose some sort of target for each shot you hit, to develop accuracy and to engage your strategic golfing mindset. Always choose a relatively small target, be it a flag, a brown spot on the fairway, or an object on the horizon. Try to visualize your ball flying right to the target. Then hit to it.

b Don't always hit your driver off the tee. Remember, although the driver hits the ball the farthest, it is also the least accurate of your clubs. When you're hitting to a narrow fairway or if all sorts of hazards abound, consider using a 3-wood, a 5-wood, or even an iron off the tee to keep your ball on the short stuff. Although you'll have a longer second shot, it will be from the short grass of the fairway instead of the rough, or worse.

■ **When setting up your shot,** *never aim for the entire fairway or the green – narrow down your focus to a flag, a spot, or even a blade of grass.*

c When in doubt, play the safe shot. Don't try to be a hero. Just get the ball onto the green and then let your putter finish the job.

d Have a "go-to" club in your bag. Every golfer has a favorite club that he or she consistently hits well with. When you have to make an important shot, use (go to) that club whenever possible. If it's a 5-wood, for example, use it to tee off on the first hole, even if it's a par-5. Your ball will land in the fairway and help inspire confidence in yourself for the rest of the round. If your go-to club is a 9-iron that you usually hit 125 yards, try to give yourself an approach shot of 125 yards to the green as often as possible so you'll have the best chance of getting on the green.

Use the entire tee box

YOU MUST TEE *your ball up in between the markers that define the tee box, and never in front of them. You do have the option, though, of teeing up your ball behind the markers, up to two-club lengths back. You do not even need to stand inside the tee box, as long as your ball is within its boundaries.*

■ **The teeing area** *encompasses a space two club-lengths back from the markers.*

Knowing where to tee up

Where you tee up your ball inside the box depends on several factors. First, find the flattest area possible so your stance and swing will be level. Second, choose the part of the tee box that will give you the best angle of attack to your target. For instance, if you are on the tee of a 148-yard par-3 hole that has the pin located in an expansive area to the left of center on the green, you may want to tee up your ball on the right side of the tee box. This will give you the best angle to the flagstick. Setting up on the left side would give you poorer access to the pin and the large, safe area surrounding it. If you are teeing up on a par-4 hole that bends sharply to the right, you should tee up as far left as you can to give yourself access to as much of the dogleg as possible.

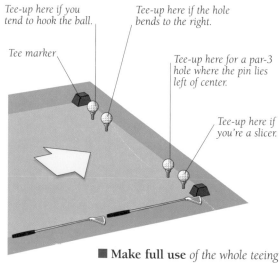

Tee-up here if you tend to hook the ball.

Tee-up here if the hole bends to the right.

Tee marker

Tee-up here for a par-3 hole where the pin lies left of center.

Tee-up here if you're a slicer.

■ **Make full use** *of the whole teeing area so that you can adapt your opening tee shot to the angle of the target.*

Teeing-up tips

Using the whole tee box can also help you if your natural shot tends to bend to the right (a slice for a right-handed golfer) or to the left (a hook for a right-handed golfer). If you consistently slice the ball, you might want to regularly tee your ball up as far to the right of the tee box as possible and then aim your shot to the left side of the fairway. Doing so will give you the largest amount of fairway possible to land your ball in. If you consistently hook the ball, you should tee up as far left as possible, for the same reason. Simple!

RATE THE HAZARDS

Knowing where all the trouble is on a hole is vital to scoring well. If you can avoid all of the pitfalls, you will always have a good lie to hit from. Some hazards are more punishing than others, however. For instance, you can easily recover from hitting your ball into a greenside bunker, but you won't fare as well if you hit your tee shot out-of-bounds or into a lake. Both of those hazards carry stiffer penalties and can really ruin a good round.

Before teeing off on a hole, first make sure you know where all the hazards are located. Then, rate each one in your head, according to the severity of the penalty. Generally, hazards are rated in the following order, from most punitive to least punitive:

1) Out-of-bounds

Hitting your ball out-of-bounds ("OB" in golfing lingo) is usually about the worst thing you can do. You have to go back and hit the shot all over again from the same spot, plus add a penalty stroke onto your score. That means the do-over shot will actually be your third, and you won't even be on the fairway yet! Do everything you can to avoid hitting your ball out-of-bounds. Study the yardage book so you know which holes are bordered by OB. Once you know that, you can make sure to play away from it at all cost.

2) Water

Although water is not quite as penal as OB, hitting your ball into a water hazard is bad news. When this happens, most players will drop another ball somewhere behind where the ball entered the water, after assessing themselves a one-stroke penalty. So if you hit your first shot into the water, the next shot you take will be your third. Although you do not need to hit from the same place, as you do with OB, you nonetheless are not as close to the hole as you would want to be on

■ **Most players** *prefer to take the penalty than attempt to play their ball out of water.*

three because of the drop. Stay away from water at all costs! Determine beforehand how far the water is from where you are hitting, and make sure the club you use cannot possibly reach that watery grave.

3) Trees and bushes

Hitting your ball into a stand of trees or bushes can be downright painful. Nothing will get your scores up and your confidence down more than constantly finding your ball nestled up to the trunk of a tree, sitting beneath a low overhang of branches, or buried within an azalea bush. Sometimes you just won't be able to play a shot at all and must declare an unplayable lie. This will cost you a penalty shot, and you'll have to drop the ball within two club-lengths of the unplayable position. Even dropping the ball in this new spot

■ **If you suspect** *you'll have problems finding your ball, you can play a provisional ball from a point where the original one was struck. You will be forced to incur one penalty stroke, however.*

doesn't guarantee you a decent lie. You could find yourself atop pine needles or in rough. Know where the most punitive trees and bushes lurk, and be sure to aim away from them, provided that doing so does not lead you into water or OB.

4) Rough

Although difficult to play out of, the rough is a preferable lie to any of the other hazards I've just mentioned. You won't be assessed any penalty, save the difficulty you'll have extricating your ball from the rough stuff. If OB, water, or ball-eating trees and shrubs lie in wait for you on the left with rough to the right, favor the right side of the fairway. If given a choice between rough and a bunker, however, most players will opt for the sand. Once you've learned how to hit a basic bunker shot, sand is actually

■ **The rough** *is one of the few hazards where you can attempt a shot and get the ball back onto the fairway without incurring a penalty.*

easier to get out of than rough. You won't be able to hit as far from the rough as you can from the fairway, and the shot will have very little if any spin on it, making it hard to hold the green. Shots hit from the sand can be made to spin and, in the case of a fairway bunker, will go as far as you want them to, provided that you make contact with the ball first.

5) Bunker

No one likes to end up in the sand, but it's one of the least troublesome hazards, provided that you have mastered the basic techniques needed to get your ball off the beach. If high rough borders the left side of a green while a bunker guards the right, favor the right side. Likewise, if OB guards one side of the fairway while a thin fairway bunker guards the other, aim away from OB. You can always get the ball out of the bunker with no penalty, and you have a good chance of continuing play without much suffering.

■ **When you get the hang** *of bunker shots you'll find that sand traps are one of the easier hazards to play out of.*

INTERNET

www.pgatour.com

Click on the "instruction" link, then click on "head game" for great advice on course strategy and other aspects of the mental side of golf.

6) Hilly lies

When you're aiming your tee shot down the fairway, take note of any hilly terrain. Even if you have to hit the ball 20 yards shorter than usual, do so if it means finding a nice flat lie for your ball. Hitting off a downhill, uphill, or sidehill lie can be tricky, so avoid them whenever possible. Remember that good position is always more important than distance.

Analyze your lie

YOUR STRATEGY ON *each shot will depend not only on the hole design and the weather, but also on what type of lie you have. If your ball is sitting up nicely on the fairway, you can take just about any shot you want. If your ball is sitting in a less-than-desirable lie, though, you may have to change your plans. For instance, a ball lying in the fairway 135 yards from the flagstick can be hit with lots of backspin because no grass will get between the ball and the club face at impact.*

Different lies call for different measures

The good backspin means you'll be able to get your ball to stop fairly quickly once it lands on the green. But put the ball into two-inch rough and the situation changes dramatically. As I described in Chapter 17, the long grass sitting behind the ball will get between it and the club face at impact, dramatically reducing the amount of backspin you can put on the ball. Called a *flier lie*, this will make the ball fly slightly farther than normal and keep rolling once it touches down on the putting surface – often ending up in rough, a bunker, or a water hazard. So that 135-yard shot from the fairway will go 140 yards from the rough and then roll still farther, if you hit it with the same club. Your strategy, therefore, has to change. Instead of hitting an 8-iron for the shot (if that's the club you would normally use to hit 135 yards), you might need to go to a 9-iron instead, or hit the 8-iron with a three-quarter swing.

> **DEFINITION**
>
> *A flier lie is what you end up with when grass comes between the club face and the ball, reducing the amount of backspin on the ball. A ball hit from a flier lie will travel farther than normal and will roll a long way after it touches down.*

Move that same 135-yard shot into three- or four-inch rough and the situation becomes even more difficult. Now the rough is long enough to really impede the club head from making decent contact with the ball. The grass grabs the club's hosel and face, slows it down, and often rotates it closed, or counterclockwise (for a right-handed golfer). This makes the shot veer off target and come up short.

■ **When your ball lands in the rough,** *examine the length of the grass before determining the best course of action for getting the ball back into play.*

Getting out of trouble

If you're presented with this situation, the smart thing to do is to cut your losses, pull out a wedge, and simply hit the ball back out onto the fairway so that you can then have a decent shot at the green. Likewise, if your ball sits atop pine needles, leaves, or an old sand-filled divot, you won't be able to confidently hit that 135-yard shot to the green. Instead, consider simply advancing the ball down the fairway far enough to give you a nice 75- or 80-yard wedge onto the green from a perfect lie in the short grass. You may end up with a bogey, but at least you won't be cursing yourself for hitting your ball into the lake from that awful lie.

Shaping the shot

AS YOU BECOME more confident and consistent with the way you strike the ball, you'll begin to notice how changes in your setup, swing, and hand and arm action can profoundly affect the direction the ball takes after it is struck. All good players eventually learn how to bend their shots left or right to varying degrees to tailor their shot to the situation at hand.

Bending and curving

Every player also has a natural shape to his or her shot. When you set up to the ball and hit it, odds are it will either bend to the right or to the left. This natural shape can be used to your advantage and should become part of your strategy when you're taking on a golf course. If your shot naturally bends to the right, for instance, you can aggressively go for flagsticks set to the right of the green. If your natural shot bends to the left, you can attack pins on the left side of the green. Once your swing becomes solid, repeatable, and reliable, you can begin to experiment with different ways of striking the ball in an attempt to purposely turn it left or right. Mastering this will enable you to maneuver your ball around obstacles or coax it into sections of the course that would be hard to get to with a straight shot.

The draw

The majority of professional golfers tend to hit the ball with a slight right-to-left curve (for a right-handed player), which – as you learned in Chapter 5 – is called a draw. This type of shot has several advantages to it. First, it tends to fly low, making it a good shot to hit into a strong wind. It also rolls very far once it comes down, due to the lower trajectory and relatively small amount of backspin. This translates to longer drives off the tee – something all golfers seek. The draw is a great shot to hit when you need to reach a target that is tucked in to the far left of your current position if you are playing into the wind or if you are hitting your tee shot on a particularly long hole.

Hitting a draw

To hit a draw, at address align your feet and shoulders slightly to the right of your target (for a right-handed golfer). Aim the club face directly at the target, which means it will be slightly closed in relation to your body.

Ball slightly back in your stance

Play the ball about a half-inch behind where you would usually play it. Then make your normal swing. The ball should start out slightly right of the target, then gently turn toward it, flying low and running a long way after touching down.

■ **When you set up to hit a draw**, *make sure your body is slightly aligned to the right so that the club face travels along an in-to-out swing path.*

Experiment with how far to the right to aim your body and how closed to make the club face in relation to your body. Some players may only need slight changes in setup angles, while others may need more. Try adjusting the position of the ball as well. Generally, the farther back you place it in your stance, the farther left the ball will draw. Placing it more than an inch behind your normal spot, however, can result in a push to the right, so be sure not to move the ball back too far.

The fade

Whenever Jack Nicklaus shoots for a flagstick that's on the back right side of a green, he will hit the ball so it turns gently to the right, allowing the ball to work itself in to the target. Called a fade (remember?), this has been Nicklaus' bread-and-butter shot throughout his career. A fade is a good shot to have in your arsenal because it tends to have a predictable trajectory, flies very high in the air, comes down softly, and doesn't roll very much after landing. Some of the best players in the world, including Ben Hogan, Sam Snead, Jack Nicklaus, and Lee Trevino, have relied on the fade as their "go-to" shot when accuracy is crucial.

Hitting a fade

Most players already hit a fade as their natural shot shape.

To hit a fade, set up to the ball with your feet and shoulders aligned slightly to the left of your target. Aim the club face directly at the target, which means it will be slightly open in relation to your body. Play the ball about a half-inch farther up in your stance than you normally would, then make your normal swing.

Ball slightly forward in your stance

The ball should start out slightly left of the target and then gently turn (or fade) toward it, flying high and landing softly. Experiment with how far left of the target you aim your body, and with how much you open up the club face. Some golfers may need to aim only a degree or two to the left, while others may need more. Just make sure that the face of the club is aimed directly at the target and that you make a normal swing once your setup is complete. Try adjusting the position of the ball as well. Typically, the farther up in your stance you place it, the more the ball will fade. Don't place it too far forward, however, because this can result in a pulled shot that goes left of the target.

■ **To hit a fade** *make sure your body is slightly aligned to the left so that the club face travels along an out-to-in path as it makes impact with the ball.*

Controlling your curves

As I've already mentioned, most of you will already have a natural shape to your shots. Whether it's a fade, a draw, or a straight shot, learn to use it to your advantage whenever you can. As long as your shot shape is controllable, there is little reason not to exploit it regularly. Think about it: If you know your tee shot will consistently fade about 20 yards to the right, why not just plan for it to do so? Aim left of the ideal landing spot, then simply swing away. Your ball will land softly, right where you want it to.

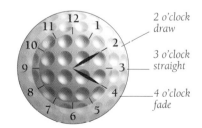

2 o'clock draw

3 o'clock straight

4 o'clock fade

■ **If you visualize** *a clockface as you strike the ball, it can help you bend the shot how you wish.*

The high shot

Suppose you have a shot to the green of about 125 yards, but your line to the flagstick is blocked by a tall tree. Your regular club for this distance might be a 9-iron. Try to hit it now, however, and the ball will most likely clip the top of the tree. So, what do you do? The answer is to hit the shot on a higher-than-normal trajectory. You do this by making a few adjustments to your setup position and your swing technique.

To hit the shot higher, choose a club that is one number lower than you would usually use for the distance. So, if the shot calls for a 9-iron, use an 8-iron instead. If you need to hit the ball higher than usual off the tee, use the same techniques and try teeing the ball up a quarter of an inch higher. Make sure at least two-thirds of the ball is above the top of your driver. The ball will fly much higher than normal and come down softly.

THE HIGH SHOT

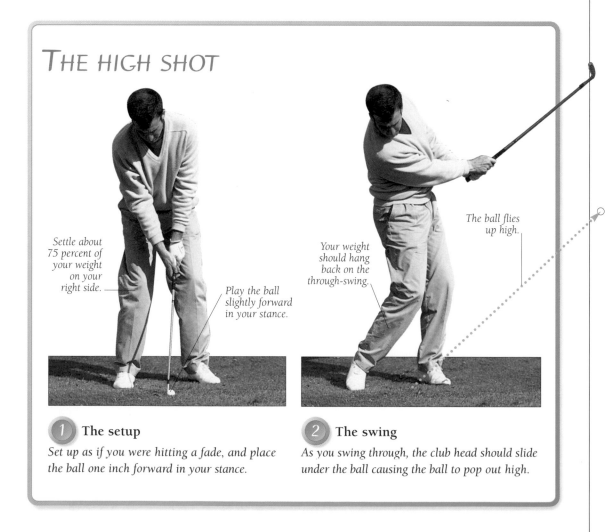

Settle about 75 percent of your weight on your right side.

Play the ball slightly forward in your stance.

Your weight should hang back on the through-swing.

The ball flies up high.

1 **The setup**
Set up as if you were hitting a fade, and place the ball one inch forward in your stance.

2 **The swing**
As you swing through, the club head should slide under the ball causing the ball to pop out high.

The low shot

The best tactic on a windy day is to hit the ball as low as possible so that it slips underneath the wind. A low shot bores through the wind much more effectively than a high shot. Also hit a low shot whenever the fairways are hard and dry to encourage lots of roll.

Choose a club that is one number lower than you would normally need for the shot (although don't use any club with less loft that a 4-iron because the ball might not get up in the air at all). When you're trying to hit a ball on a lower trajectory off the tee, follow the same directions and also try teeing the ball up at least a quarter of an inch lower than usual. Only about one-third of the ball should be above the top of your driver at address.

THE LOW SHOT

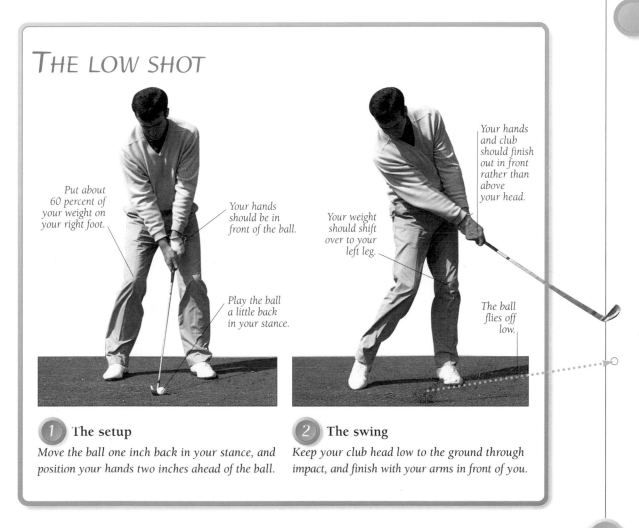

Put about 60 percent of your weight on your right foot.

Your hands should be in front of the ball.

Play the ball a little back in your stance.

Your weight should shift over to your left leg.

Your hands and club should finish out in front rather than above your head.

The ball flies off low.

1 The setup
Move the ball one inch back in your stance, and position your hands two inches ahead of the ball.

2 The swing
Keep your club head low to the ground through impact, and finish with your arms in front of you.

Measuring up

BACK IN THE LATE *1950s a professional golfer by the name of Deane Bemon began to calculate exactly how far he hit each one of his clubs under ideal conditions. Before this, most players simply selected a club according to the feel of each shot.*

Bemon is credited with being the first to decide what club to use based solely on the yardage to the target. If he had 125 yards to the pin and knew that he hit his pitching wedge exactly 125 yards, that was the club he would use. Selection became academic. Although initially frowned upon by many of the players, this method of club selection became the standard after a very short time. Jack Nicklaus learned this technique from Bemon and promptly went on to become the greatest golfer the game has ever known. You need to do the same in order to hit your ball as close as possible to the intended target.

■ **Deane Bemon** *was the first player to work out the distance he could achieve with each club.*

Without having a clear idea of just how far you hit each club in your bag, you will constantly hit shots too far or too short, causing your scores to balloon. By taking all the guesswork about distances out of the equation, you will be better able to concentrate on accuracy.

Know how far you can hit with each club

While certain clubs are intended for long shots and others are intended for short ones, the distance each individual golfer will hit a club can vary tremendously. So how do you figure out how far you hit each club? Find a large empty field, one that is long enough to contain your longest drive. Make sure it is a windless day so that your distances are not affected. Then hit seven shots with each club in your bag. After hitting each shot, pace off exactly how far each one went.

To pace off distance accurately, you will need to practice striding at one-yard intervals, which are usually a bit longer than the average person's stride. Place a yardstick down on the ground. Take a few steps back, then begin striding toward the yardstick. Try to have the toe of one foot step down right at the beginning of the yardstick and the toe of the other foot step down right at the end. It sounds simple, but it will take some time to get the feel for pacing off a distance in one-yard increments.

After you have measured all seven shots for each club, throw out the two shortest measurements, then take the average of the remaining five. That will be the average distance you hit each club. This procedure will take some time, but it's well worth doing.

Use the average distance

The first thing you will realize after measuring all those distances is that you really can't hit the ball as far as you thought you could. Amateur golfers often make the mistake of only using the longest distance measured for each club as the standard. That's just not a realistic technique. You will never be able to hit the ball perfectly square, right on the sweet spot, every time. Even the professionals know that. The great Ben Hogan once stated that, even during a winning round, he never hit more than seven perfect shots over the entire 18 holes of a course. That's why you need to use the average distance, instead of the best.

Once you have a clear idea of how far you hit each club in your bag, your strategy on the course will take on more depth and clarity. Knowing that your ball cannot possibly reach that fairway bunker if you hit the right club, or that you can clear that lake if you choose a certain club, will be a confidence-inspiring experience.

You will be able to eliminate one whole avenue of error from your game. If you are going to miss a target, it will be to the left or right and no longer long or short.

Know your distance from targets and hazards

Knowing how far you can hit each club in your bag won't do you any good if you can't figure out how far you are from your target. To take advantage of this information, you must find a way to learn how far you are from crucial areas on each hole. There are several ways to do this. If you can afford a laser range finder, by all means

Trivia...

An alternative to pacing off each shot is to buy a laser range finder at your local golf store and simply use it to measure the distance of each shot. This is a much more expensive alternative (they range from about $225 to about $400), but using the laser range finder will be more accurate and less time-consuming.

buy one. You will be able to take it onto the course and accurately measure just how far you are from any visible point on the hole. Once you know that, it will be a simple matter to choose the right club.

Make use of a yardage book

You cannot, however, use a laser range finder during tournament play. Well, you can but you'll be disqualified. So if you're competing, leave that expensive toy at home. Using a range finder is not the only way of accurately determining how far you are from any given target or hazard. As I mentioned at the beginning of this chapter, many courses sell yardage books. These small, illustrated guides have the design of each hole printed out in detail. Distances from various sprinkler heads or landmarks on the fairway to the middle of the green are given, enabling you to accurately determine just how far you will need to hit each shot. All you have to do is find the sprinkler head or landmark shown in the yardage book, pace off just how far you are from it, do a little math, then choose the right club for that distance. This is exactly what the pros do every weekend. If it works for them, it will work for you.

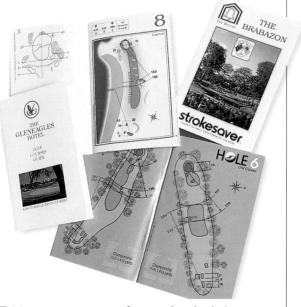

■ **Many courses provide** *a yardage book that gives exact yardages to key parts of each hole, including distances from the tee box to fairway bunkers, water hazards, and ideal landing zones.*

Try pacing off from the sprinkler

If your favorite course does not sell a yardage book, they probably will have some type of color-illustrated scorecard available that at least shows the general layout of each hole, with a few yardages printed on it. Also, almost every course these days prints yardages from the green on sprinkler heads found in mid-fairway. You should be able to find the 200-, 150-, 125-, and 100-yard sprinkler heads fairly easily. Even the most basic courses have white wooden stakes bordering the fairway at a spot exactly 150 yards from the middle of the green. Find any of these yardage markers, then simply pace off how many yards you are beyond or before it. Do the math and you'll know how far you need to hit the ball. Then choose the correct club and let it rip!

A simple summary

✓ Golf is very similar to chess, in that it requires you to plan out every move well in advance.

✓ Find out each hole's design and devise a strategy to keep your ball on the fairway, avoid the hazards, and get to the green.

✓ Always play the percentages. If the chances of successfully pulling off a difficult shot are low, don't try it. Play conservatively and take failure gracefully. Never let it get you down.

✓ Know where the hazards are on every hole. Then rate them in your mind, from the most to the least punitive. You can then choose the wisest path to the hole and onto the green.

✓ Pay close attention to the lie of your ball. If the ball is sitting up nicely on the fairway, you will be able to hit the shot you want to without reservations. If it is sitting down in the rough,

though, or atop pine needles, leaves, or an old divot, consider simply getting the ball back onto the fairway and accepting a bogey for the hole. Forget about that heroic shot; just keep it simple and get the ball back in play.

✓ As your game improves, you will want to learn how to shape your shots left or right. When you've mastered the draw and the fade, you'll be able to hit your ball around obstacles or into well-protected holes that are hiding in corners of the green.

✓ It's a good idea to have a "go-to" club – one you feel really comfortable hitting with and know exactly how far and how hard you hit.

✓ Know how far you hit each club, and learn to determine how far you are from any given target while on the course. When you know these two things, you can select the right club for the right shot, every time.

PART FIVE

A MULTI-LEVEL DRIVING RANGE IN JAPAN

IMPROVING YOUR GAME

As you progress as a player, you will quickly learn that there is always room for *improvement*. In addition to improving your technique on the course, there are many other ways to become a better golfer.

It's these other things – from golf lessons to conditioning to practice to equipment upgrades – that I want to talk about in this part. I'll also talk about what you can learn from watching *tournaments* on television and attending a professional tour event. And I'll  give you some tips about *vacationing* in golf heaven. Add all this to your swing and strategy skills, and you will become the golfer you have always wanted to be.

Chapter 19

Focus on Practice

Some golfers become completely addicted to hanging out at the local driving range pounding hundreds of balls into the sky. Other players can't stand the monotony and instead simply learn out on the course. Which is the better way to go? The truth is, it's somewhere in the middle. You shouldn't spend weeks on end aimlessly hitting balls on the range, but you do need to practice the basic shots before you go on the course.

In this chapter...

✓ The turf toupee

✓ Warming up

✓ You've got to have a goal

✓ Don't overdo it

✓ Work on your short game

301

PRACTICE MAKES PERFECT!

The turf toupee

PRACTICE RANGES AT HIGH-END *public courses or country clubs often use real grass tees. This is always preferable to artificial turf because real grass is what you hit from on the course. However, for ease of maintenance and lower cost, most ranges provide only the fake stuff. Each stall has a large square mat of synthetic grass from which to hit balls. Some of the better mats can actually come close to duplicating the type of lie you might have on the fairway, but most don't mimic the real thing very well. Golfers who spend too much time hitting balls off these mats will not transfer their skills well to real grass because the lies are so different. If it's the only facility available, though, a range with fake grass mats is far better than no practice at all.*

Hitting at the driving range

If you are lucky enough to have a real grass range nearby, by all means use it as often as possible. The skills you learn there will transfer perfectly to the golf course because the hitting surfaces are identical. Because you'll take divots at a real grass range, however, you won't be able to hit shot after shot from the same spot as you can with artificial turf. You will have to carefully manage your divots to preserve as much grass as possible on the practice tee. Try what the professionals do: After hitting, place your next ball on the grass directly behind the divot from the first shot. Repeating this procedure for the next few shots will result in one long, three-inch-wide divot. Then start another strip, placing the next ball an inch or so to the left of the front of that first long divot strip. Hit balls in the same manner, working your divots backward until you reach the back again. If you continue to use this technique, you'll end up using the least amount of grass possible.

■ **For ease of** *maintenance and lower cost, many driving ranges have mats of synthetic grass in their practice stalls.*

Warming up

NO ATHLETE EVER JUMPS RIGHT into action without first properly warming up his or her body. A good warmup is very important to prevent injury and to get you feeling loose and ready for action. Unfortunately, many golfers begin smacking balls out there the moment they get on the range. Some even choose to make their first shot with the driver, the most physically demanding club in the bag. Doing this is just asking for trouble. You might pull a muscle, hurt your back, or even sprain a wrist. Start with the simple stretching exercises shown on the next page before making practice swings with your clubs.

Start with your short clubs

Never start hitting balls at the practice range with one of your longer clubs. Your body just won't be up to it. Instead, start with a wedge and gradually work your way up to the longer clubs. No one says you have to, though; hitting a bucket of balls with just a sand or pitching wedge is great practice for your short game and will pay off when you're on the course. The professionals spend far less time hitting with their long clubs than with their wedges because they know the wedges are what bring home the bacon.

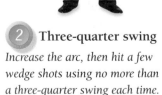

PRACTICE SWINGS

After doing your simple stretches, make a series of practice swings with one of your wedges. Gradually increase the arc until you are making three-quarter swings and hit at least ten shots like this, aiming at a target no more than 50 yards away. Then you'll be ready to begin taking full swings. These practice swings will help you swing more smoothly when play begins out on the course.

1 **Half swing**

Take one of your wedges and begin making easy half swings with it, just back and through.

2 **Three-quarter swing**

Increase the arc, then hit a few wedge shots using no more than a three-quarter swing each time.

SIMPLE STRETCHES

Warming up is vital. Before you head out onto the golf course or even swing a club, make sure you do a few simple stretches.

TORSO STRETCH

This exercise is excellent for improving trunk rotation – vital to the golf swing – and for increasing flexibility before play.

1 **Setup**
Hold a pitching wedge in front of your belly button.

2 **Rotation**
Turn your upper body to the left, then to the right, rotating a little more each time. Repeat six to eight times.

BACK STRETCH

This exercise loosens the muscles of the upper back and shoulders. Make sure your arms are fully extended throughout.

1 **Setup**
Raise a pitching wedge above your head, holding both ends.

2 **Stretch**
Bend your torso to the left, then to the right, with no rotation at all. Repeat six to eight times.

TRUNK ROTATION

This is another exercise to increase flexibility in your shoulders and torso. Regular stretching of these muscles should increase your ability to achieve a good, long backswing and follow-through.

1 **Setup**

Hold a club behind your back, keeping it in place in the crook of your elbows.

2 **Rotation**

Turn back and through at least half a dozen times, keeping a steady rhythmic pace.

SHOULDER STRETCH

The shoulder muscles are in constant use, but can become inflexible without the right kind of stretching. This simple exercise will help lengthen your turn, thereby increasing your swing arc and speed.

1 **Setup**

With no club in your hands, reach your left arm across your chest and take your left elbow with your right hand.

2 **Stretch**

Gently pull your elbow toward your chest until you feel the stretch in your left shoulder. Repeat for the right shoulder.

CAN YOU BE MORE FLEXIBLE?

If you watch today's professional golfers you will notice how far they are able to turn their shoulders in relation to their hips on the backswing. To improve your own level of flexibility and enhance your game, here are some simple stretches you can do every day. Always do stretches when your body is warm and never bounce up and down while stretching as you could damage tendons and ligaments.

Triceps stretch

This stretch loosens the muscles in your arms and shoulders. Over time, try to increase the amount you are able to bend your torso.

1 **Setup**

Place your right hand behind your neck. Reach over your head with your left hand and grasp your right elbow.

2 **Stretch**

Bend your torso slowly to the left until you feel a stretch in your shoulder and arm. Repeat on the left side.

Hamstring stretch

Keeping the hamstrings stretched will help increase your swing power and reduce the chance of pulling a muscle in your legs. Over a period of weeks, gradually try to widen the angle between your legs and the distance you bend forward at the waist. Take it slow, but try to do this stretch each day, perhaps after a run or a bike ride.

1 **Prepare**

Sit upright with your legs straight in front at a 60-degree angle to one another.

2 **Stretch**

Slowly bend forward at the waist until you feel the stretch in the back of your thighs. Hold the stretch for ten seconds and then return to an upright position. Repeat two or three times.

Latissimus stretch

This stretch lengthens the large muscles in the upper back and sides, enabling you to turn more in your backswing. Over a period of weeks, try to increase the distance that you bend to each side. Remember not to bounce!

1 Setup

Raise your hands high over your head with your palms clasped together.

2 Stretch

Slowly bend to the right until you feel a stretch in your left side, shoulder, and upper back. Hold the position for ten seconds, then release. Repeat for the other side.

Hip flexor stretch

Keeping your hips as flexible as possible is one of the best ways to increase your swing arc and speed. This simple exercise should be performed on both sides of your body. Over several weeks, try to increase the distance you can turn your torso as you pull on your knee.

1 Setup

Place your legs straight out in front of you and your hands behind you to support the upper body.

2 Positioning the legs

Cross your left leg over your right, and place your left foot on the outside of your right knee.

3 Stretch

Gently pull your left knee while turning your upper torso until you feel the stretch in your hip and lower back. Hold for ten seconds.

You've got to have a goal

WHEN YOU'RE AT THE RANGE, *you should always have a game plan. What part of your game needs work that day? Decide on a specific goal and then work toward achieving it. For instance, you might need to work on ridding yourself of a dreaded slice. If that's your goal for the day, focus on it. After warming up with some wedge shots and a few middle irons, start using the club that you seem to be having trouble with. If slicing is the culprit, that will typically be any club with more loft than a 7-iron. Take your time and work on straightening out those shots.*

A relaxed pace

Once you have hit a few perfectly, stop working on that problem for awhile and let your mind and body soak in the feeling of hitting those nice, straight shots. You should never overdo it. Allow your body to learn and correct itself at a relaxed pace. Remember, you'll be playing golf for a long time. You shouldn't expect to become a professional overnight. Keep it simple, okay?

> **INTERNET**
>
> **www.allprogreens.com**
>
> *If you're just dying to put a driving range in your backyard, a number of companies sell artificial putting greens and driving range mats, including All Pro Putting Greens.*

Aim for a target

When you're on the range, always try to hit to specific targets instead of simply banging balls through the air.

Randomly hitting balls at a driving range can be counterproductive because that wide-open hitting area does not punish you for hitting a bad shot, or ten bad shots. Without the focus of a target, you can't tell how accurately you're hitting. On the course this could translate into a nightmarish afternoon spent in the rough or out of bounds. So for every shot, choose something to hit to, and do it. How close you come will tell you if your swing and overall ball-striking technique are up to snuff.

Distance markers

Most ranges have markers indicating 50 yards, 100, 125, 150, 175, 200, 225, and 250 yards. These are perfect targets to shoot at. Some ranges even place mock greens at various locations in the field, complete with flagsticks (but not holes). The yardages to these greens are always marked, making them ideal targets, too.

When you're hitting balls, think about where you want the ball to go and not where you don't want it to go. Get used to thinking this way during practice on the range so you can take that mindset onto the course. The worst thing you can do while you're planning a shot is worry about your ball ending up in trouble. The fickle golf gods will sense your doubt and see to it that your poor little ball finds some form of trouble.

■ **Distance markers** *make ideal targets for driving practice.*

Don't overdo it

SOME GOLFERS AREN'T REALLY *golfers. Instead, they should probably be called range rovers because they spend hours and hours at the driving range and barely any time at all on the golf course. They become addicted to the repetition and the almost hypnotic control that the range can exert over you. When they're actually on the course, they barely know what to do.*

Don't become one of these range rovers. Use the range to improve your swing and perfect certain shots, but take your skills onto the course as often as you can.

Hitting hundreds of balls from artificial mats into a vast field of golf balls bears no resemblance at all to the real thing. On the course you have only one chance to hit each shot. That's it. You can't stand there and hit a dozen shots from the same spot, can you?

Head for the course

Swiping away at range balls will also teach you nothing about strategy, improvisation, or how to deal with ever-changing conditions on the course. By all means use the practice range, but never forget that the real learning takes place on the course.

Work on your short game

MANY GOOD DRIVING RANGES *also have a practice putting green and a practice chipping green. If your range has both, take a moment next time you're there to notice how many people are on them versus how many are aimlessly banging balls out into the void. Odds are that for every person practicing putting or chipping, ten will be on the range hitting drives. Visit a professional tournament, however, and things are dramatically different. Sure there are players lined up hitting shots on the range, but just as many will be working diligently on their short games over on the putting and chipping greens. They know what it takes to win tournaments. They have to because it's their business. After they work on their full swing shots, virtually all the big stars walk over to the practice putting green and work on rolling the ball for at least 20 to 30 minutes and then make their way to the chipping green to perfect all types of short shots from different distances and lies.*

■ **Head for the** *practice chipping green to work on your short game skills.*

The short salvation shot

No single factor will contribute more to lowering your scores on the course than working diligently on your short game.

With beginners, the shots that are actually supposed to land softly on the putting green instead often land on the fringe grass surrounding the green; in bunkers, the rough, or stands of trees near the green; or even remain on the fairway. To salvage situations like these, you will need to be able to chip or pitch your ball up as close as possible to the hole so you can give yourself a short, easy putt for par or bogey.

Perfecting your putting

After you have hit a bucket or two of balls at the range, go over to the practice putting green (if there is one) and begin working on your putting skills. The practice putting green, usually substantially larger than the greens found on the course, will have at least nine cups scattered all over. Some will be located in relatively flat areas, while others will be on slopes of various degrees. This gives you the chance to practice all types of putts, from slow, straight, uphill shots to fast ones with lots of break to the left or right. Each hole will have a miniature numbered flagstick in it. Some golfers will putt from hole to hole, while others will simply stake out one, putting to it from various distances.

Varying distance and position

Start out by working on your lag putting. As I explained in Chapter 12, learning to hit your putts the right distance is probably the most important aspect of putting. Begin by putting one or two balls to a hole from about 20 to 25 feet away. Never putt two balls from the same spot and distance. Instead, always vary your distance and position a bit because this is the way things will happen on the course. To whatever extent is possible, your practice sessions should mimic real playing conditions. Keep working on lagging these long putts until you can consistently get them to within two or three feet of the hole.

Getting the ball in the hole

Next, work on six- to 12-foot putts. These are your bread and butter putts – the ones you'll have to make most often on the course. You have to try to sink these putts rather than just lag them close because this is the length of putt you will regularly have for par. Hit these shots from different positions and lengths. Some should be uphill, some should be downhill. A few should break right, others left. In all cases, try to have the ball dive right into the hole. Balls that go three or four feet past are no-no's, as are those that wind up short.

One of the prime objectives of practicing putting is to never, ever three-putt a hole. Ever.

Learning to get your ball to plunk solidly into the hole will help you avoid this. It takes lots of practice, but with practice will come that elusive feel factor.

Playing under pressure

After working on those medium-range putts, end your putting practice by trying to sink 20 two-foot putts in a row into a hole with very little break to it. For each putt, set up as if it were the putt to win a championship. Try to create a sense of pressure. Each one means thrilling victory or agonizing defeat. Pretend that you will lose a $50 bet if you miss the next two-footer. This will help you replicate the kind of pressure you'll feel on the course when three other players are watching you attempt to sink that piddly little two-footer. Think you can make 20 two-foot putts in a row? You'll never know until you try.

Consummate chipping

After your practice putting session, walk over to the practice chipping green and work on these important shots. I think it's important to putt first because the feel for distances, developed from the putting session, easily transfers over to the chipping green. (For a quick refresher on basic chipping technique, go back to Chapter 13.)

DEFINITION

A shag bag is a cylindrical bag with a handle on one end and a hollow tube on the other. It's the perfect container for holding 20 or more golf balls for chipping practice.
After you chip all the balls in the bag, you can pick them up by simply placing the hollow tube over each one and pushing down on it. The shag bag saves you from having to bend over to pick up each and every ball.

Like the putting green, the chipping green will have a number of holes with small flagsticks located in various spots – some close to the edge, others farther in. You might want to buy a small bucket of range balls for chipping practice, or you could bring your own from home in a small *shag bag*

Balls for chipping

My advice is not to use range balls for chipping. They tend to have a rock-hard feel and never react the way a quality ball will on the green.

They won't spin as well and will often travel farther than a better-quality ball. Instead, buy yourself at least 15 or 20 really good golf balls and use them exclusively for chipping. The balls should be similar in design and quality to the ones you use on the course. This way, the practice sessions will be more like the real thing.

Chipping from the fringe

Start out by chipping balls from the fringe grass to a pin at least 25 or 30 feet away. Use a 7-iron or an 8-iron, and just get the ball onto the green and rolling toward the hole. Remember that whenever possible your chip shots should travel most of the distance to the hole on the ground, not in the air. Your goal should be to consistently chip the ball so it rolls to within three feet of the hole, leaving just a short putt to finish up, hopefully for par.

Next, hit some chip shots to closer pins, again from the fringe grass. Change to a higher-lofted club for these shots, perhaps a 9-iron or a pitching wedge. Concentrate on getting the ball onto the green as quickly as possible so it can roll most of the way

to the hole. When you're chipping from the fringe, a good general rule is to try to always land the ball no more than three feet onto the green so it can roll the rest of the way.

■ **Colin Montgomerie** *makes a chip shot from the fringe during the 1997 Open Championship at Royal Troon.*

Selecting a club

Your club selection will depend on the ball's original distance from the green and how far the flagstick is from the edge of the green.

If the flagstick is 50 feet away and your ball is only three feet from the green, you might use a 6-iron for the chip. If the flagstick is only ten feet away and your ball is four feet from the green, you might select a sand wedge.

Developing a feel for what's possible

Don't stop practicing until you can consistently chip a ball to within three feet of the hole.

Chipping, like putting, is largely based on feel.

Which club you select and how hard you hit the ball will depend on how fast the balls are rolling on the green that day and on your previous experience with each club. Because of this, you will need to experiment with different techniques while you're out on the practice chipping green.

Never stick with only one or two clubs when you're practicing your chipping. Seve Ballesteros, the great golfer from Spain, was a master at coming up with incredible recovery shots. One reason for his success was his willingness to use nearly every club in his bag when chipping. You should experiment too so that you can develop a feel for just what is possible when you're chipping a golf ball.

Chipping from the rough

After ten or 15 minutes of chipping from the fringe with a variety of clubs, move farther away, into the rough. From there, the two- or three-inch grass will almost always require you to use a wedge. The middle and short irons just won't have the weight or loft to get the golf ball up and out of the thick grass consistently.

Experimenting with different shots

Starting with a sand wedge, hit some shots to a flagstick that is at least 20 feet onto the green. You should immediately notice that in order to get the ball there, you'll need to land it much closer to the hole because it won't roll as far. The higher-lofted wedge will put more backspin onto the ball, making it stop sooner. Experiment with where you land the ball. Try landing it halfway to the hole or even two-thirds of the way. Also, vary the position and lie of each ball you hit. Don't hit the same shot over and over again. Remember that the objective of chipping is to get your golf ball as close as possible to the hole so that you're left with a short putt. Your chipping practice should be geared toward achieving this goal. Some professionals won't end their chipping sessions until they have holed at least one long, difficult chip. If you have the time, give it a try.

Polished pitching

For the last five or ten minutes of your short-game practice, you should work on pitching the ball. On the course, you'll need to be able to pitch your ball over hazards or other types of trouble. At least five or six times per round, it's likely that your pitching skills will be required, so you should be prepared.

Distribute your practice balls randomly in the light rough surrounding the practice chipping green. Make sure some are in relatively easy lies while others are sitting down more deeply into the rough. If there are any small hills, rises, or other obstructions, place a few balls behind them as well. The idea is to duplicate conditions on the course as closely as possible. Then, one by one, walk around and pitch each ball as close as you can to a single flagstick, perhaps located on the far side of the green.

Clubs for pitching

For each shot, use either a sand or lob wedge because the loft and weight of these clubs helps pop the ball up and out nicely. Concentrate on trying to land each ball about ten or 15 feet short of the hole, letting it roll the rest of the way. Although pitch shots are harder to regularly place inside of three feet, you should nonetheless try to do it. Keep hitting these random pitch shots until you have developed a real feel for them and are often getting the balls close to the pin. Be sure to vary the location of the flagstick when you're hitting pitches.

■ **Pitch shots** *are played when you need to loft your ball over a hazard, such as this hedge.*

Pitching drills

One of the advantages of a pitch over a chip is that you can put the ball close to a pin that is near the edge of the green on your side. The pitch lofts the ball up high and stops it quickly once it's on the green. To practice this, place a dozen or so balls in the rough about 20 yards from the pin, this time located very close to the edge of the green closest to you. Using a lob wedge, practice lofting the balls up high and landing them softly on the green close to the pin. Don't stop until you have landed one within three feet of the pin.

Mastering the pitch shot

Of the two, pitching definitely is more difficult to master than chipping for several reasons. First, the lie is almost always worse. Second, a ball that travels most of the way to the hole in the air is always harder to control than one that rolls most of the way. Third, the pitching stroke is an in-between type of movement that takes awhile to master, while the chip has a puttlike stroke. For all these reasons, don't ignore pitching when you're at your practice facility. (For a refresher on basic pitching technique, go back to Chapter 13 as often as necessary.)

■ **A pitch** *is usually played from light rough using a sand or lob wedge.*

A simple summary

✔ Don't just start banging out balls on the range merely for the sake of seeing them fly out into the void. Know exactly what your goal is for that session and work toward achieving it.

✔ When hitting practice balls, you should always aim for a target, be it a yardage marker sign, an artificial green, or a patch of brown grass.

✔ Never overdo it on the range. When you have made good progress on your goal for that day, stop and let your mind and body process the new information. Hitting too many balls can lead to boredom as well as injury.

✔ Always work on your short game at the range as much or more than your long game. If your practice facility has chipping and putting greens, use them as often as possible.

✔ Never practice your short shots from the same spot every time. Vary the angle and length of your shots so your practice will be more like the real thing.

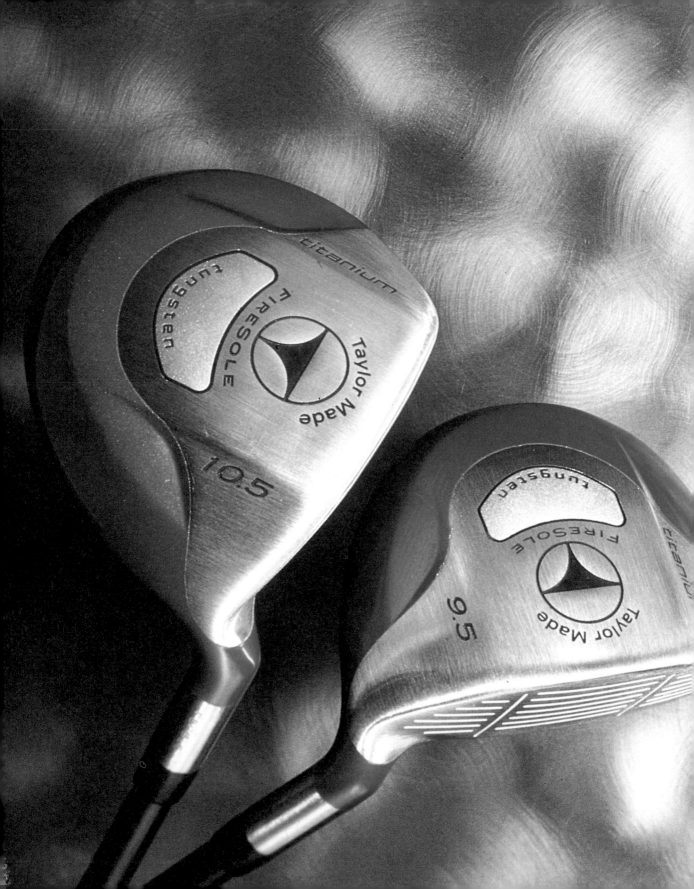

Chapter 20

Better Skills Call For Better Tools

A s a race car driver improves his or her skills on the track, odds are he or she will want to graduate to a faster, more advanced car that can take those improved driving skills to a new level. It's the same for a beginning golfer. As you become more proficient, your old equipment may end up holding you back. In this chapter I'll discuss how your needs will change and make some recommendations about updating your equipment.

In this chapter...

✓ The learning period

✓ Better clubs for a better game

✓ Buying a better ball

✓ You don't need everything in the store

TOP-OF-THE-LINE TITANIUM DRIVERS

The learning period

YOUR FIRST TWO OR THREE YEARS *of learning to play golf will have their ups and downs. Sometimes you'll experience a learning spurt, and a new idea or technique for your swing will suddenly become obvious and easy, causing your scores to take a much anticipated (and very welcome) nose dive. Instead of shooting your usual 95 for a round, you'll quickly find yourself breaking 90 or even shooting in the mid-80s. Other times, though, it will seem as if nothing is changing and your swing and overall technique aren't improving at all. In fact, your scores might actually go up, depending on how often you've been playing and what frame of mind you're in on the course.*

Stick to the fundamentals

As you work your way through all those peaks, plateaus, and valleys, just remember to stick to the fundamentals and really strive to improve each time you play. The ultimate reward for your persistence and patience will be a more consistent and much improved game, so long as you are reasonably healthy and play regularly.

Trust those old clubs!

Try not to change equipment too often while you're in the early stages of learning the game. It's a better idea to stick with the equipment you have (if it is of decent quality) so that you have some stability in your game and minimize the variables that can affect your play. Staying with the same driver for a year or two, for instance, will enable you to better identify just what factors are contributing to your better tee shots. If you change clubs too often during this learning period, you won't be able to tell if it's the better club or your better technique.

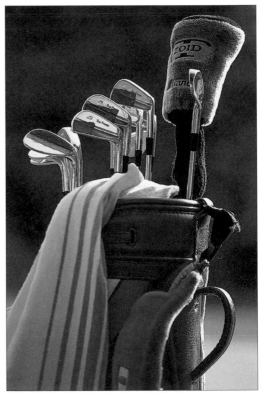

■ **Stick with** *the same set of clubs for the first year or two of play. Once you have developed good all-round game skills and your scores begin to drop, think about investing in a new set of clubs.*

During your initial learning period, the only major change you should make to your equipment is to be sure that the lengths, flexes, and lie angles of your clubs are fitted properly to your body and swing.

Doing so will simply assure that you are eliminating badly fitted clubs as a cause of poor shot making. See Chapter 6 for more on all of those club dimensions.

Minor changes are fine, such as adding an extra wedge to your bag (if you haven't already) and perhaps a lofted fairway wood or two, as well as changing your grips at least once per year, but forget about everything else. In this way, you will be able to develop your game, instead of constantly having to readjust to new clubs. Remember, keep it simple.

Better clubs for a better game

WHEN YOU HAVE *developed a repeatable, working swing and impeccable short game skills, you should begin to see your scores dropping down into the 80s. Once that happens, it might be time to reevaluate your clubs. They have served you well, but now they might begin to hold you back a bit, just like a Volkswagen would hold back that professional race car driver.*

Persimmon driver *Steel-headed driver* *Offset-headed driver*

■ **Traditional persimmon** *woods have now largely been replaced by metal-headed woods.*

Investing in a driver

Let's start with the driver. If you have only been playing for a year or two, you might not even have a driver. You may have simply been using a fairway wood off the tee because they tend to be easier to use and are more accurate. If you have gone all this time without a good driver, now might be the time to buy one. Be prepared, though. Drivers aren't cheap. In fact, many brand-name drivers can cost over $500! That's probably more than you spent on all the rest of your clubs combined. One of the reasons for the hefty price tag (apart from the huge marketing costs) is that good drivers are made of expensive materials. Most of these top-dollar clubs have a head made almost entirely of titanium, that nifty space-age metal that is stronger and lighter than steel.

Titanium drivers

Titanium is not cheap. Nor is the technology needed to machine it and turn it into the head of a driver. Still, these clubs are commonly found in the bags of professional golfers the world over. The reasons are simple. Titanium is lighter than steel or wood, so the club head can be much larger. This creates a larger sweet spot on the face, helping even off-center shots to travel straight and far.

■ **This titanium-headed** *driver was designed using the latest technology and materials, which is reflected in the price.*

The lighter weight of the titanium head means that club manufacturers can install a longer, lighter, graphite shaft, creating a larger swing arc and faster overall club-head speed.

This equates to more distance off the tee – something all golfers want.

Shopping around

If you can afford a titanium driver, go for it. It will most likely add at least a few yards to your drives. However, you don't need titanium to play a better game. These expensive drivers are definitely well made and a thrill to use, but there are many other high-quality drivers that use little if any titanium. Some are made only of steel, while others use a combination of different types of metals. Most of these clubs use an ultralight graphite shaft, enabling manufacturers to make them as long as they want. Even persimmon-headed woods (yes, real wood woods) are still manufactured today, albeit for much more money than they used to be.

You'll need to be a smart consumer when you're shopping for your driver. Visit a number of golf stores and read up on the latest equipment before you decide what to buy. You should never buy any club without first trying it out at a driving range, so try to shop at a store that has one on the premises or at least close by.

Your first driver

If you are buying your first driver, don't choose one with less than 10.5 degrees of loft because it might be too difficult for you to hit reliably. Also, if your normal swing speed is slower than 90 miles per hour (easily measurable at most well-equipped golf stores), go for a driver with at least 10.5 degrees of loft and perhaps more to ensure that you get your drives up into the air and down the fairway. If you feel you have outgrown your current driver, by all means go shopping around for a new model. But don't think you necessarily need to spend a fortune to get a good one.

If you forego the titanium, you'll probably be able to buy a quality, name-brand driver for under $300. Some well-made steel-head drivers cost even less.

Hot irons

Irons are the heart and soul of your game. If you have lowered your scores significantly but find that you aren't hitting your irons as far or as accurately as you'd like, consider a trip to your local golf store to try out a set of new irons. Many of the top manufacturers have amazing products that will help you not only hit the ball longer and higher, but with more control as well. Club heads designed with a lower center of gravity, designs that use several types of metals and alloys, and new shaft designs have all contributed to produce some really hot irons.

VIP *Take your old irons with you when you go shopping so you have something to compare the new ones with.*

You may find that the new designs hit the ball consistently crisper, farther, and higher, or you might discover that your old set performs just as well if not better. Never buy a set of irons sight unseen. Always take them for a test drive first, just as you would a new car.

THE PERFECT FIT

A brand-name set of new irons will cost you anywhere from $400 to well over $1,000, so be sure you're completely happy with the set you choose. Also verify that the store or the manufacturer offers some type of custom club-fitting service that will tailor the clubs to your unique body and swing style. There's no sense in spending money on a set of irons that doesn't fit. You wouldn't buy a suit or a dress that didn't fit, would you?

a **The club head**

If you have a tendency to hook or slice the ball, the lie angle can be adjusted to accommodate your specific swing style.

Lie angle

b **Adjusting the club size**

Grip size, shaft flex, shaft length, and total club weight can be tailored to suit your specific needs.

Shaft length

Grip size

Types of iron

Once some players have improved enough to be able to work the ball left or right at will, they decide to switch from a cavity-back iron to a forged steel blade design. Cavity-backs are designed to have most of their weight around the perimeter of the club head, which enlarges the sweet spot and allows better results on off-center hits. They also have a very low center of gravity, so the average player can get the ball high up in the air. Better players prefer using forged blade irons, though, because they can impart more left or right sidespin on the golf ball – necessary to bend the shot left or right. Forged blades also have a lower center of gravity, which enables the better player to hit lower, harder iron shots – vital to defeating the wind.

■ **Many golfers** *opt for cavity-back irons (above top) instead of the classic forged-blade design (above). The oversized club head has a larger sweet spot, making it especially popular with less experienced players.*

Shaft design

Another issue that may come up when you're shopping for a new set of irons is whether to go with steel or graphite club shafts. Traditionally, better players have always felt that steel offers slightly better control than graphite. This seems to be corroborated by the majority of professional golfers, who prefer steel-shafted irons over graphite. Steel shafts historically have suffered less from torque or twisting problems than graphite, which has developed a reputation for twisting enough to significantly affect the position of the club head at impact. This, in turn, affects ball spin and direction. Recent advances in graphite shaft design have, however, closed that gap significantly. Today's new designs tend to be just as accurate as steel and less punishing on the body.

Graphite or steel?

Graphite shafts have two distinct advantages over steel shafts.

First, they tend to be lighter than the same length and flex of steel shaft, so the graphite-shafted club can produce more club-head speed.

A faster swing speed almost always equates to more distance, something most golfers strive to achieve.

Second, graphite shafts absorb much more of the vibration produced at impact, causing less bone-jarring discomfort to the golfer.

If you have ever gotten sore wrists from too many bad shots or too much time on the practice tee, you know what I'm talking about.

Weighing up the options

If you are happy using steel shafts and feel your accuracy might be compromised by changing to graphite, then by all means stay with steel. However, if you are looking for a few extra yards and want to protect your wrists and arms from vibration and impact stress, give the graphite-shaft irons a try. On average, graphite shafts cost about $30 more per club than steel, making price another issue to consider.

The perfect putter

Putters don't usually need to be replaced too often. Most players become very attached to theirs, and wouldn't ever consider saying good-bye. If you're happy with your putter, then keep things simple and stick with it. But if you're not happy, try out a few new ones and see what you think.

Often, a new style of putter will automatically reenergize your putting.

Different weights, lengths, grips, or head styles can spark a run of luck on the greens, so by all means investigate what's out there.

Fabulous fairway woods

Fairway woods have seen a tremendous upsurge in popularity of late, due in great part to the low-profile head designs that became popular several years ago. These shallow-faced fairway woods inspire more confidence and tend to get the ball up in the air easily due to their very low center of gravity. If your set of clubs includes a 3-wood as your only fairway wood, consider trying out a 5-wood or even a 7-wood. These clubs get the ball up nicely and are much easier to hit than the long irons they replace.

■ **The lofted 7-wood** *is growing in popularity as it is suitable for shots off the tee, fairway, or out of the rough.*

If your 3-wood is an older-style, deep-faced design, consider trying out a newer, shallow-faced, low-center-of-gravity 3-wood. You may find that it hits the ball farther and higher than your old club, with fewer off-center hits.

Try those long irons

Most average golfers can't hit a long iron very well. The club face on a 1-, 2-, 3-, or 4-iron is usually smaller than that of a middle or short iron. The shaft is longer and there is much less loft, making it harder to get the ball up in the air. Long irons also tend to strike fear in the hearts of golfers. New players fear these flat-faced clubs, so they opt for the easier-to-use fairway woods instead.

But a fairway wood can't replace the long iron in every circumstance. When the wind starts gusting, for instance, the high trajectory of a ball struck by a fairway wood will leave your shot at the mercy of the wind. A long iron, however, will usually send the ball on a much lower trajectory while hitting it just as far. A long iron is also preferable to a fairway wood when the fairways are dry and firm, because the lower trajectory will enable the ball to roll much farther.

Getting a feel for your clubs

If you have no trouble hitting your 5-iron off the turf, you may want to experiment with your 3-iron and 4-iron to see if you have the same good luck. Nearly all professional players carry a 3-iron, and many carry a 2-iron as well, particularly if they'll be playing on a windy course. Few carry a 1-iron, though – even the pros can have a hard time

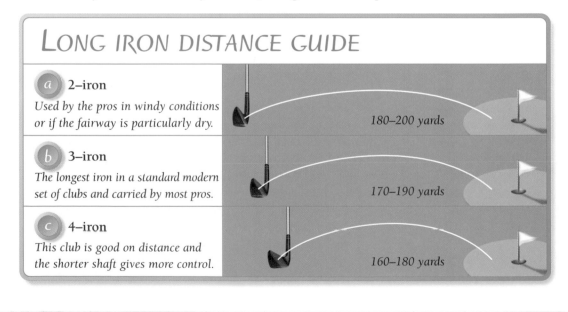

LONG IRON DISTANCE GUIDE

a) 2–iron
Used by the pros in windy conditions or if the fairway is particularly dry.

180–200 yards

b) 3–iron
The longest iron in a standard modern set of clubs and carried by most pros.

170–190 yards

c) 4–iron
This club is good on distance and the shorter shaft gives more control.

160–180 yards

with this club. If you can hit your 3-iron well, consider trying out a 2-iron at your local golf store. Hit from a tee first to get a good feel for the club. If your ball-striking skills are up to it, you may want to add a 2-iron to your set, and use it instead of a 4-wood or a 5-wood whenever the wind kicks up or when the fairways are dry and fast. Although the 1-iron can be very difficult to hit well, try one just for kicks and see what you think. Off the tee it can hit the ball as far as a 3-wood, albeit with a much lower trajectory.

Buying a better ball

THE AVERAGE *player probably benefits most from using a low-spin, long-distance ball most of the time. This type of ball offers the greatest driving distance and will spin very little, reducing the severity of slices or hooks. And keeping the ball in play is your number one priority, right?*

■ **The modern golf ball** *comes in a variety of construction types to suit players of all skill levels.*

As you improve your skills, though, your ability to draw or fade will become more and more important, as will your ability to spin the ball enough to stop it dead in its tracks after it touches down on the green. A distance ball, with its relatively hard, durable cover, will not spin enough to allow a good player (like you!) to do these things.

High-spin balls

So, when your game has improved to the point where you have excellent overall control and can reliably work the ball to the left or right, consider switching to a high-spin, soft-cover golf ball. These balls usually have a layer of resilient rubber windings (or a solid layer of resilient material) beneath a soft, synthetic balata cover. They spin much faster than any distance ball, making it easier for you to generate lots of sidespin or backspin, to fade or draw the ball, and to stop quickly on the green. You may lose a few yards off the tee, but the increase in control will be well worth it.

If you still tend to slice or hook the ball too much, avoid using a high-spin ball.

It will accentuate the unwanted slice or hook, causing you to lose many balls. High-spin balls tend to cost twice as much as distance balls, so think very carefully before making a switch.

Spin-distance balls

Most golf ball manufacturers now market an in-between ball that travels nearly as far as a pure distance ball and spins nearly as much as a high-spin ball. These spin-distance compromise balls might just be the way to go if your skills have improved but you're still not sure you can control a high-spin ball, or don't want to give up ten or more yards of distance off the tee. Priced in between the distance ball and the high-spin ball, these two- or three-piece designs are fairly easy to work and will spin enough to hold a fast, firm green. They will also travel far enough off the tee to satisfy your thirst for distance.

Consider going to your local golf store and buying a box of three high-spin balls and a box of spin-distance balls. During a round of golf, substitute them for your normal distance ball and see what you think. If your improving skills are up to it, you might discover a simple new way to lower your scores.

You don't need everything in the store

SOMETIMES A CHANGE OF EQUIPMENT *can help energize your golf game enough to drop your scores or make things more exciting. Few feelings are as great as taking that new club out onto the practice tee or course, hitting it pure, and watching the ball do exactly what the manufacturer claimed it would. Most golfers tend to believe in this type of magic a bit too often, however, thinking they can simply buy a better game. I am here to tell you that you can't really do that, unless the equipment you are currently using is so poorly designed or ill-fitted that even a professional couldn't break par with it. Your skills must be there first before your scores start dropping, and no new miracle club or ball is going to change that.*

VIP

Learn not to go equipment crazy.

Instead of buying that glitzy new titanium wonder stick you've been drooling over for the last six months, consider spending that extra $300 on five or six good golf lessons (see Chapter 21). Spending all that money on a new club won't lower your scores unless you first know how to swing the club properly. In the meantime, though, it can't hurt to look, right?

A simple summary

✓ The first few years of playing golf will be a period of learning and adjustment. You will improve in spurts. During this time, try not to change your equipment too often, but make sure that the equipment you have fits you properly.

✓ Consider getting a good driver. The ultimate driver has a graphite shaft with a titanium head, but many good drivers are a bit less high-tech and cost less too.

✓ If you are hitting with old-style fairway woods, try the new shallow-faced variety. Check out the long irons, too.

✓ Once your golfing skills improve to the point where you are hitting the ball with good distance, accuracy, and confidence, you may want to consider upgrading to clubs designed for better players to best take advantage of your developing talents.

✓ Although you'll sacrifice some distance with a high-speed ball, your overall game will improve due to the extra control it gives you. Don't make the move to a high-spin ball until your control and confidence levels are high.

✓ Consider trying a spin-distance ball, which will give you better control than a hard-cover distance ball but with nearly the same distance off the tee.

✓ Don't think for a minute that you can buy a better game. Only improving skills can lower your scores. Wait until you improve before spending a lot of money on new equipment.

Chapter 21

Can Lessons Turbocharge Your Game?

THE INFORMATION IN THIS BOOK is invaluable (of course!) and will give you a great head start in becoming a good golfer. However, many issues will undoubtedly come up for you that are related to your unique way of playing the game. No matter how well written, a book simply cannot take the place of a trained eye. In this chapter, I'll talk about the best way to seek out professional help to cure a nagging problem or simply to keep yourself on the right track.

In this chapter...

✓ Private lessons

✓ Picking your pedagogue

✓ Group lessons

✓ Golf camp

✓ Refresher courses

THE GREENBRIER GOLF ACADEMY IN WEST VIRGINIA

Private lessons

NOTHING WILL HELP IMPROVE your golf game as much as taking private lessons from a certified PGA professional. These hard-working golf teachers are trained to know what makes a great swing and what detracts from one. They can do so much more for your game than you can yourself. First and foremost, they are trained to watch you and spot obvious fundamental flaws in your technique. They also can detect those more subtle mistakes that you or your friends cannot – tiny flaws that might be causing profound problems in your game.

DEFINITION

When you hit with a cupped lead wrist, you are bending your lead hand backward. The lead hand is the one closest to the hole when you set up to swing. That's the left hand for a right-handed golfer.

Identifying common faults

Something as simple as a *cupped lead wrist*, for example, often the cause of a pesky slice, might go unnoticed by you or your friends, even with the help of videotaping.

Cupping the lead wrist causes a slice because the action tends to open up the club face during the backswing and leaves it open through impact, causing a slice rotation of the ball (for a right-handed golfer).

A teaching pro would catch that mistake in a second.

■ **An incorrect setup** *affects the path of the club head during the backswing, and is likely to result in poor contact with the ball.*

■ **A correct setup** *ensures that the club face remains parallel to the line of the shot, and a square blow is delivered to the ball.*

Trust the professionals

A good teacher will be able to look at each of your swing positions and tell you if adjustments are needed. He or she will be able to explain to you, in clear terms, not only what you are doing wrong but why your mistake is causing a problem. Having a skilled professional work with you as early on as possible will help prevent bad habits from forming. It will also improve your game enough to allow you to enjoy yourself sooner and with less aggravation than most self-taught golfers.

If you can, I strongly advise you to take at least a few private lessons with a qualified PGA professional. The one-on-one attention you receive will be an eye-opener, especially if you are completely self-taught.

■ **A qualified** *PGA professional will study your game, identify problems, and suggest changes to improve your overall technique.*

Teaching by example

Swing errors that you've adopted and come to accept as normal will be quickly spotted and corrected by the pro, who will take the time to explain why the error is holding you back. This is an important aspect of the teaching experience. Most golfers fear making any major changes to their fundamental techniques even if they know how flawed these techniques are. The teaching pro will explain how important the change is, and that it won't be all that hard to accomplish once the proper technique is ingrained. He or she will not just theorize or speak in the abstract, but will instead often teach by example, hitting a few crisp, clean, accurate shots for you to emulate (and envy).

■ **David Leadbetter** *(right) is regarded as one of the best golf instructors in the world. His students include Nick Faldo (left), Greg Norman, Ernie Els, and Florence Descampe.*

Even the pros sometimes need help!

Even professional golfers regularly take private lessons because they understand that the golf swing is an extremely dynamic and complex motion that can break down at almost any point.

They need a trained eye to observe them and to unabashedly point out a flaw or inconsistency that could lead to poor play and an unsuccessful career. Most of the major golf stars have teachers on the payroll, including Tiger Woods, who uses Butch Harmon as his swing guru.

A private, one-hour lesson with a qualified PGA professional will cost you anywhere from $25 to well over $50, depending on the teacher and the location. Although taking regular lessons could get pretty expensive, signing up for two or three will cost you less than the price of a new driver and will benefit your game immeasurably.

Committing to changes

Once you commit to taking a few private lessons, you also need to commit to trying out changes the teacher recommends for you, and sticking with them long enough for them to become good game habits. Often a new movement, grip, or stance can be very hard to get used to at first and might actually make your play worse for a little while. You need to trust your teacher and stick with the changes he or she recommends until the new movements feel natural. It takes time to forget one muscle memory and ingrain another.

Picking your pedagogue

IF YOU DECIDE TO TAKE private lessons, how do you choose the right teacher? The first way to narrow the field is to choose only from a list of certified PGA professionals, who have trained for years to know how to spot and correct flaws. Most public golf courses will have a PGA professional available to work with you, and private courses sometimes permit nonmembers to take lessons from their resident pro. Just ask at the pro shop. Even your local driving range will most likely have a certified pro available for lessons.

DEFINITION

*A certified **PGA professional** is a qualified teaching professional who meets or exceeds the teaching standards set by the Professional Golfers' Association of America. In addition to being able to play near-flawless golf, these teachers must take numerous business and teaching classes and apprentice under an established PGA professional.*

■ **Vivien Saunders** *joined the PGA in 1969 and in 1972 became the first woman to qualify as a PGA professional.*

Points to consider

Try to choose a teacher who has a good reputation among the golfers in your area. If a friend of yours has recently taken a few lessons and is now beating you soundly on the course, consider trying his or her teacher. Also, consider a teacher who uses videotape as a teaching tool. When you first see your swing on tape, you might laugh or cry but your teacher will be able to use it to show you precisely what you are doing wrong.

Don't go with a teacher you feel uncomfortable with.

No matter how good he or she is at their craft, you won't learn much if your personalities clash. Look for someone who communicates well and doesn't mind if you ask lots of simple questions. Avoid impatient, crabby teachers like the plague.

What to look for in a teacher

Steer clear of teachers who insist that there is one and only one way to do something. That's nonsense. Watch 20 different professional players hit the ball and you'll see 20 different swings. All that counts is that a technique is repeatable and that you make good contact every time. Look for a teacher who is willing to work within your limitations and natural abilities instead of one who insists you do it either his or her way or no way at all.

Trivia...

One of the best-loved of all golf instructors was Harvey Penick, an Austin, Texas, native who taught the game of golf for over 60 years and helped develop and train some of the best golfers the world has ever known. His list of students includes PGA superstars Tom Kite and Ben Crenshaw, and LPGA superstars Mickey Wright, Betsy Rawls, and Kathy Whitworth. The Teacher of the Year Award, given each year by the Golf Teachers' Association, is called the Harvey Penick Award.

Working with your teacher

When you do take a lesson, be sure to tell your teacher what you think your major problems are and if you have any physical problems he or she should know about, such as a bad back or knee, arthritis, or any problems with your vision. Then, be as open as possible to the teacher's suggestions, two of which should be to set goals for yourself and not to over-practice, and work on them with patience and confidence. Listen carefully to everything and don't be afraid to ask questions. With time and the right teacher-student relationship, your golf game should take off like never before.

INTERNET

www.espn.go.com/golf

This site from ESPN features a wealth of knowledge from technical consultants, together with an exclusive list of GOLF magazine's top 100 teachers in the United States.

Group lessons

PRIVATE, ONE-ON-ONE *lessons can be too expensive for many golfers. If this is the case for you, don't fret. Many facilities offer golf classes to the public in which one or two instructors teach a class of anywhere from five to 15 students. Although you won't get quite the same amount of personal attention from the teacher, you'll get enough to learn the fundamentals. Plus, you'll also be with a group of golfers who play at about the same level you do.*

The camaraderie, plus the opportunity to compare your skills to those of others, will be a great help to your own game.

And once you graduate you'll have a group of ready-made partners to play golf and implement your new-found knowledge with.

■ **Group lessons** *are a cheaper alternative to one-on-one tuition and a great way to meet players with similar skill levels to your own.*

What's involved?

Many driving ranges offer group classes, as do some courses and country clubs. Prices vary, but you should expect to pay anywhere from $60 to $120 for a five- to seven-session class that meets once or twice a week.

Each session should last about an hour, and all aspects of the game should be covered, including the fundamentals, putting, chipping, pitching, and the long game. For the price of two or three private lessons, in the group class you'll get more than twice the time, all the golf balls you could possibly hit, plus the company of other golfers at your skill level.

Golf camp

VIRTUALLY EVERY PART OF *the United States now has a number of quality golf schools you can attend. Catering for beginners as well as intermediate and advanced players, a three- to five-day golf school may be a great way for you to learn the game or to improve to the next level. Usually set up as a combination vacation-*

■ **The Greenbrier Golf Academy** *in West Virginia has three championship courses and offers professional training programs to players of all levels.*

school, most of these exclusive facilities arrange room, board, instruction, and several rounds of quality golf, all for one price. These package deals tend to be on the expensive side, but most attendees rave about the experience. They not only improve their game, but they have a great vacation in the process.

Everything you need

The teacher-to-student ratio in these schools is usually four or five to one, giving you enough personal attention to improve dramatically and enough time alone to work on the drills you've been taught. Most of the time the package includes a nice hotel room or condo close to the golf course/training facility. The facility itself is usually top-notch, as are the instructors.

The learning experience

Most golfers substantially improve their game due to the intensity of the school experience. For three or more days you are totally immersed in golf with quality instructors there by your side. After the day's instruction, you can play a round of golf with your fellow students (if you have the energy). The vacation atmosphere allows you to relax despite the intensity – one of the keys to playing well at any time.

INTERNET

www.golfschoolinfo.com

You can find some of the best golf schools in the country at this site. It also features instruction and tips from top instructors.

Choosing your location

Most golf magazines carry advertisements for golf schools across the country. They do tend to be pricey, often reaching up into the thousands for a week-long experience. Others offer prices not much higher than an average golf vacation would cost, so shop around. If you have the time and the money, consider it seriously. Choose a school in a desirable golfing destination such as Hawaii, Arizona, Michigan, or Las Vegas, and you'll have the time of your life. You will learn more than you ever imagined and will probably come home with a tan.

■ **The Pinehurst Resort** *is regarded by many as the "Golf Capital of America."*

Refresher courses

EVEN PROFESSIONAL GOLFERS *get regular refresher lessons from their instructors. Most set up a two- or three-day training period at the beginning of the competitive season when they and their teachers go over the fundamentals and swing mechanics, and then troubleshoot any area of the game that needs work. In addition, many players have their teachers accompany them to important tournaments, partly as a confidence booster but also to keep their basic mechanics intact.*

■ **In addition to** *receiving refresher lessons from their own instructors, many pros teach refresher courses themselves. Here, Nick Faldo uses his technical expertise to coach a group of young enthusiasts.*

If you took a few lessons when you first started playing golf and have been playing without additional help ever since, it's a great idea to consider taking a few lessons again to refresh your skills and to have a trained, objective eye take a look at your swing and your overall game.

You may have developed a few ingrained swing problems that a teacher could instantly pick up but that you are unaware of. You may have also improved substantially but need a gentle nudge to take your game up another notch. Going for one or two quick lessons might be just the thing to jolt your game into overdrive. Try to take a refresher lesson at least once each year, to ensure improvement and to turbocharge your love for the game.

A simple summary

✓ A great way to speed up the learning process is to take a few lessons from a certified PGA instructor. Most club professionals are PGA certified and are available at your local golf course for lessons.

✓ Taking a few private lessons is the best way to put your game on track. Although they tend to be expensive, the money you spend on them will be less than the cost of a new driver, and the results will be dramatic.

✓ Group lessons are a good option if private ones are a bit pricey for you. You'll still get plenty of attention, plus a chance to meet new golfing buddies.

✓ Choose a teacher you feel comfortable with and who doesn't mind answering your questions.

✓ Stick with the changes your teacher suggests, even if they feel awkward at first. As you ingrain better habits, your game will improve.

✓ Golf schools are the ultimate in lessons. These resortlike facilities offer a week of intensive golf tuition in a vacation setting, and often on championship courses.

✓ Consider taking a refresher lesson every year or so to identify any potential problems and to keep you sharp.

Chapter 22

Are You Ready to Compete?

COMPETITION BRINGS OUT the best and the worst in all of us. In this chapter I'll discuss how competition just might improve your game and how you can compete, at your own level, in golf tournaments in your area or across the country. I'll also talk about what it takes to turn professional and how to establish and use a USGA handicap to your advantage when you're competing against other golfers.

In this chapter...

✓ Competition might be the best way to get better

✓ Entering an amateur tournament

✓ The handicap system

✓ Golfing for a living

TOM KITE CELEBRATING HIS WIN AT THE 1992 U.S. OPEN

Competition might be the best way to get better

■ **Thousands of spectators** *attend golf tournaments each year and, for many, there is no greater thrill than watching a professional at work.*

GOLF MAY BE *the most psychological of all the outdoor games. I mean, your performance on the course will be affected as much or more by your mental outlook as it is by your physical abilities. You know the feeling. When you're at the driving range, you hit ball after ball perfectly while no one is watching. Step up to the first tee of a round of golf, though, with three other people watching you, and you choke big time. Why? You know you are capable of hitting the ball well. What's different? Pressure to perform, that's what.*

Sharpen your focus

You don't want to choke in front of others. And that pressure plays games with your head. A little self-doubt creeps into the equation, and – next thing you know – you top your tee shot, sending it dribbling weakly into the right rough 20 yards away while everyone else's drives are 200 yards down the middle of the fairway.

VIP

Golf is a mind game. If you think you might hit a shot badly, odds are you will.

If you feel comfortable over the ball, though, chances are good you'll hit it right down the middle. You know the feeling of being in that comfort zone. When you have confidence in your ability to hit the ball, a calm shroud covers you. Nothing else can creep into the moment. You simply swing and watch the ball sail away to its target. Playing a competitive round of golf ups the mental ante. You have more on the line. You want to win and every shot counts. This added pressure will break down your game at first, much the same way that lifting heavier weights at the gym will break down your muscle fibers more quickly than the lighter weights you have been using.

But eventually those muscles rebuild and become stronger. That's what playing golf on a competitive level can do for your game. It will sharpen your focus and help improve your strategic abilities on the course. After playing in a few amateur tournaments, a round of golf with your chums will seem like a walk in the park.

Even playing competitively with a friend will help to sharpen your game. Don't believe it? Play for a dollar a hole and see what happens!

■ **Focus on a clear** *idea of your intended shot, and have confidence in your ability to hit the ball.*

Performing under pressure

■ **The pressure** *on professional players is immense during the most prestigious events of the golfing calendar, such as the U.S. Masters Tournament at Augusta National Golf Club, above.*

Professional golfers know the importance of playing in a competitive atmosphere. It's one of the reasons they are so much better than the rest of us. Week after week, they bare their skills and egos to the world and to over a hundred other competitors. That kind of pressure hones their games to a much sharper point than we could ever achieve playing our buddies just for the fun of it. You are also more highly motivated to win, because more is at stake.

Competition will improve your game like no other drill or exercise can because it teaches you to deal with pressure and to think carefully and shrewdly about every shot.

Get it in perspective

At first you may find that the pressure adds strokes to your game, simply because you are not used to the heat. Eventually, though, you'll learn to put the pressure aside and begin to play a better, more focused, and confident game. Play in a tournament or two, and fun rounds will become a breeze. It's all a matter of perspective.

Entering an amateur tournament

ONCE YOU ARE REGULARLY *shooting rounds in the low 90s, you're ready to compete with other golfers at a similar level. Your game will be pressed harder than it ever has been, eventually raising all your golf skills. And who knows – you might just win the tournament!*

Where to find information

There are many local amateur tournaments around the country every year, and it's likely that at least one or two are held at your home course. Go into the pro shop at your course sometime in the early spring and ask what amateur tournaments are scheduled for the season. These contests are geared to different levels of skill, and there should be one you are eligible to play in. Call around to nearby courses to find out about their upcoming amateur tournaments too. Local golf publications always advertise amateur tournaments as well.

Join a local golf club

Another great way to learn about upcoming tournaments is to join a local golf club or group. Your favorite course probably has one, and usually the annual fee is moderate. Perks of belonging include entry to a variety of tournaments and outings, as well as meeting and befriending other golfers. Joining a local golf club will help improve your game and will introduce you to scores of golf aficionados as crazy for the game as you are.

■ **Joining a local** *golf club is a great way to meet other players, improve your game, and gain your first taste of competitive pressure, even if its simply playing a round with friends.*

Entry requirements

Most amateur tournaments charge an entry fee, which covers the cost of the round as well as a cart and lunch. You have to be able to play reasonably well, and most tournament organizers require you to have an official USGA *handicap* too so they can group together players of similar skill levels.

The handicap system

A HANDICAP IN GOLF *is a way of leveling the playing field. Having a handicap is not a bad thing. In fact, it benefits you by enabling you to go head to head with better players and sometimes come out on top. As far as I know, golf is the only sport that uses this system.*

Calculating your handicap

Basically, a player's handicap is calculated by taking your average score of ten or more rounds of golf, then comparing this to what would be par for a normal 18-hole course.

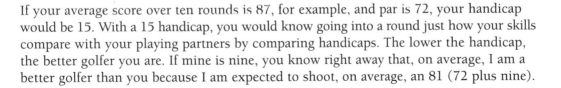

If your average score over ten rounds is 87, for example, and par is 72, your handicap would be 15. With a 15 handicap, you would know going into a round just how your skills compare with your playing partners by comparing handicaps. The lower the handicap, the better golfer you are. If mine is nine, you know right away that, on average, I am a better golfer than you because I am expected to shoot, on average, an 81 (72 plus nine).

Scratch players

When you're first starting to play, it's a good idea to team up with golfers who have similar handicaps, instead of playing with low handicappers or *scratch players*. That way, you won't slow down the better players by taking a lot of shots to complete a hole, and you won't feel intimidated by them either.

Should you get a handicap?

Most recreational golfers don't ever bother to get a handicap. They simply play golf and compare their total score with those of their playing partners to see who did the best. That's fine if you don't ever want to compete in amateur tournaments or become eligible to belong to certain golf clubs. But most tournaments require you to have a certified USGA handicap to determine if you are good enough to be there and to know who to pair you up with on the course. Golf clubs also want to know that you can play well enough to keep up with the other members, so they require you to show a valid handicap before joining.

Having a certified USGA handicap is a good idea, even if you don't plan to compete or join a club.

To get one, you must keep an accurate score of every round you play. It's not a bad idea to do this anyway, because careful scoring will help you become a better golfer as you track your improvement from day to day.

How to get a handicap

Until you're able to consistently get around a full-size golf course in under 100 strokes, you don't really need to go for an official handicap. Shooting below 100 means you're able to hit the ball fairly straight and able to drive it at least 160 yards regularly. Once you can do that, you are ready to get a handicap.

The USGA states that you must play at least ten rounds of golf before an official handicap can be assigned to you. You will then get a nifty little embossed card from the USGA that clearly states what your handicap is so that you can just whip it out of your wallet when necessary.

Witnessing scores

To meet the USGA's requirements, you must have a witness along during any round you intend to use to calculate your handicap. Your witness (usually a playing partner) must keep score for you, add up your scores on every hole, and sign your scorecard after the round. You then take the scorecard back from him or her, verify the scores on each hole and sign it yourself. You should keep your playing partner's score in the same way. This method ensures that the scores are as accurate and truthful as possible.

■ **Even professional** *players like Jack Nicklaus (above) must complete a scorecard and have it verified at the end of each round of a tournament.*

Keep it truthful!

Never be less than truthful about your score.

Golf is an easy game to cheat at, and as such it depends greatly on the honesty and integrity of the people playing it. Besides, if you lie about your scores, you'll end up receiving an artificially low handicap. Then, when you compete against a player who's better than you, you won't be able to subtract as much from your score, perhaps enabling your competitor to win. Telling the truth about all your scores will guarantee that your handicap is accurate, and it may enable you to beat players of higher skill.

The handicap card

Once you take your scorecard back from your playing partner, check to see that the scores on each hole are correct, sign beneath your partner's signature, and hand it in to the appropriate employee at the pro shop of your home course. Most courses have a handicap computer where they input all the scores, making the process easy for you. There's usually a nominal fee, but it shouldn't be very much. After handing in ten verified scores, you'll receive an official handicap card, complete with your up-to-date handicap and a history of your most recent scores. Each time you play after that, your handicap is adjusted to account for the new score. Your handicap might rise or fall, depending on what shape your game is in at any given time. And that's all there is to it!

■ **The first national handicapping** *system was developed by the USGA. Their headquarters (above) are located in New Jersey.*

Playing with your handicap

Once you have your handicap, you can use it whenever you play a friendly, competitive round with a friend.

At the end of the round, simply subtract your handicap from your score to get your adjusted net score. Your playing partner does the same. Then you compare net scores to see who wins.

So if you shoot a 98 and have a handicap of 24, your net score would be 74. If your partner shoots 100 and has a handicap of 28, his or her net score would be 72. You lose!

DIFFERENT WAYS TO PLAY

Strokeplay events

Strokeplay, also called medalplay, is the most common way of scoring any game of golf. Basically, you keep track of how many strokes you take, and at the end of 18 holes the player with the fewest strokes wins. However, many amateur competitions are organized in formats other than regular strokeplay.

■ **Walter Hagen,** *famous for his stylish attire, was the master of both strokeplay and matchplay events during the 1920s.*

Best ball and scramble

Instead of each player competing separately, sometimes teams play other teams in competitions called best ball, or scramble. In best ball, the best individual score from a team of players on any given hole is used as the team score for that hole. In a scramble, all team members hit their tee shots, then play their next shots from wherever the best tee shot of the team landed. Subsequent shots are always played from wherever the best shot landed. These two games are fun to play and are not quite as stressful as strokeplay, in which players' individual scores are the deciding factor in the tournament. In best ball or a scramble, you always have someone to fall back on if you don't hit a great shot.

■ **The Ryder Cup,** *a biennial competition between the United States and Europe, is probably the best known matchplay event.*

Matchplay events

Some competitions are held as matchplay events. In matchplay, two players compete against each other hole by hole, instead of comparing their total score for the entire round. The player who scores lowest on each hole wins that hole. The first competitor to win more holes than are left to play wins the match. Matchplay is challenging and fun because each hole is a new competition. If you shot a nine on the last hole, it doesn't matter; you start all over again on the next hole and don't add that terrible nine to your score, as you would in regular strokeplay.

Golfing for a living

AT ANY GIVEN TIME, *only a few hundred golfers regularly get to play golf for a living. Professional golfers must be able to consistently shoot below-par rounds on courses they might have played only a few times before. They also must travel all over the country or the world, endure the rigors of time-zone changes, and jump right into a tournament with many of the world's best players.*

It's tough at the top

Being a professional golfer means being an independent contractor who must play well, day in and day out, in order to continue playing. Pro golfers do not get signed to a lucrative contract the way team athletes do. If Mark McGwire has a bad month at the plate, he still gets to collect those big, sweet paychecks. If David Duval or Tom Lehman has a bad month, they make nothing. In fact, they lose money because they don't work for a multi-million-dollar sports franchise and must pay their own expenses for transportation, meals, and housing. Even the biggest winners in golf make far less at their sport than do middle-of-the-road athletes in baseball, football, and basketball.

> ### Trivia...
> *Sports management agencies became big business in the 1980s and 90s. Perhaps the biggest of them all is the International Management Group, founded by attorney Mark McCormack more than 30 years ago when he took on his first sports celebrity client, Arnold Palmer.*

■ **Although under** *constant pressure to perform, professional golfers have a lifestyle that most amateur players only dream of.*

The major tours

Don't get me wrong. If given a choice, I'd rather be a professional golfer than nearly anything else I can think of. Imagine being able to play golf for a living! Unfortunately, only a few talented individuals get to do so regularly. The major tours for professional golfers include:

- PGA Tour
- LPGA Tour
- Senior Tour
- Buy.com Tour
- Futures Tour
- European Tour
- Asian Tour

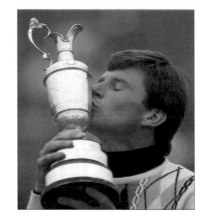

INTERNET

www.pgatour.com

This page from the Professional Golf Association has information on the PGA Tour and the Senior Tour.

■ **Nick Faldo** *kisses golf's most famous trophy after winning the 1987 Open Championship, one of four "Majors" on the PGA Tour.*

Getting that big break

In addition to these well-known tours, there are numerous regional mini-tours all over the United States, Europe, and Asia, giving players of less experience or talent the opportunity to break into the sport. To have any chance at fame and fortune, however, you must make it big on one of the tours listed above.

Players get onto one of the major tours in a variety of ways.

Some work their way up through local and regional mini-tours until they become eligible for the Buy.com Tour (for men) or the Futures Tour (for women). These two tours act as preparatory stages for the PGA and LPGA Tours, while giving up-and-coming golfers a chance to make a living at the sport. Others play amateur or college tournaments and work their way up through the ranks of the elite amateur players, perhaps getting a chance to compete in prestigious tournaments that offer the winners a chance to compete in selected professional tournaments. For example, the winner and second-place finisher of the U.S. Amateur Championship and the winner of the U.S. Public Links Championship both get a one-time entry to the Masters Tournament.

■ **Karrie Webb** *qualified for the LPGA Tour after finishing second in a qualifying tournament, even though she had a broken bone in her wrist!*

A chance in a million

Other players attempt to qualify to join the PGA or LPGA tours by entering regional, sectional, and final qualifying tournaments held at various locations around the country. To qualify this way usually costs thousands of dollars, making it a tough choice for players who lack financial support. The competition is fierce, too. Only a few players out of many hundreds ever finish high enough in the standings to earn a starring spot on either the PGA or LPGA Tours.

INTERNET

www.lpga.com

This is the site for the Ladies Professional Golf Association Tour.

Go pro, or play for fun?

Yes, it is extremely difficult to become a successful professional golfer, in this or any other country. But that's okay. The players you and I watch every weekend on television will give us plenty of entertainment because they really are the cream of the crop. After all, you wouldn't want to watch a bunch of hackers shooting in the 90s, would you?

If you can consistently shoot at or around par on challenging courses (from the championship tees, way in the back), you might want to consider going pro – if you are young enough and have enough money to give it a go. Otherwise, just play golf for the fun of it, like the rest of us. Keep it simple, right?

A simple summary

✓ Competing against other golfers can be a great way to hone your game and learn to master the effects of pressure.

✓ You can enter a local or regional amateur tournament, provided you have a certifiable handicap and can afford the entrance fee. The thrill of competing in an official tournament will give you an idea of what the professionals go through every week.

✓ Establishing and using a USGA-certified handicap can help make competing with other golfers of differing skill levels possible.

✓ Though becoming a professional golfer is a dream that many of us would love to realize, the odds of actually doing so are against us. If you can consistently shoot par or better on difficult courses, however, you might want to consider giving it a try.

Chapter 23

Golf as a Spectator Sport

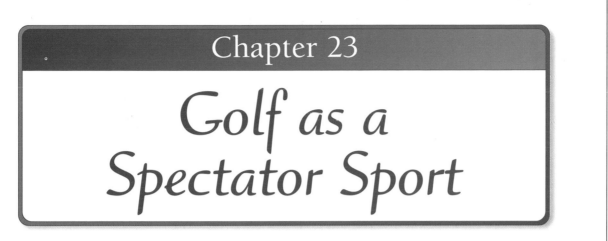

THE PROFESSIONAL GOLF SEASON lasts virtually year-round. This is because important tournaments are played all over the world. They are definitely worth watching, in person if you can and on television if you can't. You can learn a lot by watching a great golfer play. Even if you only pick up on his or her timing and rhythm, it will be time well spent. In this chapter I'll tell you how to find the tournaments to watch, as well as what the pros can teach you about your own game.

In this chapter...

✓ The different tours

✓ Golf on the TV

✓ The fine art of watching a professional tournament

✓ Watching the pros will improve your game

THE MASTERS, AUGUSTA NATIONAL GOLF CLUB, GEORGIA

The different tours

LUCKILY FOR US, THERE are several organizations *that sponsor professional golf tournaments nationwide. As I've already mentioned, they include the PGA, LPGA, and Senior Tours, as well as the Futures and Buy.com Tours (sort of the minor leagues of professional golf). Additionally, there are many regional mini-tours that put on tournaments for professional players attempting to break into the more prestigious tours. Wherever you live, odds are that, particularly during the summer, a professional golf tournament is about to be held nearby. The PGA Tour holds nearly 50 official tournaments each year, plus a number of unofficial ones. The LPGA and Senior Tours each hold more than 40 tournaments, while the Buy.Com and Futures Tours each hold more than 30. Add the many regional mini-tour events, and you have well over 200 professional tournaments you can attend.*

> ## Trivia...
> *The longest consecutive winning streak in PGA history was in 1945 when the legendary Byron Nelson won an incredible 11 straight tournaments, including the PGA Championship. He went on to win a total of 18 tournaments that year, a record that has so far proven impossible to beat.*

Climate considerations

Of course the climate in your area will determine when and if a professional tournament is scheduled to be held. In the early months of the year most tournaments are held on the West Coast or in Hawaii. In the spring they tend to move to Florida and some of the other southern states. By early summer professionals are playing in the Midwest and Northeast, and by mid- to late summer in the Rocky Mountain states and the Northwest. Don't expect the pros to come into town in early March while you're still shoveling snow in suburban Denver.

■ **The beautifully** *manicured fairways and greens of Augusta, Georgia, are home to the Masters tournament, which is held each year during the warm southern spring.*

Pro players in action

Of all the pro players, those on the PGA Tour are probably the most impressive to watch. Headlined by marquee players such as Tiger Woods, David Duval, Davis Love III, and Phil Mickelson, PGA tournaments are a blast to attend. Just hanging out at the practice range and watching them bomb 325-yard drives out into space, or drop ten straight 65-yard lob wedge shots right next to a

■ **Phil Mickelson** *started hitting golf balls when he was just 18 months old. He is now the most famous and successful left-handed player on the PGA Tour.*

INTERNET

www.pgatour.com/stats

This site provides interesting statistics of the players on PGA and Senior Tours.

practice pin will get your golf game revving. Then, when you actually get to see these guys performing under pressure, you'll feel humbled and inspired. Watching them bend a low-hit 2-iron around a huge oak tree, or loft an 8-iron over a lake and onto the green 165 yards away will just blow you away.

The Senior Tour players are fun to watch too even though they don't hit the ball quite as far as the younger guns. Remember, these men used to play on the PGA Tour. Players like Tom Watson, Tom Kite, Lanny Wadkins, and Hale Irwin are no duffers.

Simply watch and learn

I really enjoy watching the women of the LPGA play golf. Their style of play is more familiar to the average golfer. And although they're more talented than most of us amateurs could ever hope to be, the women actually hit shots with clubs that I might use. For instance, when Tiger Woods has a 200-yard approach shot into a green, he'll often hit a 5-iron or even a 6-iron! Ridiculous, but true. When Se Ri Pak or Karrie Webb have to hit the same shot, they are both more likely to use a 5-wood or perhaps a 2-iron – the same clubs that an average golfer would use.

INTERNET

www.lpga.com

The official site of the LPGA, this site gives you the year's schedule of LPGA events, and information regarding the Futures Tour.

Because the professional women's game is closer to the kind of game we play, we can learn more about our own game from them.

The smaller tournaments

The Buy.com and Futures Tours also hold tournaments all over the country. Although players competing on these tours aren't necessarily as skilled as those on the more prestigious tours, they are all great golfers and have a hunger to succeed that the established superstars can only vaguely remember. If any Buy.com or Futures Tours events are scheduled for your region, do yourself a favor and attend a few. As a plus, the crowds will be smaller, which means you can get close to the action.

Regional tournaments

INTERNET

www.golfweek.com

To check on scheduling for regional mini-tours, go to this site, or pick up a copy of Golfweek magazine.

Mini-tours – regional tournaments held for players just starting out in the professional ranks – are another possibility when you want to see some decent competition. Although the participants are usually a step down in talent and experience from the national tours, the play will nevertheless be exciting. Plus, there is almost always a mini-tour event being held somewhere near you during good weather.

Golf on the TV

IN THE MID-1950S GOLF *hadn't yet caught on with the masses. All of that changed with the introduction of two things: television and Arnold Palmer. At the same time that televisions began to find their way into living rooms all over the nation, a brash, young, exciting golfer was changing the way the game was played, tackling revered golf courses like a linebacker, and developing a tremendously loyal group of fans called Arnie's Army. They followed him around each course in droves, cheering him on as he'd drive to the green on a par-4 or hack his ball out of the rough and onto the green just feet from the pin. Television was right there to cover the young star, causing a golf renaissance, particularly among the middle classes.*

■ **Arnold Palmer** *is one of the greatest and best-loved names in the history of golf. He is pictured with the Crestar Classic trophy, his 60th PGA Tour victory since turning professional in 1954.*

Simply sit back and relax!

Today television transports us to a beautiful, lush, green place while snow is mounting up outside our homes. It's a good reason to sit back and watch talented young golf pros play the game on courses you and I can only dream of one day playing.

Tournament coverage

Professional golf tournaments typically last four days (except the Senior Tour events, which last three), starting on Thursday and ending on Sunday. The Thursday and Friday rounds are usually not covered by the major networks due to the relatively small potential audiences on those days. But they are covered by ESPN or the Golf Channel, two excellent cable networks that do a great job of broadcasting golf from all the major tours.

■ **The arrival of television** *revolutionized the way professional golf was played. Many tournaments abandoned matchplay in favor of the longer strokeplay formula to maximize advertising revenues.*

The big networks bid for the rights to cover the Saturday and Sunday rounds of the important tournaments. These include not only the four majors, but also tournaments such as the Ryder Cup, the Presidents Cup, the U.S. Amateur Championship, the U.S. Women's Amateur Championship, and the Women's U.S. Open.

Trivia...

First held in 1916, the PGA Championship was originally a matchplay event. It remained so until 1968 when it was finally switched over to strokeplay. The reason? The strokeplay format usually takes much longer, affording television advertisers as much time as possible to run commercials.

Twenty-four-hour golf

If you have cable television (and who doesn't these days?), you may have the Golf Channel, a 24-hour cable station dedicated solely to all matters golf.

From tournaments to advice to product reviews, if it's golf, the Golf Channel's got it. Particularly valuable is the station's coverage of lower-profile tournaments, such those sponsored by the Buy.com Tour and the Futures Tour. Amateur golf is also covered, as are a number of celebrity golf events.

TV masterclasses

The Golf Channel regularly broadcasts helpful instruction and advice by some of golf's leading teachers, making this station a "must have" for beginners and advanced players alike. I recommend watching this channel whenever you can, especially if you're addicted to golf. Just be sure your family doesn't disown you for spending so much time in front of the tube!

TOURNAMENTS DEFINED

The majors

The four tournaments known collectively as the majors are the Masters, the U.S. Open, the British Open, and the PGA Championship. All are scored by strokeplay.

Matchplay events

The Ryder Cup is an international matchplay golf competition between the United States and Europe, which take turns hosting the event. Held every two years, usually on a famous course, it is often thought of as the Olympics of golf.

■ **Carnoustie,** *on the east coast of Scotland, hosted the 1999 British Open Championship – one of four major tournaments on the PGA Tour.*

The Presidents Cup is an international matchplay competition between the United States and the rest of the world, excluding Europe. The location of the event varies.

RYDER CUP **1999** OFFICIAL
EUROPEAN PROGRAM

The U.S. Amateur Championship, a matchplay event, is held in the United States each year and determines who is the best amateur male player. Most winners of this championship go on to have a great career in professional golf.

Tournaments for women

The U.S. Women's Amateur Championship, also a matchplay event, determines the best female amateur player. The Women's U.S. Open, a strokeplay event, decides who the best professional female golfer in the world is. Any professional female golfer in the world who qualifies for the event can play. It is always held in the United States on various famous courses.

Television is good for your game!

When you watch a golf tournament on television, not only will you get to witness great fundamentals and techniques, but you will also see the successful strategies the pros use to make their way around tough courses. Their shot selections – like your own – are based on conditions and yardages and on what will be the highest percentage choice for any given moment. Professionals rarely make major blunders in strategy, so picking up on how they manage the course will help make your own game plans that much smarter.

■ **This caddie** *uses a yardage meter to measure the distance between targets. This determines club and shot selection.*

Top tips

Pay attention to the pre-shot routines of the pros. See how they set up to the ball the same way every time? Watch how their setups change when the wind is howling or when the ball is in a terrible lie. Also pay attention to how precise they can be to how focused they become when they're getting ready to hit the ball. If you can take these techniques to heart and make them part of your game, your scores will drop.

In addition, most of the play-by-play announcers usually have very insightful commentary that can help you better understand the intricacies of the game.

Particularly helpful are the comments and analyses of former great players-turned-announcers, such as Johnny Miller, Ken Venturi, and Curtis Strange.

The fine art of watching a professional tournament

SOMETIMES WATCHING GOLF on television just isn't enough. You can't really experience the depth and beauty of the course or the emotions of the players. You don't get to smell the flowers or the freshly mown grass. And there is nothing quite like standing just a few yards behind a professional golfer and watching him or her let loose on a 300-yard drive with a bullet that splits the fairway and lands in what seems like the next county. Everyone in love with the game of golf should attend a professional golf tournament at least once to see up close the awesome talent of today's golf pros.

Simply cut to the action

Watching from home has its advantages, though. When you're sitting on your cushy sofa, the tournament is fed to you in polished, understandable bits. The cameras make it easy to jump from one player to another even though they might be on opposite sides of the course. As soon as you watch David Duval's approach shot to the 8th green, the camera deftly switches over to Sergio Garcia's drive on the 4th hole and then cuts again to Tiger Woods' lob shot on the 6th. At the tournament, you wouldn't be able to see all three of those shots – unless you can run at light speed around the course.

Seeing it live

Following the action live at the course has a couple of disadvantages. First, the game takes longer. Most courses are, well, big, and it takes the players time to walk from hole to hole. Second, hundreds, sometimes thousands, of other fans are milling about, following their favorite players or camping out at a strategic spot on the course that provides a view of several holes at once. How can you enjoy watching a golf tournament with all those people in the way?

Getting there

Okay, so you've decided to attend a PGA Tour event close to your home. It's not a major tournament, but at least 5,000 people are expected to attend each day. The first thing you usually have to do is find a parking space. Fortunately, many tournament organizers now provide a remote parking facility and shuttle buses to take you to and from the course. Your next task is to decide which days you want to attend.

Most tournaments last about a week and consist of one or two practice days, a **pro-am** tournament on Wednesday, and then the competition itself, which runs from Thursday through Sunday. You can buy a ticket for the entire week, for just the competition days, or for the single day of your choice.

■ **This painting** *by LeRoy Nieman depicts Jack Nicklaus, Tom Watson, Clint Eastwood, and Gerald Ford at the 1983 Bing Crosby Pro-Am tournament.*

Be prepared!

Remember that even though you will not be playing golf, you still must walk up and down all the hills on the course in either the warm sunshine or nasty weather. Watch the weather reports and be prepared.

Dress the way you would for a round of golf under those conditions, and be sure to bring along some water and perhaps a sandwich and some fruit. Some fans even take a small folding chair.

The warm-up

The first place you want to go when you arrive is the practice tee. There you will be able to watch your favorite players warming up for that day's round. Watch carefully and you'll learn the right way to warm up, which you should do before each of your own rounds of golf. You won't see the pros beating ball after ball out into the range. Rather, you'll see them spend much more time on their wedge and middle-iron games and hit just enough long-iron and wood shots to confirm that there are no glaring problems. Then they'll go over to the practice chipping and putting greens and put in lots of time working on the true scoring shots that make the difference between 1st place and 20th.

Never bother the pros when they are practicing.

This time is crucial for them and they don't like interruptions. After all, golf is their job. Many pros will schedule a time for autographs before or after practice or a round. Wait for those times.

Staking your spot

Golf courses cover a lot – and I mean a lot – of ground, and you can't be everywhere at once. So you'll need to decide on a plan of attack for watching the tournament. Some fans park themselves at one spot, say the 12th tee, and watch every player who passes through. Others find a spot on the course that allows them to see the action on several holes at once. They might be able to see approach shots to one green, tee shots from another, and layups on a third. If camping out is your cup of tea, bring a camp chair and go for it.

■ **The 18th hole** *always draws a large crowd, as can be seen here at Wentworth during the 1989 World Matchplay event.*

Planning your viewing

I usually use a different plan. First, I choose three or four players I really like and concentrate on them for the day. I get a *pairing sheet* when I arrive so that I can find out exactly what time my favorite players are teeing off. There's usually an appreciable amount of time separating each pair, so I often watch the earliest one tee off and follow him or her for six or seven holes to get a good feel for his or her methods and skills. Then I stay put and watch a few groups pass through, until another one of my favorites approaches. I follow him or her for another six or seven holes, and then again stay put. After watching a few more groups pass through, I latch on to yet another favorite of mine, following him or her to the 18th hole. Then, if there are any players still coming through, I stay at the 18th and watch them all.

DEFINITION

A *pairing sheet* is *a list of the groups of golfers playing that day, arranged chronologically. Each two- or three-member group is assigned an exact time to tee off at the 1st tee. The pairing sheet gives you those times, so you can plan your viewing accordingly.*

■ **Many spectators** *choose a vantage point close to the green where they can see their favorite player take several shots.*

Following the players

That's just my method. It works well for me, but you may come up with another that suits your own needs better. Keep it simple. Whatever you do, just be prepared to walk a few miles!

One additional tip:

Try not to follow the premiere players all the time because they'll have the largest crowds in tow.

With so many heads and bodies standing around, it's often impossible to see anything at all. Instead, try to follow some of the lesser-known players. You'll still see some great golf but without the massive crowds.

INTERNET

www.pebble-beach.com

If you can't get to any of the big tournaments, visit this site for a virtual tour of the course at Pebble Beach in California, which has staged a number of major tournaments.

Watching the pros will improve your game

I KNOW I'VE SAID IT BEFORE, but it's really true: Going to a professional tournament and watching closely will improve your own golfing skills. Pay attention to how the pros manage the course. Watch player and caddie go through the routine of calculating yardage, determining what club to hit, and how to shape the shot. Look for changes in ball position and how the player deals with a lousy lie. Even look at the arc and timing of the swing. Does the player have a steep swing arc or a shallow one? What type of shot does each produce? Why does player A always hit the ball low, while player B consistently hits it high? Seeing first hand how setup, swing arc, and tempo directly affect the flight of the ball will be a real eye-opener.

■ **Jack Nicklaus,** *master of course strategy, is renowned for his excellent judgment on what type of shot to play.*

Playing it safe

Notice, too, when the pros take big chances and when they play conservatively. Unless the championship is on the line, most of them will play the safest shot possible. Learn from that! Watch Justin Leonard pitch the ball back out into the fairway from a bad lie – instead of going for the green – when there is perhaps only a 15-percent chance of getting it there. He knows that a bogey is not a bad score when you get into a bad situation.

Work on that short game!

Watch how good their short games are. Check out how well they play out of the bunkers. Rarely do the pros fail to get a chip, pitch, or bunker shot close enough to the pin to putt it in with one stroke. They are superb inside of 50 yards because they practice those shots all the time. The moral here is practice that short game!

VIP

Finally, watch how rarely the pros lose their tempers on the course.

Sure, a few do, but most simply let the anger go and move on. They can't afford to take it with them to the next tee because it will ruin that shot too. Remember, golf is very much a mental game. Lose your cool and you'll lose the match.

Do's and don'ts at the tournament

Don't hound a player for his or her autograph. Wait for the player to say, "Okay, I'll sign some now," before you approach. Nothing can ruin a player's mental game faster than having hundreds of fans storming him or her for autographs in the middle of a round. Remember that they are there to compete, not socialize.

Don't talk or move while a player is getting ready to make a swing.

Don't go inside of the ropes separating spectators from players.

Don't take photographs while a player is concentrating. Most tournament organizers will not even allow you to bring in a camera, so consider leaving yours at home.

Don't get drunk, rowdy, or insolent on the course grounds. Golf is supposed to be the last courteous sport, so try to keep it that way.

Don't be rude while you're trying to procure a good spot from which to see the action.

Don't walk across a fairway until a course marshal tells you it's okay to do so.

Don't heckle a player, ever.

Don't litter on the course. And yes, cigarette butts are litter.

Don't ever say "You da man!"

Do approach a player for an autograph if and when he or she says it's okay to do so.

■ **A course marshal** *will signal when it is safe to cross the fairway. One spectator in this crowd has taken extreme measures to ensure a clear view of action on the course!*

Do point out to a course marshal where a player's ball landed, if it looks like it will be difficult to find.

Do speak to a player if he or she seems willing.

Do applaud and cheer after a shot has been made.

Do take children with you, provided they can control themselves and keep quiet and still at the appropriate times.

■ **Thunderous applause** *greets Jack Nicklaus at Augusta's 18th hole after a critical final-round putt wins him the 1986 Masters Tournament.*

A simple summary

✓ Most areas in the country have a professional golf tournament scheduled sometime during the year. In addition to the PGA, LPGA, and Senior Tours, the Buy.com and Futures Tours hold tournaments all over the country. Smaller, regional mini-tours have tournaments as well. No matter where you live, there will be at least one professional tournament scheduled close by.

✓ You can learn a lot about golf by watching professional tournaments on television. Just make sure you budget some time into your day to interact with family members.

✓ Attending a professional golf tournament is a great way to improve your own skills as well as a fun way to spend a few days.

✓ Don't forget to watch the players at the practice tees. I bet you'll see them working on the short game.

✓ Whenever you're attending a tournament, be courteous and respectful to the players, who are there trying to make a living.

Chapter 24

Golf Vacations

Everybody loves to have some time off, and we all need to get away now and then. But something has changed for you, hasn't it? Now that you're a golfer, all you want to do is play golf. Think of it: traveling to Hawaii, Arizona, Florida, or Europe and getting to tee off in the glorious sun on a perfectly manicured course. Your family comes along too and has lots of fun enjoying all the amenities the resort has to offer. It's a perfect vacation.

In this chapter...

✔ The perfect destination

✔ Resorts and package deals

✔ What to pack for a golf vacation

✔ Golf as a side trip

✔ Visiting the great courses

SUNSET OVER VALDERRAMA GOLF COURSE, SPAIN

The perfect destination

JUST WHERE YOU DECIDE to go on your golf vacation has more to do with personal preferences than anything else. You may prefer the warm, sunny climate of Arizona or the cool, windswept shores of northern Scotland. To each his or her own. Once you decide on a general region for your destination, though, you should ask yourself a few questions so you can narrow down your choices.

■ **Scotland** is world famous for it's beautiful golf courses, many of which are set in wild and dramatic scenery.

Choosing your destination

First, how good of a golfer are you? If you're a beginner, you probably won't want to choose a destination with an extremely difficult course. You can figure that out by looking up the *course rating* and *slope*.

If the rating of the course is 72 or less, you should be able to get around it fairly well. If the slope of the course is lower than 115, you should also be okay.

Avoid a course with a very high course rating and slope, because you'll lose lots of balls and patience.

DEFINITION

I know you remember from Chapter 3 that the course rating is the score that a scratch player (one with a zero handicap) would be expected to shoot at that course. If the course is rated 68, for example, it is a relatively easy course and can be played by beginners. A rating of 72 would make it an average course. A high rating, say a 76, means that the course is a tough one and should be avoided by beginners. The slope is just another measurement of a course's level of difficulty. The higher the slope, the more difficult the course. The average slope for courses in the United States is around 113. Anything below that is relatively easy; anything above that can be challenging. Beginners should stay away from courses with slopes of more than 115. Remember, keep it simple.

Value for money

The next consideration should be price. What will you be able to afford? Some posh golf resorts can cost thousands of dollars per person, making them too expensive for most of us. Others are much more reasonably priced and offer special package deals that make it possible for the whole family to come along.

Or you can avoid the resorts completely by booking a few tee times at a reasonably priced course in a desirable spot and then simply reserving a room in a nearby budget hotel. Combine that with a discounted airfare, and you could come up with a real deal.

Some airlines will set up a golf vacation package deal for you, including airfare, hotel, rental car, and greens fees, all for a very reasonable price.

Ask your travel agent about it, or check with the airline's reservation service or web site.

Entertainment for all the family

When you're deciding on a destination for your golf vacation, don't forget to factor in your family and their needs. If you're taking your significant other and children, what will be available for them to do while you are playing golf? (The ideal, of course, is to have an entire family that plays golf, but it's not always possible.) For instance, choosing a golf destination in or near Orlando, Florida, would give you access not only to great golf, but to Disneyworld and a zillion other theme parks as well, plus great outlet shopping. Going to a golf resort in Telluride, Colorado, would also give you and your loved ones access to wonderful summer hiking trails and breathtaking scenery.

GRAND CYPRESS (New Course)

Hole	Yards	Par	Hole	Yards	Par
1	362	4	10	330	4
2	514	5	11	430	4
3	179	3	12	207	3
4	440	4	13	431	4
5	393	4	14	371	4
6	496	5	15	570	5
7	182	3	16	190	3
8	440	4	17	485	5
9	382	4	18	371	4
Out	3,388	36	In	3,385	36

TOTAL 6,773 YARDS; PAR 72

■ **Grand Cypress** (New Course) near Orlando, Florida, was designed by Jack Nicklaus. Some holes have features reminiscent of the Old Course at St. Andrews.

Staying closer to home

A golf vacation needn't be thousands of miles away, either. You could drive to a nearby state or even stay in your own. The advantage of staying close to home is that you can get away for just a day or two and still have a good time for a lot less money than you'd spend on a golf trip to Hawaii.

For instance, golfers living in Seattle who might be getting tired of the endless rain can simply take a drive out to the sunnier eastern portions of Washington State that are almost always very dry at that time of year. Spokane, the second largest city in Washington, has great golf courses at very reasonable prices, and you can get there by car from Seattle in a day. If you live in Detroit, Michigan, you can drive north several hundred miles and play golf at one of many beautiful courses in the northern parts of the state. Whatever part of the country you live in, great vacation golf is only a car ride away.

Resorts and package deals

GOLF RESORTS ARE EVERYWHERE. *You can find them in the United States, Mexico, Brazil, Bermuda, Puerto Rico, Greece, Malta, Scotland, Spain. Even Turkey and Poland have them. Golf resorts are big business, and for good reason. They have wonderful golf courses that are usually available only to guests of the resort. This means the fairways and greens will not be overused and scarred. Plus, the conditions are almost always perfect, ensuring you a great experience.*

Golf for all

Most resorts have at least 27 holes of golf available, while many provide 36 or more. There's usually one challenging 18-hole course and a less difficult nine or 18-hole course for those who don't care so much for a confrontation with the golf gods.

TRYALL GOLF CLUB, JAMAICA

It's all at your fingertips

The beauty of a golf resort is the convenience of having everything you want within walking distance. You probably won't even need to rent a car. Fine dining, shopping, swimming, tennis, and a gymnasium or massage facilities are almost always located on the premises or nearby. Some golf resorts even have an accredited golf school.

A good golf resort will provide you with excellent accommodations, often right next to a course. Some, such as the ones in and around Las Vegas and Reno, Nevada, also have nightly shows and gambling. Conference rooms are available at many resorts, making them a great place to hold business seminars.

INTERNET

www.travelguides.com

Use the navigator to access details of golf courses and resorts in the United States and around the world.

What's included?

Most golf resorts offer several types of package deal depending on how long you stay, your level of accommodation, and the time of year. At least one round of golf per day is usually included in the price, although many resorts will let you play two. After playing 36 holes, I think you'll be ready for a shower, a change of clothes, and a great dinner.

One word of advice when you're planning to go to a golf resort:

Never assume a service is included in the package price!

Always ask in advance exactly what amenities at the resort are included in your vacation plan. If you don't ask, you might end up getting stuck paying for greens fees and other costs on top of the package price.

THE PINEHURST RESORT

Trivia...

Built in 1925, the Pinehurst Golf Resort in North Carolina is the oldest golf resort in the United States. Designed by Donald Ross, who worked on the Old Course at St. Andrews, Pinehurst's eight courses are set among woodland and shady pines and offer some of the finest golf imaginable.

What to pack for a golf vacation

OF THE MILLIONS OF GOLFERS *planning to take a golf vacation this year, more than a few will fail to pack everything they'll need while others will lug more than they need through airports across the world. Exactly what will you need? Basically, you need to keep it simple.*

SHORT-SLEEVE SHIRT

Clothing considerations

Be sure to pack a selection of appropriate clothing.

Even if you are planning a trip to a desert course, take rain gear, long pants, at least one long-sleeve tee-shirt or turtleneck, and a good hat, preferably one with a wide brim if you're going to a sunny spot. If you're going to a place with a seasonal climate, take layers of light clothing so you can adjust to whatever the temperature is. Always take an extra golf glove or two, as well as some extra socks. A light windbreaker pullover would also be a good idea.

Essential extras

Make sure to pack sunscreen. Don't wait to get to the vacation spot to buy it because sunscreen is one of those things that always costs twice as much as you'd pay at home. Take along lip balm that offers protection from the sun, and pack a few Band-Aids in case you get a blister. (Do I sound like your mom yet?) Take your golf umbrella with you and some extra spikes for your shoes, just in case you break or lose some. And don't forget that spike wrench! Pack plenty of golf balls too. You won't want to spend the high prices that pro shops charge for them. Take a bunch of tees and a marker pen, too, to mark your balls so you can identify them quickly on the course.

LONG-SLEEVE JERSEY

SPARE GLOVE

LONG PANTS

SPIKE WRENCH AND SPIKES

Be sure to call in advance to find out if the courses you'll be playing on require you to use soft-spike shoes.

If they do (and if you have traditional metal spikes in your shoes), change over to soft spikes before you leave.

Transporting your clubs

It's a good idea to have a sturdy, wheeled traveling case for your golf clubs.

Wheels are essential, especially if you have to walk any appreciable distance inside an airline terminal with your bags. Consider getting a hard-shell case instead of a soft one for better protection. Although the soft cases are lighter and collapsible, they don't offer the same level of protection. You paid a lot of money for those clubs, so you need to protect them from rough handling while they're being loaded or unloaded by baggage handlers.

Golf as side trip

NO ONE SAYS GOLF has to be the focal point of your vacation. You might prefer to go on a sightseeing or camping trip with your family or friends. You may decide to take a road trip to a nearby national park and do some hiking and camping out under the stars. By all means, plan to take a trip like this. But there's no rule against taking your clubs along with you, is there?

Pack your clubs, just in case...

Before you leave on your non-golf vacation, do a little checking to see if there are any good courses close to where you are headed.

You never know – a great golf course might be ten minutes away from your destination. If you forget to take your clubs, you'll want to kick yourself when you pass that beautiful course on your way to somewhere else. Take my advice and pack those clubs. You just never know!

If you leave home without your clubs and then find a course you *must* play, stop in and see if they have clubs to rent in the pro shop. Pro shops sometimes have a few sets for the clubless guest.

Visiting the great courses

GOLF HAS A RICH PAGEANT *of history that goes back hundreds of years. Much of it is enshrined within the boundaries of a few dozen renowned golf courses around the world. Some of these hallowed courses are in the United Kingdom, and others are right here in the United States – the country with the most courses, by far.*

Fulfilling your dreams

Most of us work for a living and may never have the time and money to visit some of these courses. Even if you could, a good number of them are private country clubs that won't even allow you on the grounds, let alone play a round. Such is the nature of privilege and wealth. Luckily, some of these historic courses are open to the general public, provided you can pay the often high green fees. Think of it: vacationing in Scotland and actually getting to play a round of golf on the Old Course at St. Andrews! It can be done. St. Andrews is actually open to the public. You can arrange a package trip to the area and play golf on the mother of all courses. Now that would be a vacation!

INTERNET

www.gto.com

Check out Golf Travel Online for access to nearly anything you need to know about taking a golf vacation.

■ **Founded in 1754,** *the Royal and Ancient Golf Club of St. Andrews is widely regarded as the home of golf. This view up the 18th fairway toward the magnificent clubhouse is recognized the world over.*

The 20 most famous courses in the world

Most of these famous golf courses are not open to the public, but as an avid golfer you ought to know about them anyway. That way, when you win the lottery you can join one of them and disappear forever within the confines of its lush, rolling fairways.

In the following list, the name of the course is listed first, followed by the city and state, or city and country, where it's located. For those venues with more than one course, the individual course name has been placed in parentheses.

Augusta: *Augusta, Georgia*
Perhaps the most well-known of the famous U.S. courses, immaculate Augusta was the brainchild of Bobby Jones, the greatest amateur golfer of all time. Don't even think of trying to get a tee time at this extremely private course.

BALLYBUNION (OLD COURSE), IRELAND

Ballybunion (Old Course): *Ballybunion, Ireland*
Another timeless course, Ballybunion is a public venue that costs only about $70 to play.

Baltusrol Golf Club (Lower): *Springfield, New Jersey*
Built in 1895 by A. W. Tillinghast, this private beauty has undulating greens and tree-lined fairways. Baltusrol was the scene of many PGA competitions during the 20th century.

Carnoustie (Championship Course): *Carnoustie, Scotland*
Located along the east coast of Scotland, this famous course was designed, in part, by a legendary Scottish golfer named Old Tom Morris. The site of the 1999 British Open, Carnoustie is a public venue and will cost you about $85 to play.

The Country Club: *Brookline, Massachusetts*
Over 100 years old, this beautiful private course has small greens and beautiful tree-lined fairways. The Country Club hosted the 1999 Ryder Cup Championship.

Cypress Point Club: *Pebble Beach, California*
A beautiful seaside course, Cypress Point's beauty and challenge may be unmatched. It, too, is a private course.

CYPRESS POINT CLUB, CALIFORNIA

Merion Golf Course (East):
Ardmore, Pennsylvania
A private, parkland-style course, Merion was the site of many great PGA tournaments in the 20th century.

Muirfield: Gullane, Scotland
This historic private course in golf's mother country is as difficult and venerable as it is beautiful.

MUIRFIELD, SCOTLAND

National Golf Links of America: Southampton, New York
A course with water in play on some holes, this superb private venue on the shores of Peconic Bay, Long Island, is an American classic.

Oakmont Country Club: Oakmont, Pennsylvania
A parkland course rich in competitive history, Oakmont is a private club.

Olympic Club (Lake Course): San Francisco, California
A true test of a golfer's skills, the tree-lined holes of the Lake Course at Olympic are beautiful, but – oddly – no water comes into play despite the name. This is a private venue.

Pebble Beach: Pebble Beach, California
Located close to Cypress Point, this is perhaps the most legendary course in the United States. The nearby Pacific Ocean makes Pebble Beach both breathtaking and difficult to play. It's a resort, which means the public can play there, although the greens fee is now approaching $300 a round.

PEBBLE BEACH, CALIFORNIA

Pinehurst Country Club #2: Pinehurst, North Carolina
This beautiful, traditionally designed, pine-laden course is a resort destination that you can play on, provided you are willing to part with several hundred dollars for the greens fee alone.

Pine Valley: Clementon, New Jersey
A private course, Pine Valley reeks of tradition and golf nostalgia. Built in 1918, it has both sand and grass bunkers and the highest slope rating in the country – a whopping 153!

Royal Birkdale: Southport, England
The site of the 1998 British Open, this windswept course is famous for its huge sand dunes. Royal Birkdale is a private facility.

Royal Melbourne: Melbourne, Australia
Beautiful and treacherous, this private course is regularly rated as the finest course in Australia and one of the world's top ten.

Shinnecock Hills: Southampton, New York
This old, windswept layout is steeped in tradition and beauty. Shinnecock Hills is a private course.

St. Andrews (Old Course): St. Andrews, Scotland
The cradle of golf as we know it, this course on the east coast of Scotland is treeless, stark, and beautiful, as well as challenging. Fortunately, it is a public course, with a greens fee of about $120.

Turnberry (Ailsa Course): Turnberry, Scotland
This historic course is a resort that can be played by the public for about $135.

Winged Foot Golf Course (West): Mamaroneck, New York
This picturesque private course in suburban New York was designed and built by the famous A. W. Tillinghast in 1923. It has narrow, tree-lined fairways that make accuracy a must.

TURNBERRY, SCOTLAND

Twenty famous courses you can play

Many of the world's most famous courses are private and don't want the likes of us around. So what? Who needs them? Many legendary U.S. courses are open to the public, so you and I can play them. Most of them are pretty expensive, but a few are actually reasonable and allow you to play the course more than once for the same fee.

Because fees change, I've given a price range for each course rather than a specific amount. I'll mark the range like this:

◉	under $25
◉◉	$25 to $50
◉◉◉	$50 to $100
◉◉◉◉	$100 to $150
◉◉◉◉◉	more than $150

■ Nothing can surpass *the thrill of taking your first tee shot on a world famous course.*

Pinon Hills Golf Course: Farmington, New Mexico
◉

This municipal course, built by Ken Dye in 1989, is a remarkably well-designed high desert course that players just can't say enough good things about. Generally thought to be the best course for the least amount of money in the country, Pinon Hills charges a mere $13 per round. If you are ever in the area, it is a must play.

Bethpage State Golf Course (Black Course): Farmingdale, New York
◉◉

Possibly the finest municipally run course in the nation, the Black course, built by A. W. Tillinghast in 1936, is a true test of any golfer's skills. With lots of hills and a course rating of 75.4, this course is not for the beginner but is a great bargain at less than $30. The Black course will host the U.S. Open in 2002.

Edinburgh, USA Golf Course: Brooklyn Park, Minnesota
◉◉

A beautiful, challenging course with scenic lakes in play on many holes, this public course is a gem at a bargain price.

Torrey Pines Golf Course, San Diego, California
◉◉

A great municipal course, Torrey Pines has beautiful views of the Pacific Ocean. It hosts the PGA Buick Invitational each year. Try it if you're ever in the area – the price won't bankrupt you.

Cog Hill #4: Lemont, Illinois

Known for its large oak trees and sloping greens, this course hosts the annual Motorola Western Open for the PGA Tour players. Played from the championship tees, Cog Hill #4 is a real challenge for even the scratch golfer.

La Cantera Golf Club: San Antonio, Texas

Designed by Tom Weiskopf and Jay Moorish, this breathtakingly beautiful venue uses streams and waterfalls as water hazards. It also is home to a golf school.

Pumpkin Ridge (Ghost Creek Course): Cornelius, Oregon

A beautiful public course with an artificial creek meandering through it, this layout has trees, water, and lots of hilly lies to make a round here challenging as well as memorable.

World Woods: Brookville, Florida

Tight, difficult, and beautiful, this Tom Fazio design has lots of pine trees and large waste areas that must be cleared on a number of tee shots.

Coeur D'Alene Golf Resort: Coeur D'Alene, Idaho

This beautiful course is famous for its floating 14th green, as well as its watery driving range, which uses floating range balls. The course is perfectly manicured and beautiful.

Kapalua Plantation Course: Maui, Hawaii

A scenic, hilly course, the Lincoln Mercury Kapalua International PGA Tournament is held here each year. A splendid layout, it deserves a try if you are a good golfer with deep pockets.

La Quinta Resort: La Quinta, California

A Pete Dye design, the courses at this beautiful resort are challenging due to extensive bunkering and the hilly terrain. If you have the money and the time, go to La Quinta.

■ **Be sure to** *consider the course rating, as some have hazards that challenge even the top players.*

■ **Follow in the footsteps** *of the professionals and play at courses that have hosted famous tournaments.*

Pasatiempo Golf Course: Santa Cruz, California
◉◉◉◉

Built by the famed Alister MacKenzie in 1929, this beautiful public venue has rolling hills and trees that make it an extremely challenging 18 holes of golf.

The Tournament Player's Course at Sawgrass: Ponte Vedra, Florida
◉◉◉◉

This Pete Dye-designed course hosts the annual Player's Championship each year, a hotly contested tournament of the world's best players. You can play here if you stay at the resort.

Harbour Town Golf Links Course: Hilton Head Island, South Carolina
◉◉◉◉◉

Home to the annual MCI Heritage Classic tournament, this wonderful, challenging course has lots of water, sloping greens, and spectacular scenery.

The Links at Spanish Bay: Pebble Beach, California
◉◉◉◉◉

A Robert Trent Jones Jr. design, this splendid ocean-side course has all the beauty that the Monterey coast has to offer. Spanish Bay also has the unique privilege of being an official Audubon Society bird sanctuary.

Pebble Beach: Pebble Beach, California
◉◉◉◉◉

I already described this course for you in the world-famous list. The 18th hole is one of the classic finishers. It curves around Monterey Bay, so the Pacific Ocean is in play all the way from the tee.

Pinehurst Country Club #2: Pinehurst, North Carolina
◉◉◉◉◉

The site of the 1999 U.S. Open, #2 is a par-72 course. This course was described in the world-famous list.

Pinehurst #7: Pinehurst, North Carolina
◉◉◉◉◉

A modern Rees Jones design with lots of sloping terrain, the #7 course is a tough, fair test of any golfer's skills. Rated at 75.6 from the championship tees, you had better be a decent golfer if you plan a trip to this public resort course.

Spyglass Hill: Pebble Beach, California

A sister course to Pebble Beach, Spyglass is a gem that plays up and down a steep slope known as Spyglass Hill. Water is in play on numerous holes. Like Pebble Beach, Spyglass is a resort course.

Troon North: Scottsdale, Arizona

A spectacular high desert course, Troon North may be the most well-maintained public venue in the country. Though pricey, it is worth the expense.

A simple summary

✓ Whatever part of the world you want to vacation in, there is probably a great golf course waiting for you.

✓ Make sure to call in advance and find out if your golf game is good enough to be allowed to play the vacation course you want to visit. Most courses will accommodate beginners, but some might be a bit too challenging for those just starting out in the game.

✓ Golf resorts have popped up all over the world. Package deals abound, making the price of a week in paradise affordable for most of us.

✓ Pack light, but be sure to bring your protective golfing gear and pack up your clubs in a special case so they don't get bashed around in transit.

✓ Even if you decide not to make golf the main theme of your vacation, there is usually a good course close to most vacation destinations. Consider bringing your clubs along just in case.

✓ Golf's legendary courses have helped shape the game. If you have the opportunity, visit a few to see what golfing tradition is all about.

✓ A good number of famous courses are open to the public. If you have the money, you can play a round or two on one of these historic venues. You won't soon forget it.

More Resources

Golf organizations

Association of Disabled American Golfers
P.O. Box 280649
Lakewood, CO 80228-0649
(303) 922-5228
discovercolorado.com

Golf Writers Association of America
P.O. Box 328054
Farmington Hills, MI 48332
(313) 442-1481
www.gwaa.com

Ladies Professional Golf Association
2570 W. International Speedway Blvd.
Suite B
Daytona Beach, FL 32114
(904) 254-8800
www.lpga.com

Minority Golf Association of America
P.O. Box 1081
Westhampton Beach, NY 11978
(516) 288-8255
www.mgaa.com

PGA Tour
112 TPC Blvd., Sawgrass
Ponte Vedra Beach, FL 32082
(904) 285-3700
www.pgatour.com

Professional Golfers' Association (PGA)
100 Avenue of the Champions #109601
Palm Beach Gardens, FL 33410
(407) 624-8400
www.pga.com

United States Golf Association (USGA)
P.O. Box 708
Far Hills, NJ 07931
(908) 234-2300
www.usga.com

Magazines

Golf magazines are fun to read and will help you stay in touch with what's going on in the sport. Subscriptions to the best golf magazines are relatively inexpensive and are well worth the price. Timely commentary on recent or upcoming tournaments, player profiles, instruction and advice from well-known players, and monthly reviews of the latest clubs, balls, and other equipment are provided in these publications.

Be careful not to take every little piece of advice you read in books and magazines to heart. Sometimes a piece of advice can be wrong for you. Each golfer's swing is like a fingerprint, and it's not wise to try to make everyone fit into the same precise form. If the book or article is written by a player or teacher you trust, then give what he or she says a try. Always bow to the information your own teacher gives you, though, because he or she is much more familiar with your own individual swing and the challenges you alone face.

VIP

Golf Digest
P.O. Box 2029
Harlan, IA 51537-2029
(800) 727-4653
www.golfdigest.com

Golf Illustrated
5300 CityPlex Tower
2448 E. 81st St.
Tulsa, OK 74137-4207
(918) 491-6100
www.golfillustrated.com

Golf Magazine
2 Park Ave.
Harlan, IA 51537-2029
(800) 727-4653
www.golfdigest.com

Golf Tips
Werner Publishing Corporation
12121 Wilshire Blvd., 12th Floor
Los Angeles, CA 90025-1176
(310) 820-1500
www.golftipsmag.com

Golfweek
7657 Commerce Center Dr.
Orlando, FL 32819-8923
(407) 345-5500
www.golfweek.com

Golf World
P.O. Box 2029
Harlan, IA 51537-2029
(800) 727-4653

Books

For the beginner, it's probably a good idea to buy a few books covering the fundamentals of the game (this book is a good first choice). Books can only give you a general idea of technique, though. To really learn the game, you should take some lessons, play, and practice.

Look for books written by a player or teacher you look up to. Although most books "written" by players are, in fact, written by an anonymous co-author, most of the information in them comes directly from the player or teacher, who always makes sure that every sentence is true to his or her philosophy.

Ben Hogan's Five Lessons: The Modern Fundamentals of Golf
by Ben Hogan, Simon & Schuster, 1990

Corey Pavin's Shotmaking
by Corey Pavin, Pocket Books, 1997

Golf My Way
by Jack Nicklaus, Fireside Press, 1998

Harvey Penick's Little Red Golf Book: Lessons and Teachings From a Lifetime in Golf
by Harvey Penick, Simon & Schuster, 1992

How to Play Your Best Golf All the Time
by Tommy Armour, Simon & Schuster, 1995

The Pocket Guide to Golf Practice Drills
by Peter Ballingall, Dorling Kindersley Publishing, 1995

Faldo: A Swing for Life
by Nick Faldo, Viking Penguin Books, 1995

Ultimate Golf Techniques
by Malcolm Campbell, Dorling Kindersley Publishing, 1998

Golf schools

The Academy of Golf at the
PGA National Resort and Spa
  1000 Avenue of the Champions
  Palm Beach Gardens, FL 33418
  (800) 832-6235
  www.pgagolfacademy.com

America's Favorite Golf Schools
  P.O. Box 3325
  Fort Pierce, FL 34948
  (800) 365-6640
  www.afgs.com

Arnold Palmer Golf Academy
  Bay Hill Club
  9000 Bay Hill Blvd.
  Orlando, FL 32819
  (800) 523-5999
  www.apga.com

Balance Point Golf Schools
  65278 Stockton Rd.
  Enterprise, OR 97828
  (800) 898-4563
  www.balancepointgolf.com

Bill Skelley School of Golf
  1847 E. John Sims Pkwy.
  Niceville, FL 32578
  (800) 541-7707
  www.billskelley.com

Brad Dean Golf Academy
at Crystal Mountain Resort
  12500 Crystal Mountain Dr.
  Thompsonville, MI 49683
  (800) 968-7686
  www.crystalmtn.com

Classic Swing Golf School
    1705 Platt Blvd.
    Surfside Beach, SC 29575
    (800) 827-2656
    www.classicswing.com

Dave Pelz Short Game School
    Boca Raton Resort and Club
    P.O. Box 5025
    Boca Raton, FL 33431
    (800) 833-7370
    www.davepelz.com

David Leadbetter Golf Academy
    5500 34th St. West
    Bradenton, FL 34210
    (941) 755-1000
    www.leadbetter.com

Faldo Golf Institute by Marriott
    11501 International Dr.
    Orlando, FL 32821
    (888) GO-FALDO
    www.gofaldo.com

Golf Digest Schools
    5520 Park Ave.
    Trumbull, CT 06611
    (800) 243-6121
    www.golfdigest.com

Golf University of San Diego
    17550 Bernard Oaks Dr.
    San Diego, CA 92128
    (800) 426-0966
    www.golfuniversity.com

Harvey Penick Golf Academy by Golfsmith
    11000 N. IH 35
    Austin, TX 78753
    (800) 500-9536
    www.golfsmith.com

John Jacobs' Golf School
    7825 E. Redfield Rd.
    Scottsdale, AZ 85260
    (800) 472-5007
    www.jacobsgolf.com

Ken Venturi Golf Academy
    3200 S.R. 546
    P.O. Box 7010
    Haines City, FL 33844
    (800) 543-7084
    www.kenventuri.com

Mike McGetrick Golf Academy
    Meridian Golf Club
    9742 Meridian Blvd.
    Englewood, CO 80112
    (800) 494-1818
    www.mcgetrickgolf.com

Natural Golf Schools
    2400 W. Hassell Rd.
    Hoffman Estates, IL 60195
    (888) NAT-GOLF
    www.naturalgolf.com

Nicklaus/Flick Golf Schools
    11780 U.S. Highway One
    North Palm Beach, FL 33408
    (800) 642-5528
    www.nicklaus.com

Stratton Golf School
    RR1, Box 145
    Stratton Mountain, VT 05155
    (800) 787-2886
    www.stratton.com

Golf on the Web

THE INTERNET OFFERS YOU *countless sites where you can learn about all things golf. Type "golf" (without the quotes) into your favorite search engine and see what you get. When I tried, I got 1,533,453 web sites — more than you could ever check in a lifetime. When I did the same for football, I got 1,291,250 sites, but only 634,180 for fishing. Ha! I guess it's clear what the world's most popular recreational sport is!*

The Internet can be a wild, free-for-all kind of place with both good guys and bad guys. The bad guys are known to create and distribute computer viruses to as many home users as possible, often through e-mail programs. To combat these evil lunatics, be sure to have a good antivirus program installed on your hard drive right from the start. The best programs will automatically search for, quarantine, and destroy all known viruses trying to infect your system, allowing you to sleep easier at night. You will be able to get regular virus updates from the manufacturer over the Internet, keeping your system as protected as possible from emerging viruses.

VIP

www.allprogreens.com
If you're just dying to put a driving range in your backyard, a number of companies sell artificial putting greens and driving-range mats, including All Pro Putting Greens.

www.buygolf.com
This great online retail store, provides visitors with the best golf equipment at reasonable prices. As a bonus, they also provide information on the PGA Tour. BuyGolf has a nifty fantasy golf game that lets you play against the pros, too.

www.cegolf.com
Check out this site for great information on all aspects of the game, including ways to improve.

www.cheapgolfballs.com
Reconditioned golf balls are sold here.

www.dmcsoft.com/sgts/
If you want to make a pilgrimage to the birthplace of golf, Tayleur Mayde's web site offers golf vacations to Scotland's legendary courses.

www.duffer.com
For a complete list of instructional golf books and videos that will help you learn proper alignment, as well as other important fundamentals, check out this site.

www.global-fitness.com
At Global Fitness you can find just about any information you seek relating to strength training, aerobic conditioning, nutrition, or any other exercise topic.

www.globalgolfguide.com
Global Golf Guide is a worldwide golf course locator. You can also make golf travel plans through this site. It provides a panoramic, virtual reality tour option, enabling you to see courses, resorts, and planned golf communities as you have never seen them before.

www.golf.com
This site has a comprehensive collection of golf information, including advice, tournament results and statistics, equipment reviews, golf real estate,

course descriptions, golf for kids, golf classified ads, and travel info. Nearly anything you are looking for can be found right here or through the links provided.

www.golfacademy.com
Golf Academy has plenty of instructional information on chips, pitches, and all other aspects of the game.

www.golfball.com
You'll find tips on golfing fundamentals, information on new equipment, and articles on virtually every aspect of the game at this site.

www.golfballs.com
You can buy a huge assortment of golf balls in just about every color and material you can think of from this site.

www.golfballzone.com
This site sells a huge assortment of new and reconditioned golf balls.

www.golfcourse.com
This directory of thousands of courses in the United States includes brief course descriptions, fees, yardage, slope, par, and course rating for every course.

golfcircuit.com
A comprehensive site, Golfcircuit also provides golf fans with a search engine specifically geared to golf sites.

www.golfdigest.com
The web version of today's most comprehensive golf magazine, this site is arranged in a magazine-style format and tells visitors all they need to know about professional golf, as well as instruction, product reviews, great golf vacations, and upcoming trends in the industry. Links to many other sites are also included.

www.golfdirect.com
The North American Golf Directory lists golf courses, resorts, schools, and even golf condos for all 50 states.

www.golfonline.com
This jam-packed, comprehensive site also covers the editorial side of competitive golf and has a magazine-style format similar to its very successful print sister, *Golf Magazine*. Instructional information, product reviews, and trends are all covered here.

www.golfresorts.com
There are more than 600 links to golf resorts around the world on this site. Information is provided by the individual resorts.

www.golfschoolinfo.com
You can find some of the best golf schools in the country at this site.

www.golfsmith.com
One of the best retail online sites, Golfsmith has just about everything you need, at very reasonable prices. Come here to check out the latest equipment.

www.golftipsmag.com
Golf Tips magazine's site offers information on all the fundamentals, including proper setup, stance, and ball position.

www.golfweb.com
Focusing on the professional side of the sport, Golfweb also offers visitors information about traveling and provides access to golf games. A newsletter is provided, as is an interactive question-and-answer feature.

www.golfweek.com
One of the country's premiere online and print golf magazines, *Golfweek* provides the reader with more up-to-date statistical data on the players than any other site. It uses a magazine format and specializes in covering all of the professional golf tours.

www.gto.com
Check out Golf Travel Online for access to nearly anything you need to know about taking a golf vacation.

www.igogolf.com
The International Golf Outlet sells a lot of everything to do with golf, including clothes. There are pictures of all the merchandise, so you can see before you buy.

www.linkstime.com
You can plan your next golf outing from this new Internet reservation site, which is tied into thousands of golf courses across the country and overseas. By logging on, you'll be able to reserve a tee time on your favorite local course or on that great resort course you've been dreaming about for years. The fee for doing so is only $1.50 each time. Using this site saves

you the hassle of waiting on the phone, and it also lets you reserve a tee time much further in advance than is allowable over the phone.

www.lpga.com

The official site of the LPGA Tour, which is the home organization for female golf professionals in the United States. You'll find everything you need to know about LPGA tournaments or players is here.

www.missilegolf.com

For something completely different, Peace Missile offers golf clubs made from Russian and U.S. nuclear missile parts. Then you can really nuke the balls.

www.mrgolf.com

This is the homepage of Mr. Golf Etiquette, who will tell you everything you need to know about playing by the rules and being courteous on the course.

www.npursuit.com

This is the home page of N-Pursuit, which makes George Low Silver Wiz putters with silver inserts in the face. Obviously, this is a high-ticket item.

www.pelzgolf.com

You'll find great advice and instructions on putting, as well as other aspects of the short game, at this site.

www.pgacom

The PGA (Professional Golf Association) of America, one of the two biggest golf governing bodies in America, hosts this site. Here you'll find news on equipment, tournaments, rule changes, player info, and a ton of other interesting tidbits.

www.pgatour.com

This is the official site for the PGA Tour. You can find anything you want to know on tournament results, instruction, or player profiles. Senior Tour information is also available.

www.putt.com

From this site of links (sorry about the pun!), you can access zillions of other golf web pages.

www.shippeddirect.com

If you want to find a job in the golfing industry, visit this site. It provides all sorts of information and listings to help you do just that.

www.st-duffer.com

Learn about Saint Duffer, patron saint of frustrated golfers, who has been known to work miracles on the course.

www.teachkidsgolf.com

This site shows video clips of all the basic swing elements. Although it's designed with the younger golfer in mind, it's the perfect primer for adults as well.

www.thegolfballplace.com

You can buy golf balls in just about every color and material you can think of from the huge assortment available on this site.

www.usagolflinks.com

This is a great site for those looking for information on just about any golf course in the nation. It also provides a newsletter, as well as information on the history of golf.

www.usga.org

This official site of the United States Golf Association includes a complete rule book, an explanation of the handicap system, tournament structures, and a virtual tour of the golf museum. You can also find out how to join the USGA, which has millions of members.

www.virtual-fairway.com

New and reconditioned golf balls are sold on this site.

www.worldgolf.com

World Golf is a huge site with information on golf tournaments and courses around the world. It also offers a good section on the history of golf.

www.xgolf.com

Chat with fellow golfers; sound off about the rules, equipment, and what ticks you off; and learn the lingo and more on this somewhat unorthodox site.

Your Scores

PHOTOCOPY THIS PAGE *and use it to record your score after each game you play. This information will be invaluable for assessing your progress. Watch your scores come tumbling down as your skills improve!*
After each game remember to note:

1. The name of the course
2. Par on the day you played
3. Total number of strokes you took
4. Total number of putts you took
5. Weather conditions

Course Name	Par	Strokes	Putts	Sun	Rain	Wind
_____				○	○	○
_____				○	○	○
_____				○	○	○
_____				○	○	○
_____				○	○	○
_____				○	○	○
_____				○	○	○
_____				○	○	○
_____				○	○	○
_____				○	○	○
_____				○	○	○
_____				○	○	○
_____				○	○	○
_____				○	○	○
_____				○	○	○
_____				○	○	○
_____				○	○	○
_____				○	○	○

A Simple Glossary

Ace A hole-in-one.

Address The unique way you position your body just before hitting the ball.

Alignment How you aim your club face and body at address.

Amateur A person who does not earn any money for playing golf.

Approach shot A shot that brings your ball onto the green.

Away Being farthest from the hole.

Baby shot When you hit a shot softer and shorter than is usual for a particular club.

Back nine The second half of your 18-hole round.

Backspin Reverse spin put on the golf ball when it is hit.

Backswing The first part of the swing, which ends when the club stops above your head.

Bag What you carry your clubs in. Usually cylindrical, most bags have pockets added on, enabling you to carry everything you need for the day.

Balata Tree sap that was once used to make covers for golf balls.

Ball marker Any small, flat object used to mark the position of your ball on the green.

Ball-mark repair tool A forked tool used to fix the mark your ball leaves on the green when it lands.

Baseball grip A way to hold the club that keeps all ten fingers in contact with the grip of the club.

Best ball A game using the best score from a two-person team as the score that counts.

Birdie Playing a hole in one stroke less than par.

Blade An iron's club head. Also, striking the ball on its equator with the bottom of the blade.

Blocked shot Hitting the ball straight and to the right of the target (for a right-handed golfer).

Bogey Playing a hole in one stroke more than par.

Bounce The metal hump that hangs down below the leading edge of a sand wedge.

Break The amount of turn a putted ball makes on the green.

Breaking down When your wrist bends during a putt.

Bump-and-run A type of shot that flies part of the way to the target, then bounces and rolls the rest of the way.

Bunker A sand-filled hazard near the green or on the fairway.

Caddie A person paid to carry your golf bag and give you advice on how to play a hole.

Carry How far a ball flies in the air.

Cart Either a small motorized vehicle used to drive around the course, or a small two-wheeled dolly you can strap your bag to and pull around the course. The manually operated cart is usually referred to as a pull-cart.

Casual water Water that has collected on the course, other than in a hazard.

Cavity-back iron A type of iron that has most of the weight of the club head located around its perimeter, to create a larger head and a larger sweet spot on the face. The back of the club head is essentially a large cavity, which reduces mass in the center and back of the head.

Certified PGA professional A qualified teaching professional who meets or exceeds the teaching standards set by the Professional Golfer's Association of America.

Check When the ball stops rolling because of the backspin on it.

Chip A low-running shot typically played from near the edge of the green toward the hole.

Closed face When the club face is pointing to the left of the intended target (for a right-handed golfer).

Closed stance When your body alignment is pointing to the right of the intended target (for a right-handed golfer).

Club face The part of the club head that makes contact with the ball.

Clubhouse The large building on the grounds of a golf course that usually houses the pro shop, a restaurant, restrooms, and some type of meeting room.

Collar A strip of grass around the green that is longer than the grass of the putting surface. *See* Fringe.

Coming over the top When, on the downswing, the path of the club head tends to move in a right-to-left motion across the ball (for a right-handed golfer). Also called an out-to-in blow.

Compression The squeezing or flattening of the golf ball at impact.

Course rating A number that defines a course's level of difficulty. Higher is harder.

Crossed over Having your club shaft pointing to the right of your target at the top of your backswing (for a right-handed golfer).

Cross-handed A putting grip that puts the left hand below the right (for a right-handed player).

Cup The hole in the putting green that you strive to put your ball into.

Cupped lead wrist When you hit with a cupped lead wrist, you are bending your lead hand backward.

The lead hand is the one closest to the hole when you set up to swing. That's the left hand for a right-handed golfer.

Cut Another term for a shot that bends to the right (for a right-handed golfer).

Deloft Decreasing the loft of a club face by tilting the club shaft toward the target.

Dimple One of hundreds of small indentations on the golf ball.

Divot A small strip of turf removed by the club head during a swing.

Dogleg A hole where the path from tee to cup turns left or right.

Double bogey Finishing a hole in two more shots than par.

Double eagle Finishing a hole in three shots less than par on a par-5 hole.

Downhill lie A lie in which your front foot is below your rear foot at address.

Draw A shot that bends slightly to the left (for a right-handed golfer).

Drive The shot taken off the tee.

Driver The longest club in your bag. The driver usually hits the ball the farthest.

Driving range A place to hit practice balls.

Drop Placing a ball back into play after it was deemed unplayable.

Duff To completely miss or mess up a shot.

Eagle Finishing a hole in two under par for a par-4 or par-5. It's also possible to eagle a par-3, but that's called an ace. *See* Ace.

Executive course A nine-hole, par-3 course that can be played in about 90 minutes.

Explosion shot A shot from a bunker that displaces a large amount of sand.

Fade A shot that bends slightly to the right (for a right-handed golfer).

Fairway The closely mown area of grass running from the tee to the green.

Fat Hitting the ground before you strike the ball.

Flagstick The flagged pole that sticks out of the hole on each green.

Flex The amount of bend in a club shaft.

Flier lie What you end up with when grass comes between the club face and the ball, reducing the amount of backspin on the ball.

Flop shot A type of pitch shot that travels high up into the air and lands softly.

Follow-through The path of your swing after you have made impact with the ball.

Fore A warning call you should shout when your ball is headed for a person.

Forged steel blade A club where the head is made of softer forged steel, instead of the harder cast steel cavity-back irons are made of.

Fringe The collar of grass surrounding the green, usually shorter in length than the fairway but longer than the green itself. *See* Collar.

Front nine The first nine holes on an 18-hole golf course.

Gimme A very short putt that your playing partners do not require you to hit because it's so obvious that it will go in.

Glove Usually worn on the lead hand (the left hand for a right-handed golfer) to enhance your grip and prevent blisters.

Grain The direction in which grass is growing.

Green The closely mown round or oblong area of grass that surrounds the cup; the putting surface.

Green in regulation Putting your ball onto the green of a par-3 hole in one shot, onto a par-4 green in two, or onto a par-5 green in three.

Greens fee The amount of money you must pay to play a round of golf.

Grip The manner in which you hold the club. Also, the rubber covering on the club shaft where you hold it.

Grooves The etched-in lines on the face of a club, there to impart backspin on the ball.

Ground under repair An area of a course under repair, from which you may get relief. *See* Relief.

Handicap A score adjustment system allowing those of differing skill levels to compete.

Hard pan Hard-packed ground or turf.

Hazard A penalizing area of sand or water in which you may not ground your club.

Hole *See* Cup.

Holed out When the ball falls into the cup.

Honor The privilege of going first.

Hook A shot that bends to the left (for a right-handed golfer).

Hosel The part of the club head that attaches to the club shaft.

Impact The moment at which the club face contacts the ball.

Impediment Any loose debris that can be moved away from your ball.

Interlocking grip A grip linking the index finger of one hand and the pinky of the other.

Iron Any club with a metallic blade for a club head. Most players carry at least nine or ten irons, ranging from a 2- or 3-iron to a sand wedge. The different clubs provide different degrees of loft.

Lag putt A long putt intended to end up within a foot or two of the hole.

Laid off When your club shaft points to the left of the target at the top of your backswing (for a right-handed golfer).

Lay up A shot intentionally hit short of the green to avoid trouble.

Lie The condition of the ground that your ball sits on (or in). Also, the spot where your ball rests on the course after a shot.

Lip out When the ball enters the hole on the very edge and, instead of dropping in, swirls around the circumference of the cup and pops back out due to excess centrifugal force.

Loft The angle a club face makes with the ground. Also, how high up in the air a particular club will hit a ball.

Matchplay The original way golf was played. The game is played hole by hole. If you score lower on the first hole than your opponent, you win the hole, and go "one up." If you win the second hole, you go two up, and so on. If you lose a hole, you go "one down." If you tie a hole, you "halve" the hole. The outcome of the match is decided when you are either up or down by more holes than there are left to play. For instance, if you are four up with only three holes left, you win the match.

Mulligan An illegal second attempt at a botched shot; often used in a casual round of golf among friends.

Municipal course A course owned and operated by a local government. Also called a muni.

Muscle memory A physical phenomenon that enables your body to perform an action repeatedly in exactly the same way every time without consciously thinking about it.

Nuked shot When you hit a shot harder and longer than is usual for a particular club.

Neutral grip A grip in which a right-handed player can see two knuckles of the left hand when looking down at the grip itself while addressing the ball.

Neutral stance When your feet are on a line parallel to the target line.

Open face A club face aligned to the right of the target (for a right-handed player).

Open stance When your body alignment is pointing to the left of the target (for a right-handed golfer) at setup.

Out-of-bounds An area outside the grounds of a course, usually marked by white stakes.

Out-to-in blow *See* Coming over the top.

Overlapping grip A grip fitting the pinky finger of the top hand over the index finger of the bottom hand.

Pairing sheet A list of the players in each group of a tournament, and what time those groups are scheduled to tee off.

Par What a good player should shoot on a hole, or for a round.

Pin Another word for flagstick.

Pitch A lofted short shot to the green with a little run at the end of its flight.

Pitch-mark Repair tool. *See* Ball-mark repair tool.

Plumb-bob A technique used to help determine the break of a putt.

Pre-shot routine The ritualistic procedure performed before every shot.

Primary rough The first cut of longer grass you encounter when leaving the fairway.

Private club A golf club open only to members and their guests.

Pro-am A tournament that teams up professionals and amateurs.

Professional Someone who is paid for playing golf.

Pro shop The store in the clubhouse where you check in to play and can buy equipment.

Provisional shot A second shot, hit when you think the first ball might be lost. If you find the ball, the provisional shot does not count.

Public course A golf course that anyone can play on for a fee. *See* Greens fee.

Pull A straight shot that goes to the left of the target (for a right-handed player).

Punch shot A low recovery shot, usually hit out of some type of trouble.

Push A straight shot hit to the right of the target (by a right-handed golfer).

Putter A straight-faced club normally used to hit the ball on the putting green.

Range A practice area, often located on or near the course.

Release The moment during the downswing when your wrists uncock.

Relief The right to move a ball away from trouble without incurring a penalty stroke.

Reverse overlap grip A standard putting grip that places the index finger of the left hand over the pinky of the right (for a right-handed golfer).

Rough Grass allowed to grow longer than that of the fairway.

Round A complete course of nine or 18 holes of golf.

Run How far a ball bounces and rolls after touching down.

Score How many shots you took to play the course.

Scorecard The card on which you keep score, and on which you find course statistics.

Scramble A game in which four players on a team tee off, then choose the best shot of the four as the spot from which all players will take their next shot. This continues until the ball is holed out.

Scratch golfer A golfer who regularly shoots par on a course.

Secondary rough The thicker rough you encounter after the primary rough.

Setup *See* Address.

Shaft The long, thin part of the club that provides most of the energy of a golf shot.

Shag bag A bag for holding practice balls. The bag is designed so that you can pick up your balls without bending over.

Shank A shot where the hosel of the club head makes impact with the ball, instead of the face.

Short game Shots played less than 50 yards from the green.

Sidehill lie A lie in which the ball is either above or below your feet at address

Skied A tee shot that goes almost straight up in the air.

Slice A shot that bends to the right of the target line (for a right-handed player).

Slope A number given to every golf course describing its level of difficulty. The average slope of courses in the United States is 113. The various contours of a putting green are also referred to collectively as the slope.

Spikes Special shoes you wear that prevent your feet from slipping and sliding during a swing. Small plastic, rubber, or metal cleats are fastened to the sole of the shoe.

Square stance When your club head is perpendicular to the target line and your feet, hips, and shoulders are all parallel to the same line.

Splash The standard bunker shot, in which the sand wedge splashes out a divot of sand and with it the ball.

Stance The position of your feet at address.

Starter The person in charge of sending players out onto the course.

Stroke One swing of the club.

Stroke play The most common way to determine the winner in a round of golf. Whoever takes the fewest strokes to complete the course wins.

Strong grip A grip in which a player sees more than two knuckles of the left hand; it is used to turn the ball to the left.

Surlyn An artificial material used to make the covers of most golf balls.

Sweet spot The small center portion of the club face where the ball should make contact for maximum distance and accuracy.

Swing plane The angle of the club shaft relative to your body during the swing.

Tap-in A short, easy putt of no more than a foot.

Target line The imaginary line running from the ball to your intended target.

Tee A wooden, rubber, or plastic device used to prop the ball up for the first shot of a hole.

Tee box The area from which you hit the first shot of a hole.

Tee shot The shot you take off the tee.

Tee time The time at which you and your group begin your round.

Ten-finger grip *See* Baseball grip.

Texas wedge A putter.

Thin Hitting the ball on its equator, causing it to have a low trajectory.

Through the green The entire course, not including the hazards, tee boxes, and putting greens.

Top Hitting the ball above its equator, causing it to travel only a short distance.

Torque The amount of twisting a club shaft undergoes at impact.

Tour A succession of tournaments played by professionals.

Trajectory The unique flight characteristics of a golf ball after it is hit.

Trap *See* Bunker.

Triple bogey Finishing a hole in three more than par.

Turn Going from the ninth green to the tenth tee of a golf course.

Unplayable lie A lie out of which you cannot possibly hit a ball.

Uphill lie A lie in which your front foot is higher than your rear foot at address.

Vardon grip *See* Overlapping grip.

Waggle Back and forth warm-up movements of the club prior to hitting the ball.

Water hazard A body of water, identified by yellow or red stakes. If your ball goes into one and you can't hit it out, you must take a one-shot penalty.

Weak grip A grip in which a player sees one knuckle of the left hand; it is used to turn the ball to the right.

Wedge A short iron with a loft of at least 48 degrees, used to hit very short shots or to get out of the sand. A pitching wedge has the least amount of loft for a wedge; a gap wedge has more, followed by a sand wedge, and then finally the lob wedge, which has the most loft of any golf club.

Whiff The sound the club makes as it whips through air above the ball – and misses the ball entirely.

Wood A golf club that uses a large, pear-shaped head to hit the ball. Made of metal or wood, woods generally are longer than irons and are used to hit the ball longer distances. A driver is considered a wood, as is a 3-wood. Many golfers now carry 5-, 7-, and even 9-woods instead of long irons (those marked with smaller numbers, such as 2 or 3), because the woods tend to be slightly easier to hit. The higher the number of the club, the more loft it has.

Wristy A stroke is one in which the wrists break down. *See* Breaking down.

Yips A nervous affliction that causes the hands and arms to move in a jerky manner while putting.

Index

Acknowledgements

Author's acknowledgements

This book is dedicated to Nicki, whose support and friendship are surpassed only by her beautiful golf swing.

I would like to thank my editors, Beth Adelman and LaVonne Carlson-Finnerty, for all their help in getting this book to press. Thank you also to my agent, Laura Peterson, for her help, not only with contracts, but with all of the minutia she is always so good at taming. Kudos also to Laura's assistant, Laura Weed, for her timely help with so many aspects of the endeavor. I must also thank Nicki for the use of her kitchen table, and my dog Louie for helping to get me out of the house.

Publisher's acknowledgements

Dorling Kindersley would like to thank our European consultant Peter Ballingall, Lillywhites of London for loaning us golf clubs to photograph, Steve Gorton for additional photography, Mark Newcombe and Matthew Harris for providing step-by-step photography, Andrew Ainsworth and his assistants at Asheridge Golf Club, Justin Clow for his template development and additional artworks, Alistair Carlisle and Simeon Shoul for design help, Andrea Hill and Louise Waller for DTP assistance, Hilary Bird for compiling the index, and Neal Cobourne and Louise Candlish for the jacket design and text.

Picture credits

2: Corbis; 5: Allsport; 14/15: Brian Morgan Golf Photography; 16/17 Peter Dazeley; 16tl: Allsport/David Cannon; 17br: Allsport/David Duval; 18/19: Peter Dazeley; 20: Golf Photography International; 22: The Art Archive; 24b: Eric Hepworth Photography; 25cr: The Golf Picture Library; 27c: Bridgeman Art Library, London/New York; 28cl: Action Plus/M. Glyn Kirk; 28tr: Phil Sheldon; 30cl: Action Plus/Mike Hewitt; 31cl: Bridgeman Art Library London/New York; 32tr: David Cannon; 32bl: Action Plus/M. Glyn Kirk; 38tr: Eric Hepworth Photography; 39bl: Phil Sheldon; 40tr: Phil Sheldon; 41tr: Eric Hepworth Photography; 41bl: Peter Dazeley; 43cr: Allsport/David Cannon; 44: Phil Sheldon; 45: Peter Dazeley; 46: Allsport/Pascal Rondeau; 48: Peter Dazeley; 50: Golf Photography International; 54b: Peter Dazeley; 58: M. Glyn Kirk; 59: Phil Sheldon; 61br: Golf Picture Library; 62: Golf Picture Library; 63bl: Phil Sheldon; 63tr: Peter Dazeley; 65: Phil Sheldon; 68: Action Plus/M. Glyn Kirk; 71: Phil Sheldon; 72bl: Peter Dazeley; 73: Peter Dazeley; 74: Phil Sheldon; 75: Action Plus/Neil Tingle; 76tr: Peter Dazeley; 76br: Phil Sheldon; 78: All Sport/Paul Severn; 80: Action Plus/Neil Tingle; 82: Brian Morgan Golf Photography; 88: Action Plus/M. Glyn Kirk; 94: Action Plus/Mike Hewitt; 105bl: Peter Dazeley; 106cr: Allsport/Casey Martin; 114: The Golf Picture Library; 115c: Allsport/David Cannon; 115l: Peter Dazeley; 115r: Allsport/Andrew Redington; 122: Phil Sheldon; 124: Phil Sheldon; 132: Phil Sheldon; 134: All Sport/Dave Concannon;

135: The Golf Picture Library; 136: Hobbs Golf Collection; 139bl: Action Plus/Chris Brown; 142: Golf Photography International; 144: Allsport/Stephen Munday; 145: Action Plus/Chris Brown; 160: Peter Dazeley; 162: Action Plus/R. Francis; 166: Dave Concannon; 167: Peter Dazeley; 174: Phil Sheldon; 175: Allsport/Matthew Stockmam; 176/177: Golf Photography International; 178: Phil Sheldon/Jan Traylen; 180: Phil Sheldon; 182: Peter Dazeley; 184: Peter Dazeley; 187: Eric Hepworth Photography; 188: Peter Dazeley; 189tr: Golf Photography International; 190: Golf Photography International; 192bl: Eric Hepworth Photography; 192tr: Phil Sheldon; 194: Eric Hepworth Photography; 196: Phil Sheldon; 199: Action Plus/Neil Tingle; 200/1: Golf Photography International; 203cl: Allsport/David Duval; 204: Phil Sheldon; 205: Phil Sheldon; 206/7: Golf Photography International; 208: Phil Sheldon; 210: Action Plus/M. Glyn Kirk; 212: Allsport/David Cannon; 215: Peter Dazeley; 220/221: Visions in Golf/Mark Newcombe; 222: Eric Hepworth Photography; 224: Phil Sheldon; 226: Science Photo Library/Stephen Dalton; 229: Golf Photography International; 230: Golf Photography International; 232bl: Peter Dazeley; 236: Action Plus/ R. Francis; 238: Allsport/Craig Jones; 240: Golf Photography International; 243: Golf Photography International; 244: Golf Photography International; 248: Phil Sheldon/Karina Hoskyns; 250: Visions in Golf/Mark Newcombe; 251: Visions in Golf/Mark Newcombe; 254: Golf Photography International; 256tr: Phil Sheldon; 256bl: Phil Sheldon; 257: Phil Sheldon; 269: Allsport/Harry How; 270: Phil Sheldon/Jan Traylen; 271: Allsport/Craig Jones; 272: Phil Sheldon; 274: Phil Sheldon; 276cl: Phil Sheldon; 278: Phil Sheldon; 281: Action Plus/Mike Hewitt; 282: Phil Sheldon; 284: Golf Photography International; 285: Phil Sheldon; 286t: Action Plus/Neil Tingle; 287: Phil Sheldon; 294: Phil Sheldon; 295: Phil Sheldon; 296: Peter Dazeley; 298: Allsport/Pascal Rondeau; 299: Peter Dazeley; 300: Corbis; 302: Eric Hepworth Photography; 303: Golf Photography International; 304/5: Golf Photography International; 306/7: Golf Photography International; 309: Eric Hepworth Photography; 310: Peter Dazeley; 312: Golf Photography International; 313: Phil Sheldon/Jan Traylen; 314: Phil Sheldon; 315: Phil Sheldon; 316: Taylor Made; 318: Visions in Golf/Mark Newcombe; 320: Allsport/David Cannon; 323: Golf Photography International; 325: Peter Dazeley; 330bl: The Golf Picture Library; 330br: The Golf Picture Library; 331bl: Peter Dazeley; 331tr: Allsport/David Cannon; 334: Phil Sheldon; 335: Brian Morgan Golf Photography; 336b: Phil Sheldon; 336tr: The Golf Picture Library; 338: Allsport/David Cannon; 340: Phil Sheldon; 341cl: Allsport/David Cannon; 344: Phil Sheldon; 345: United States Golf Association; 346tr: Hulton Getty; 346bl: Phil Sheldon/Jan Traylen; 347: Phil Sheldon/David Duvall; 348tl: Phil Sheldon; 348br: Eric Hepworth Photography; 350: Corbis; 352: Phil Sheldon; 353: The Golf Picture Library; 354: Golf Photography International; 355: Eric Hepworth Photography; 356: Hobbs Golf Collection; 356bl: Hobbs Golf Collection; 356tr: Phil Sheldon; 357: Action Plus/Mike Hewitt; 358: Hobbs Golf Collection; 359: Phil Sheldon; 360: Action Plus/Mike Hewitt; 361: Phil Sheldon; 362: Phil Sheldon; 363: Phil Sheldon; 364: Eric Hepworth; 366: Action Plus/Peter Tarry; 368: Allsport/David Cannon; 369: Allsport/Craig Jones; 372: Phil Sheldon; 373cl: Phil Sheldon; 373br: Allsport; 374b: The Golf Picture Library; 374tr: Eric Hepworth Photography; 375: The Golf Picture Library; 376: Action Plus/Steve Bardens; 377: Peter Dazeley; 378: Peter Dazeley.